Practical Data Analysis Using Jupyter Notebook

Learn how to speak the language of data by extracting useful
and actionable insights using Python

Marc Wintjen

BIRMINGHAM - MUMBAI

Practical Data Analysis using Jupyter Notebook

Commissioning Editor: Amey Varangaonkar
Acquisition Editor: Devika Battike
Content Development Editor: Nazia Shaikh
Senior Editor: Ayaan Hoda
Technical Editor: Manikandan Kurup
Copy Editor: Safis Editing
Project Coordinator: Aishwarya Mohan
Proofreader: Safis Editing
Indexer: Priyanka Dhadke
Production Designer: Shankar Kalbhor

First published: June 2020

Production reference: 1180620

Published by Packt Publishing Ltd.
Livery Place
35 Livery Street
Birmingham
B3 2PB, UK.

ISBN 978-1-83882-603-1

www.packt.com

Packt.com

Subscribe to our online digital library for full access to over 7,000 books and videos, as well as industry leading tools to help you plan your personal development and advance your career. For more information, please visit our website.

Why subscribe?

- Spend less time learning and more time coding with practical eBooks and Videos from over 4,000 industry professionals

- Improve your learning with Skill Plans built especially for you

- Get a free eBook or video every month

- Fully searchable for easy access to vital information

- Copy and paste, print, and bookmark content

Did you know that Packt offers eBook versions of every book published, with PDF and ePub files available? You can upgrade to the eBook version at www.packt.com and as a print book customer, you are entitled to a discount on the eBook copy. Get in touch with us at customercare@packtpub.com for more details.

At www.packt.com, you can also read a collection of free technical articles, sign up for a range of free newsletters, and receive exclusive discounts and offers on Packt books and eBooks.

Foreword

It has been stated in many ways that society is producing more data than we have ever before and that we have just scratched the surface on figuring out how to make use of it. Whether it is truly the oil, or gold, of the 21st century, only time will tell but it is clear that being able to read it, mold it, and tell a story with it are skills that will be in demand for the foreseeable future. These skills turn data, facts, and figures, into information, knowledge, and insights gained from that data.

With the media grasping on buzzwords in the last few years, it may lead one to believe that working with data is a pretty new field. However, techniques have been introduced and perfected over decades on how to glean insight from the digital world. In a sense, it is only in the past decade that we have been able to apply these techniques at scale. These old but true best practices are almost technology agnostic and will help with whatever language or solution you are implementing. As you read on, it is exciting that you will not only get to learn the exciting technology used to gain intuition from data but also the knowledge of someone who has applied these lessons in a business setting. It is only by asking the right questions of the data does one get valuable information.

Some of these concepts that get lost in practice become the most important part of any data role. One learns quickly how asking where the source of the data is could be a key to understanding if one's visualization makes sense. Missing or malformed data can lead to wrong conclusions and mistrust from the audience of any analysis. Applying the tools that you learn, will help in being confident that any artifact from your analysis will be sound and truthful.

Marc is a true advocate for data literacy and transparency. He knows the tricks to get the most out of the data and the questions to ask even before you get hands-on. I am confident that he will lead you through the journey well, and I wish you luck on your adventure.

Andrew Vlahutin
Data Scientist and Machine Learning Engineer

About the author

Marc Wintjen is a risk analytics architect at Bloomberg L.P. with over 20 years of professional experience. An evangelist for data literacy, he's known as the data mensch for helping others make data-driven decisions. His passion for all things data has evolved from SQL and data warehousing to big data analytics and data visualization.

I want to thank the many people who have supported me throughout my career. My inspiration comes from my colleagues, with whom I have shared long hours spent solving complex problems and gaining some wisdom along the way (hopefully). Also, this would not have been possible without the support of my family's love and sacrifice. To my wife, Debra, my daughter, Rebecca, and my son, Seth – thank you! To my parents and extended family, thank you!

About the reviewers

Juan Jose Morales Urrutia has a Masters's degree in computer science from Georgia Tech. He is currently a senior software engineer at Bloomberg LP. Juan Jose is passionate about all things related to data. He enjoys designing data warehouses on the cloud, implementing scalable data pipelines, and building advanced analytics solutions using machine learning. Needless to say, he thinks this book will give you a fantastic introduction to the wonderful world of data.

Khaled Tannir has a Master of Research and a Master of Computer Science degree. He has more than 25 years of technical experience as a big data architect. He leads IT projects in multiple industries, such as banking, finance, and insurance. Creative and forward-thinking, and author of two books, he has focused for 10 years on big data, data mining, and machine learning. With significant experience in big data technologies, Khaled has implemented many Proofs of Concept that need different skills. Khaled is a big data trainer and mentor. He is the instructor of the *Data at Scale* module at McGill University (Montréal, Canada). He is the founder of dataXper, a company that focuses on delivering high-quality big data consulting and training services.

Packt is searching for authors like you

If you're interested in becoming an author for Packt, please visit authors.packtpub.com and apply today. We have worked with thousands of developers and tech professionals, just like you, to help them share their insight with the global tech community. You can make a general application, apply for a specific hot topic that we are recruiting an author for, or submit your own idea.

Table of Contents

Preface

Welcome, and thank you for taking the time to read this book. Throughout this book, I will take you on a journey through the **evolution of data analysis** in a very simple and easy-to-understand manner. The book will introduce you to modern tools, such as **Jupyter Notebook** and various **Python** libraries, to teach you how to work with data. In the process, you will learn about the many different types of data and how to clean, blend, visualize, and analyze data to gain useful insights.

Data literacy is the ability to read, work with, analyze, and argue with data. Data analysis is the process of cleaning and modeling your data to discover useful information. This book combines both concepts by sharing proven techniques and hands-on examples, so you can learn how to communicate effectively with data.

Complete with hands-on tutorials and real-world examples, this easy-to-follow guide will teach you concepts of data analysis using SQL, Python, and Jupyter Notebook.

Who this book is for

This book is for anyone who is looking to develop their skills to become data-driven, personally and professionally. No prior knowledge of data analysis or programming is required to get started with this book. Anyone looking for a new career working with data will enjoy reading the book.

What this book covers

Chapter 1, *Fundamentals of Data Analysis*, is a straightforward introduction to what data analysis is and how a blend of traditional and modern techniques can be used for data analysis.

Chapter 2, *Overview of Python and Installing Jupyter Notebook*, provides an introduction to the Python programming language using an open source data analysis tool called Jupyter Notebook.

Chapter 3, *Getting Started with NumPy*, is where you will learn about the key functions used for analysis with a powerful Python library named NumPy; You will also explore arrays and matrix data structures.

Chapter 4, *Creating Your First pandas DataFrame*, teaches you what a pandas DataFrame is and how to create them from different file type sources, such as CSV, JSON, and XML.

Chapter 5, *Gathering and Loading Data in Python*, shows you how to run SQL SELECT queries from Jupyter Notebook and how to load them into DataFrames.

Chapter 6, *Visualizing and Working with Time Series Data*, explores the process of making your first data visualization by breaking down the anatomy of a chart. Basic statistics, data lineage, and metadata (data about data) will be explained.

Chapter 7, *Exploring, Cleaning, Refining, and Blending Datasets*, focuses on essential concepts and numerical skills required to wrangle, sort, and explore a dataset.

Chapter 8, *Understanding Joins, Relationships, and Aggregates*, delves into constructing high-quality datasets for further analysis. The concepts of joining and summarizing data will be introduced.

Chapter 9, *Plotting, Visualization, and Storytelling*, continues to teach you how to visualize data by exploring additional chart options, such as histograms and scatterplots, to advance your data literacy and analysis skills.

Chapter 10, *Exploring Text Data and Unstructured Data*, introduces **Natural Language Processing (NLP)**, which has become a must-have skill in data analysis. This chapter looks at the concepts you'll need to know in order to analyze narrative free text that can provide insights from unstructured data.

Chapter 11, *Practical Sentiment Analysis*, covers the basics of supervised machine learning. After that, there's a walk-through of sentiment analysis.

Chapter 12, *Bringing It All Together*, brings together many of the concepts covered in the book using real-world examples to demonstrate the skills needed to read, work with, analyze, and argue with data.

To get the most out of this book

This book is for anyone who is absolutely new to the field of data analysis. No prior knowledge or experience of working with data or programming is required. The book is a step-by-step guide that walks you through installations and exercises.

Only basic technical acumen is required. The ability to download files, access websites, and install applications on your computer is all that is needed in this regard.

Software/hardware covered in the book	OS requirements
Software: Jupyter Notebook, Anaconda, Python 3.X, NLTK	Any OS (tested on Windows 10 and macOS X)
Hardware: Any (tested on Intel Core i7, 16 GB, 235 GB HD)	

If you are using the digital version of this book, we advise you to type the code yourself or access the code via the GitHub repository (link available in the next section). Doing so will help you avoid any potential errors related to the copying and pasting of code.

Download the example code files

You can download the example code files for this book from your account at www.packt.com. If you purchased this book elsewhere, you can visit www.packtpub.com/support and register to have the files emailed directly to you.

You can download the code files by following these steps:

1. Log in or register at www.packt.com.
2. Select the **Support** tab.
3. Click on **Code Downloads**.
4. Enter the name of the book in the **Search** box and follow the onscreen instructions.

Once the file is downloaded, please make sure that you unzip or extract the folder using the latest version of:

- WinRAR/7-Zip for Windows
- Zipeg/iZip/UnRarX for Mac
- 7-Zip/PeaZip for Linux

The code bundle for the book is also hosted on GitHub at https://github.com/PacktPublishing/Practical-Data-Analysis-using-Jupyter-Notebook. In case there's an update to the code, it will be updated on the existing GitHub repository.

We also have other code bundles from our rich catalog of books and videos available at https://github.com/PacktPublishing/. Check them out!

Download the color images

We also provide a PDF file that has color images of the screenshots/diagrams used in this book. You can download it here:
`https://static.packt-cdn.com/downloads/9781838826031_ColorImages.pdf`.

Conventions used

There are a number of text conventions used throughout this book.

`CodeInText`: Indicates code words in text, database table names, folder names, filenames, file extensions, pathnames, dummy URLs, user input, and Twitter handles. Here is an example: "So, `purchase_data.iloc[0]` or `purchase_data.ix[0]` will both return the same results."

A block of code is set as follows:

```
product_data = {
 'product a': [13, 20, 0, 10],
 'project b': [10, 30, 17, 20],
 'project c': [6, 9, 10, 0]
}
```

Any command-line input or output is written as follows:

```
>cd \
>cd projects
>jupyter notebook
```

Bold: Indicates a new term, an important word, or words that you see onscreen. For example, words in menus or dialog boxes appear in the text like this. Here is an example: "Depending on the OS, such as Linux, a CSV would only include a **line feed** (**LF**) and not a **carriage return** (**CR**) for each row."

 Warnings or important notes appear like this.

 Tips and tricks appear like this.

Get in touch

Feedback from our readers is always welcome.

General feedback: If you have questions about any aspect of this book, mention the book title in the subject of your message and email us at customercare@packtpub.com.

Errata: Although we have taken every care to ensure the accuracy of our content, mistakes do happen. If you have found a mistake in this book, we would be grateful if you would report this to us. Please visit www.packtpub.com/support/errata, selecting your book, clicking on the Errata Submission Form link, and entering the details.

Piracy: If you come across any illegal copies of our works in any form on the Internet, we would be grateful if you would provide us with the location address or website name. Please contact us at copyright@packt.com with a link to the material.

If you are interested in becoming an author: If there is a topic that you have expertise in and you are interested in either writing or contributing to a book, please visit authors.packtpub.com.

Reviews

Please leave a review. Once you have read and used this book, why not leave a review on the site that you purchased it from? Potential readers can then see and use your unbiased opinion to make purchase decisions, we at Packt can understand what you think about our products, and our authors can see your feedback on their book. Thank you!

For more information about Packt, please visit packt.com.

Section 1: Data Analysis Essentials

In this section, we will learn how to speak the language of data by extracting useful and actionable insights from data using Python and Jupyter Notebook. We'll begin with the fundamentals of data analysis and work with the right tools to help you analyze data effectively. After your workspace has been set up, we'll learn how to work with data using two popular open source libraries available in Python: NumPy and pandas. This will lay the foundation for you to understand data so that you can prepare for *Section 2: Solutions for Data Discovery*.

This section includes the following chapters:

- Chapter 1, *Fundamentals of Data Analysis*
- Chapter 2, *Overview of Python and Installing Jupyter Notebook*
- Chapter 3, *Getting Started with NumPy*
- Chapter 4, *Creating Your First pandas DataFrame*
- Chapter 5, *Gathering and Loading Data in Python*

Fundamentals of Data Analysis 1

Welcome and thank you for reading my book. I'm excited to share my passion for data and I hope to provide the resources and insights to fast-track your journey into data analysis. My goal is to educate, mentor, and coach you throughout this book on the techniques used to become a top-notch data analyst. During this process, you will get hands-on experience using the latest open source technologies available such as Jupyter Notebook and Python. We will stay within that technology ecosystem throughout this book to avoid confusion. However, you can be confident the concepts and skills learned are transferable across open source and vendor solutions with a focus on all things data.

In this chapter, we will cover the following:

- The evolution of data analysis and why it is important
- What makes a good data analyst?
- Understanding data types and why they are important
- Data classifications and data attributes explained
- Understanding data literacy

The evolution of data analysis and why it is important

To begin, we should define what data is. You will find varying definitions but I would define data as the digital persistence of facts, knowledge, and information consolidated for reference or analysis. The focus of my definition should be the word *persistence* because digital facts remain even after the computers used to create them are powered down and they are retrievable for future use. Rather than focus on the formal definition, let's discuss the world of data and how it impacts our daily lives. Whether you are reading a review to decide which product to buy or viewing the price of a stock, consuming information has become significantly easier to allow you to make informed data-driven decisions.

Data has been entangled into products and services across every industry from farming to smartphones. For example, America's Grow-a-Row, a New Jersey farm to food bank charity, donated over 1.5 million pounds of fresh produce to feed people in need throughout the region each year, according to their annual report. America's Grow-a-Row has thousands of volunteers and uses data to maximize production yields during the harvest season.

As the demand for being a *consumer* of data has increased, so has the supply side, which is characterized as the *producer* of data. Producing data has increased in scale as the technology innovations have evolved. I'll discuss this in more detail shortly, but this large scale consumption and production can be summarized as big data. A National Institute of Standards and Technology report defined big data as consisting of *extensive datasets—primarily in the characteristics of volume, velocity, and/or variability—that require a scalable architecture for efficient storage, manipulation, and analysis.*

This explosion of big data is characterized by the **3Vs**, which are **Volume**, **Velocity**, and **Variety**, and has become a widely accepted concept among data professionals:

- **Volume** is based on the quantity of data that is stored in any format such as image files, movies, and database transactions, which are measured in gigabytes, terabytes, or even zettabytes. To give context, you can store hundreds of thousands of songs or pictures on one terabyte of storage space. Even more amazing than the figures is how much it costs you. Google Drive, for example, offers up to 5 TB (terabytes) of storage for free according to their support site.
- **Velocity** is the speed at which data is generated. This process covers how data is both produced and consumed. For example, batch processing is how data feeds are sent between systems where blocks of records or bundles of files are sent and received. Modern velocity approaches are real time, streams of data where the data flow is in a constant state of movement.
- **Variety** is all of the different formats that data can be stored in, including text, image, database tables, and files. This variety has created both challenges and opportunities for analysis because of the different technologies and techniques required to work with the data.

Understanding the 3Vs is important for data analysis because you must become good at being both a consumer and producer of data. The simple questions of how your data is stored, when this file was produced, where the database table is located, and in what format I should store the output of my analysis of the data can all be addressed by understanding the 3Vs.

There is some debate—for which I disagree—that the 3Vs should increase to include **Value**, **Visualization**, and **Veracity**. No worries, we will cover these concepts throughout this book.

This leads us to a formal definition of data analysis which is defined as *a process of inspecting, cleansing, transforming, and modeling data with the goal of discovering useful information, informing conclusion, and supporting decision-making,* as stated in *Review of business intelligence through data analysis.*

Xia, B. S., & Gong, P. (2015). Review of business intelligence through data analysis. Benchmarking, 21(2), 300-311. doi:10.1108/BIJ-08-2012-0050

What I like about this definition is the focus on solving problems using data without the focus on which technologies are used. To make this possible there have been some significant technological milestones, the introduction of new concepts, and people who have broken down the barriers.

To showcase the evolution of data analysis, I compiled a few tables of key events from the years of 1945 until 2018 that I feel are the most influential. The following table is comprised of innovators such as Dr. E.F. Codd, who created the concept of a database to the launch of the iPhone device that spawned the mobile analytics industry.

The following diagram was collected from multiple sources and centralized in one place as a table of columns and rows and then visualized using this dendrogram chart. I posted the CSV file in the GitHub repository for reference: `https://github.com/PacktPublishing/python-data-analysis-beginners-guide`. Organizing the information and conforming the data in one place made the data visualization easier to produce and enables further analysis:

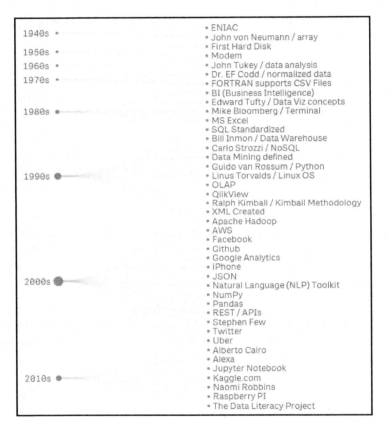

That process of collecting, formatting, and storing data in this readable format demonstrates the first step of becoming a *producer* of data. To make this information easier to consume, I summarize these events by decades in the following table:

Decade	Count of Milestones
1940s	2
1950s	2
1960s	1

1970s	2
1980s	5
1990s	9
2000s	14
2010s	7

From the preceding summary table, you can see that the majority of these milestone events occurred in the 1990s and 2000s. What is insightful about this analysis is that recent innovations have removed the barriers of entry for individuals to work with data. Before the 1990s, the high purchasing costs of hardware and software restricted the field of data analysis to a relatively limited number of careers. Also, the costs associated with access to the underlying data for analysis were great. It typically required higher education and specialized careers in software programming or an actuary.

A visual way to look at this same data would be a trend bar chart, as shown in the following diagram. In this example, the height of the bars represents the same information as in the preceding table and the **Count of Milestone** events is on the left or the *y* axis. What is nice about this visual representation of the data is that it is a faster way for the *consumer* to see the upward pattern of where most events occur without scanning through the results found in the preceding diagram or table:

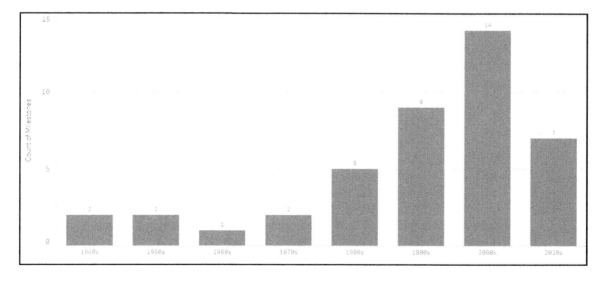

The evolution of data analysis is important to understand because now you know some of the pioneers who opened doors for opportunities and careers working with data, along with key technology breakthroughs, significantly reducing the time to make decisions regarding data both as *consumers* and *producers*.

What makes a good data analyst?

I will now break down the contributing factors that make up a good data analyst. From my experience, a good data analyst must be eager to learn and continue to ask questions throughout the process of working with data. The focus of those questions will vary based on the audience who are consuming the results. To be an expert in the field of data analysis, excellent communication skills are required so you can understand how to translate raw data into insights that can impact change in a positive way. To make it easier to remember, use the following acronyms to help to improve your data analyst skills.

Know Your Data (KYD)

Knowing your data is all about understanding the source technology that was used to create the data along with the business requirements and rules used to store it. **Do research ahead of time** to understand what the business is all about and how the data is used. For example, if you are working with a sales team, learn what drives their team's success. Do they have daily, monthly, or quarterly sales quotas? Do they do reporting for month-end/quarter-end that goes to senior management and has to be accurate because it has financial impacts on the company? Learning more about the source data by asking questions about how it will be consumed will help focus your analysis when you have to deliver results.

KYD is also about data lineage, which is understanding how the data was originally sourced including the technologies used along with the transformations that occurred before, during, and afterward. Refer back to the 3Vs so you can effectively communicate the responses from common questions about the data such as where this data is sourced from or who is responsible for maintaining the data source.

Voice of the Customer (VOC)

The concept of VOC is nothing new and has been taught at universities for years as a well-known concept applied in sales, marketing, and many other business operations. VOC is the concept of understanding customer needs by learning from or listening to their needs before, during, and after they use a company's product or service. The relevance of this concept remains important today and should be applied to every data project that you participate in. This process is where you should interview the consumers of the data analysis results before even looking at the data. If you are working with business users, listen to what their needs are by writing down the specific points on what business questions are they trying to answer.

Schedule a working session with them where you can engage in a dialog. Make sure you focus on their current pain points such as the time to curate all of the data used to make decisions. Does it take three days to complete the process every month? If you can deliver an automated data product or a dashboard that can reduce that time down to a few mouse clicks, your data analysis skills will make you look like a hero to your business users.

 During a tech talk at a local university, I was asked the difference between KYD and VOC. I explained that both are important and focused on communicating and learning more about the subject area or business. The key differences are prepared versus present. KYD is all about doing your homework ahead of time to be prepared before talking to experts. VOC is all about listening to the needs of your business or consumers regarding the data.

Always Be Agile (ABA)

The agile methodology has become commonplace in the industry for application, web, and mobile development **Software Development Life Cycle (SDLC)**. One of the reasons that makes the agile project management process successful is that it creates an interactive communication line between the business and technical teams to iteratively deliver business value through the use of data and usable features.

The agile process involves creating *stories* with a common theme where a development team completes tasks in 2-3 week *sprints*. In that process, it is important to understand the *what* and the *why* for each story including the business value/the problem you are trying to solve.

The agile approach has *ceremonies* where the developers and business sponsors come together to capture requirements and then deliver *incremental value*. That improvement in value could be anything from a new dataset available for access to a new feature added to an app.

See the following diagram for a nice visual representation of these concepts. Notice how these concepts are not linear and should require multiple iterations, which help to improve the communication between all people involved in the data analysis before, during, and after delivery of results:

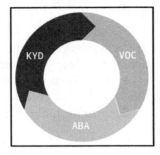

Finally, I believe the most important trait of a good data analyst is a passion for working with data. If your passion can be fueled by continuously learning about all things data, it becomes a lifelong and fulfilling journey.

Understanding data types and their significance

As we have uncovered with the **3Vs**, data comes in all shapes and sizes, so let's break down some key data types and better understand why they are important. To begin, let's classify data in general terms of *unstructured*, *semi-structured*, and *structured*.

Unstructured data

The concept behind **unstructured** data, which is textual in nature, has been around since the 1990s and includes the following examples: the body of an email message, tweets, books, health records, and images. A simple example of unstructured data would be an email message body that is classified as **free text**. *Free text* may have some obvious structure that a human can identify such as free space to break up paragraphs, dates, and phone numbers, but having a computer identify those elements would require programming to classify any data elements as such. What makes free text challenging for data analysis is its inconsistent nature, especially when trying to work with multiple examples.

When working with unstructured data, there will be inconsistencies because of the nature of free text including misspellings, the different classification of dates, and so on. Always have a peer review of the workflow or code used to curate the data.

Semi-structured data

Next, we have semi-structured data, which is similar to unstructured, however, the key difference is the addition of *tags*, which are keywords or any classification used to create a natural hierarchy. Examples of semi-structured data are XML and JSON files, as shown in the following code:

```
{
  "First_Name": "John",
  "Last_Name": "Doe",
  "Age": 42,
  "Home_Address": {
    "Address_1": "123 Main Street",
    "Address_2": [],
    "City": "New York",
    "State": "NY",
    "Zip_Code": "10021"
  },
  "Phone_Number": [
    {
      "Type": "cell",
      "Number": "212-555-1212"
    },
    {
      "Type": "home",
      "Number": "212 555-4567"
    }
  ],
```

```
    "Children": [],
    "Spouse": "yes"
}
```

This JSON formatted code allows for free text elements such as a street address, a phone number, and age, but now has *tags* created to identify those fields and values, which is a concept called **key-value** pairs. This key-value pair concept allows for the classification of data with a structure for analysis such as filtering, but still has the flexibility to change the elements as necessary to support the unstructured/free text. The biggest advantage of semi-structured data is the flexibility to change the underlining schema of how the data is stored. The schema is a foundational concept of traditional database systems that defines how the data must be persisted (that is, stored on disk).

The disadvantage to semi-structured data is that you may still find inconsistencies with data values depending on how the data was captured. Ideally, the burden on consistency is moved to the **User Interface (UI)**, which would have coded standards and business rules such as required fields to increase the quality but, as a data analyst who practices KYD, you should validate that during the project.

Structured data

Finally, we have **structured** data, which is the most common type found in databases and data created from applications (apps or software) and code. The biggest benefit with structured data is consistency and relatively high quality between each record, especially when stored in the same database table. The conformity of data and structure is the foundation for analysis, which allows both the producers and consumers of structured data to come to the same results. The topic of databases, or **Database Management Systems (DBMS)** and **Relational Database Management Systems (RDMS)** is vast and will not be covered here, but having some understanding will help you to become a better data analyst.

The following diagram is a basic **Entity-Relationship (ER)** diagram of three tables that would be found in a database:

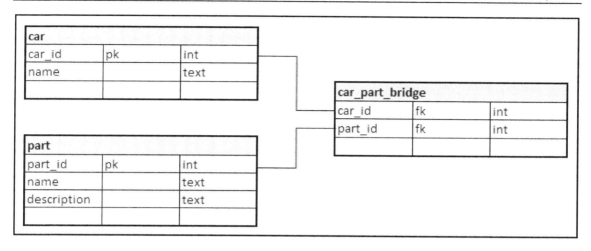

In this example, each **entity** would represent physical tables stored in the database, named `car`, `part`, and `car_part_bridge`. The relationship between the car and part is defined by the table called `car_part_bridge`, which can be classified by multiple names such as `bridge`, `junction`, `mapping`, or `link` table. The name of each field in the table would be on the left such as `part_id`, `name`, or `description` found in the `part` table.

The `pk` label next to the `car_id` and `part_id` field names helps to identify the primary keys for each table. This allows for one field to uniquely identify each record found in the table. If a **primary key** in one table exists in another table, it would be called a **foreign key**, which is the foundation of how the relationship between the tables is defined and ultimately joined together.

Finally, the text aligned on the right side next to the field name labeled as `int` or `text` is the data type for each field. We will cover that concept next and you should now feel comfortable with the concepts for identifying and classifying data.

Common data types

Data types are a well-known concept in programming languages and is found in many different technologies. I have simplified the definition as, the details of the data that is stored and its intended usage. A data type will also create consistency for each data value as it's stored on disk or memory.

Data types will vary depending on the software and/or database used to create the structure. Hence, we won't be covering all the different types across all of the different coding languages but let's walk through a few examples:

Common data type	Common short name	Sample value	Example usage
Integers	`int`	`1235`	Counting occurrences, summing values, or the average of values such as sum (hits)
Booleans	`bit`	`TRUE`	Conditional testing such as if sales > 1,000, *true* else *false*
Geospatial	`float` or `spatial`	`40.229290,` `-74.936707`	Geo analytics based on latitude and longitude
Characters/string	`char`	`A`	Tagging, binning, or grouping data
Floating-point numbers	`float` or `double`	`2.1234`	Sales, cost analysis, or stock price
Alphanumeric strings	`blob` or `varchar`	`United States`	Tagging, binning, encoding, or grouping data
Time	`time`, `timestamp`, `date`	`8/19/2000`	Time-series analysis or year-over-year comparison

Technologies change and legacy systems will offer opportunities to see data types that may not be common. The best advice when dealing with new data types is to validate the source systems that are created by speaking to an **SME (Subject Matter Expert)** or system administrator, or to ask for documentation that includes the active version used to persist the data.

In the preceding table, I've created a summary of some common data types. Getting comfortable understanding the differences between data types is important because it determines what type of analysis can be performed on each data value. Numeric data types such as integer (`int`), floating-point numbers (`float`), or `double` are used for mathematical calculations of values such as the sum of sales, count of apples, or the average price of a stock. Ideally, the source system of the record should enforce the data type but there can be and usually are exceptions.

As you evolve your data analysis skills, helping to resolve data type issues or offer suggestions to improve them will make the quality and accuracy of reporting better throughout the organization.

String data types that are defined in the preceding table as characters (`char`) and alphanumeric strings (`varchar` or `blob`) can be represented as text such as a word or full sentence. `Time` is a special data type that can be represented and stored in multiple ways such as `12 PM EST` or a date such as `08/19/2000`. Consider geospatial coordinates such as latitude and longitude, which can be stored in multiple data types depending on the source system.

The goal of this chapter is to introduce you to the concept of data types and future chapters will give direct, hands-on experience of working with them. The reason why data types are important is to avoid incomplete or inaccurate information when presenting facts and insights from analysis. Invalid or inconsistent data types also restrict the ability to create accurate charts or data visualizations. Finally, good data analysis is about having confidence and trust that your conclusions are complete with defined data types that support your analysis.

Data classifications and data attributes explained

Now that we understand more about data types and why they are important, let's break down the different classifications of data and understand the different data attribute types. To begin with a visual, let's summarize all of the possible combinations in the following summary diagram:

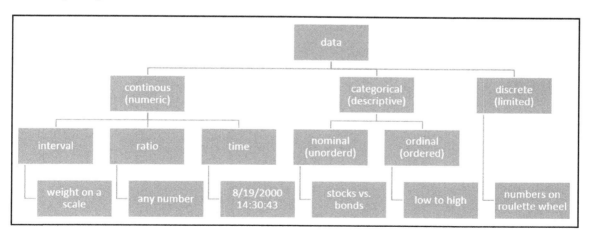

In the preceding diagram, the boxes directly below **data** have the three methods to classify data, which are **continuous**, **categorical**, or **discrete**.

Continuous data is measurable, quantified with a numeric data type, and has a continuous range with infinite possibilities. The bottom boxes in this diagram are examples so you can easily find them for reference. Continuous data examples include a stock price, weight in pounds, and time.

Categorical (descriptive) data will have values as a `string` data type. Categorical data is *qualified* so it would describe something specific such as a person, place, or thing. Some examples include a country of origin, a month of the year, the different types of trees, and your family designation.

Just because data is defined as categorical, don't assume the values are all alike or consistent. A month can be stored as `1`, `2`, `3`; `Jan`, `Feb`, `Mar`; or `January`, `February`, `March`, or in any combination. You will learn more about how to clean and conform your data for consistent analysis in `Chapter 7`, *Exploring Cleaning, Refining, and Blending Datasets*.

A `discrete` data type can be either continuous or categorical depending on how it's used for analysis. Examples include the number of employees in a company. You must have an integer/whole number representing the count for each employee, because you can never have partial results such as half an employee. Discrete data is continuous in nature because of its numeric properties but also has limits that make it similar to categorical. Another example would be the numbers on a roulette wheel. There is a limit of whole numbers available on the wheel from `1` to `36`, `0`, or `00` that a player can bet on, plus the numbers can be categorized as red, black, or green depending on the value.

If only two discrete values exist, such as `yes`/`no` or `true`/`false` or `1`/`0`, it can also be classified as binary.

Data attributes

Now that we understand how to classify data, let's break down the attribute types available to better understand how you can use them for analysis. The easiest method to break down types is to start with how you plan on using the data values for analysis:

- **Nominal data** is defined as data where you can distinguish between different values but not necessarily order them. It is qualitative in nature, so think of nominal data as labels or names as *stocks* or *bonds* where math cannot be performed on them because they are string values. With nominal values, you cannot determine whether the word *stocks* or *bonds* are better or worse without additional information.

- **Ordinal data** is *ordered* data where a ranking exists, but the distance or range between values cannot be defined. Ordinal data is qualitative using labels or names but now the values will have a natural or defined sequence. Similar to nominal data, ordinal data can be counted but not calculated with all statistical methods.

  An example is assigning 1 = low, 2 = medium, and 3 = high values. This has a natural sequence but the difference between low and high cannot be quantified by itself. The data assigned to *low* and *high* values could be arbitrary or have additional business rules behind it.

  Another common example of ordinal data is natural hierarchies such as state, county, and city, or grandfather, father, and son. The relationship between these values are well defined and commonly understood without any additional information to support it. So, a son will have a father but a father cannot be a son.

- **Interval data** is like ordinal data, but the distance between data points is uniform. Weight on a scale in pounds is a good example because the difference between the values from 5 to 10, 10 to 15, and 20 to 25 are all the same. Note that not every arithmetic operation can be performed on interval data so understanding the context of the data and how it should be used becomes important.

Temperature is a good example to demonstrate this paradigm. You can record hourly values and even provide a daily average, but summing the values per day or week would not provide accurate information for analysis. See the following diagram, which provides an hourly temperature for a specific day. Notice the *x* axis breaks out the hours and the *y* axis provides the average, which is labeled **Avg Temperature**, in Fahrenheit. The values between each hour must be an average or mean because an accumulation of temperature would provide misleading results and inaccurate analysis:

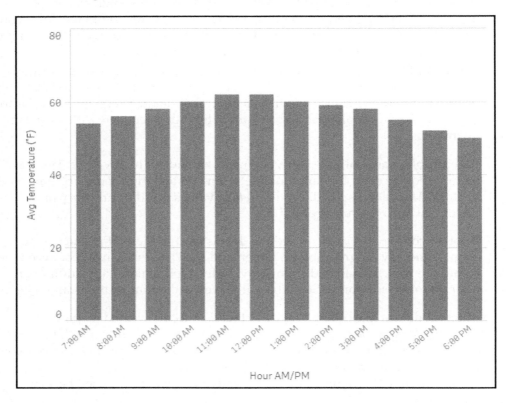

- **Ratio data** allows for all arithmetic operations including sum, average, median, mode, multiplication, and division. The data types of `integer` and `float` discussed earlier are classified as ratio data attributes, which in turn are also numeric/quantitative. Also, `time` could be classified as ratio data, however, I decided to further break down this attribute because of how often it is used for data analysis.

Note that there are advanced statistical details about ratio data attributes that are not covered in this book, such as having an absolute or true zero, so I encourage you to learn more about the subject.

- **Time data** attributes as a rich subject that you will come across regularly during your data analysis journey. Time data covers both date and time or any combination, for example, the time as HH:MM AM/PM, such as 12:03 AM; the year as YYYY, such as 1980; a timestamp represented as YYYY-MM-DD hh:mm:ss, such as 2000-08-19 14:32:22; or even a date as MM/DD/YY, such as 08/19/00. What's important to recognize when dealing with time data is to identify the intervals between each value so you can accurately measure the difference between them.

It is common during many data analysis projects that you find gaps in the sequence of time data values. For example, you are given a dataset with a range between 08/01/2019 to 08/31/2019 but only 25 distinct date values exist versus 30 days of data. There are various reasons for this occurrence including system outages where log data was lost. How to handle those data gaps will vary depending on the type of analysis you have to perform, including the need to fill in missing results. We will cover some examples in Chapter 7, *Exploring Cleaning, Refining, and Blending Datasets*.

Understanding data literacy

Data literacy is defined by Rahul Bhargava and Catherine D'Ignazio as *the ability to read, work with, analyze, and argue with data*. Throughout this chapter, I have pointed out how data comes in all shapes and sizes, so creating a common framework to communicate about data between different audiences becomes an important skill to master.

Data literacy becomes a common denominator for answering data questions between two or more people with different skills or experience. For example, if a sales manager wants to verify the data behind a chart in a quarterly report, having them fluent in the language of data will save time. Time is saved by asking direct questions about the *data types* and *data attributes* with the engineering team versus searching for those details aimlessly.

Let's break down the concepts of data literacy to help to identify how it can be applied to your personal and professional life.

Reading data

What does it mean to read data? Reading data is consuming information, and that information can be in any format including a chart, a table, code, or the body of an email.

Reading data may not necessarily provide the consumer with all of the answers to their questions. Having domain expertise may be required to understand how, when, and why a dataset was created to allow the consumer to fully interpret the underlying dataset.

For example, you are a data analyst and your colleague sends a file attachment to your email with the subject line as FYI and no additional information in the body of the message. We now know from the *What makes a good data analyst?* section that we should start asking questions about the file attachment:

- What methods were used to create the file (human or machine)?
- What system(s) and workflow were used to create the file?
- Who created the file and when was it created?
- How often does this file refresh and is it manual or automated?

Asking these questions helps you to understand the concept of *data lineage*, which can identify the process of how a dataset was created. This will ensure reading the data will result in understanding all aspects to focus on making decisions from it confidently.

Working with data

I define *working with data* as the person or system that creates a dataset using any technology. The technologies used to create data are vastly varied and could be as simple as someone typing rows and columns in spreadsheets, to having a software developer use loops and functions in Python code to create a pipe-delimited file.

Since writing data varies by expertise and job function, a key takeaway from a data literacy perspective is that the producer of data should be conscious of how it will be consumed. Ideally, the producer should document the details of how, when, and where the data was created to include the frequency of how often it is refreshed. Publishing this information democratizes the metadata (data about the data) to improve the communication between anyone reading and working with the data.

For example, if you have a timestamp field in your dataset, is it using **UTC (Coordinated Universal Time)** or **EST (Eastern Standard Time)**? By including assumptions and reasons why the data is stored in a specific format, the person or team working with the data become good data citizens by improving the communication for analysis.

Analyzing data

Analyzing data begins with modeling and structuring it to answer business questions. Data modeling is a vast topic but for data literacy purposes, it can be boiled down to **dimensions** and **measures**. Dimensions are distinct nouns such as a person, place, or thing, and measures are verbs based on actions and then aggregated (sum, count, min, max, and average).

The foundation for building any data visualization and charts is rooted in data modeling and most modern tech solutions have it built in so you may be already modeling data without even realizing it.

One quick solution to help to classify how the data should be used for analysis would be a *data dictionary*, which is defined as *a centralized repository of information about data such as meaning, relationships to other data, origin, usage, and format.*

You might be able to find a data dictionary in the help pages of source systems or from GitHub repositories. If you don't receive one from the creator of the file, you can create one for yourself and use it to ask questions about the data including assumed data types, data quality, and identifying data gaps.

Creating a data dictionary also helps to validate assumptions and is an aid to frame questions about the data when communicating with others. The easiest method to create a *data dictionary* would be to transpose the first few rows of the source data so the rows turn into columns. If your data has a header row, then the first row turns into a list of all fields available. Let's walk through an example of how to create your own data dictionary from data. Here, we have a source **Sales** table representing **Product** and **Customer** sales by quarter:

Product	Customer	Quarter 1	Quarter 2	Quarter 3	Quarter 4
Product 1	Customer A	$ 1,000.00	$ 2,000.00	$ 6,000.00	
Product 1	Customer B		$ 1,000.00	$ 500.00	
Product 2	Customer A		$ 1,000.00		
Product 2	Customer C	$ 2,000.00	$ 2,500.00	$ 5,000.00	

Product 3	Customer A		$ 1,000.00	$ 2,000.00			
Product 4	Customer B		$ 1,000.00	$ 3,000.00			
Product 5	Customer A					$ 1,000.00	

In the following table, I have transposed the preceding source table to create a new table for analysis, which creates an initial data dictionary. The first column on the left becomes a list of all of the fields available from the source table. As you can see from the fields, **Record 1** to **Record 3** in the header row now become sample rows of data but retain the integrity of each row from the source table. The last two columns on the right in the following table, labeled **Estimated Data Type** and **Dimension or Measure**, were added to help to define the use of this data for analysis. Understanding the data type and classifying each field as a dimension or measure will help to determine what type of analysis we can perform and how each field can be used in data visualizations:

Field Name	Record 1	Record 2	Record 3	Estimated Data Type	Dimension or Measure
Product	Product 1	Product 1	Product 2	varchar	Dimension
Customer	Customer A	Customer B	Customer A	varchar	Dimension
Quarter 1	$ 1,000.00			float	Measure
Quarter 2	$ 2,000.00	$ 1,000.00	$ 1,000.00	float	Measure
Quarter 3	$ 6,000.00	$ 500.00		float	Measure
Quarter 4				float	Measure

Using this technique can help you to ask the following questions about the data to ensure you understand the results:

- What year does this dataset represent or is it an accumulation of multiple years?
- Does each quarter represent a calendar year or fiscal year?
- Was Product 5 first introduced in Quarter 4, because there are no prior sales for that product by any customer in Quarter 1 to Quarter 3?

Arguing about the data

Finally, let's talk about how and why we should argue about data. Challenging and defending the numbers in charts or data tables helps to build credibility and is actually done in many cases behind the scenes. For example, most data engineering teams put in various checks and balances such as alerts during ingestion to avoid missing information. Additional checks would also include rules to look into log files for anomalies or errors in the processing of data.

From a consumer's perspective, *trust and verify* is a good approach. For example, when looking at a chart published in a credible news article, you can assume the data behind the story is accurate but you should also verify the accuracy of the source data. The first thing to ask would be: does the underlying chart include a source to the dataset that is publicly available? The website `fivethirtyeight.com` is really good at providing access to the raw data and details of methodologies used to create analysis and charts found in news stories. Exposing the underlining dataset and the process used to collect it to the public opens up conversations about the how, what, and why behind the data and is a good method to disprove misinformation.

As a data analyst and creator of data outputs, the ability to defend your work should be received with open arms. Having documentation such as a data dictionary and GitHub repository and documenting the methodology used to produce the data will build trust with the audience and reduce the time for them to make data-driven decisions.

Hopefully, you now see the importance of data literacy and how it can be used to improve all aspects of communication of data between consumers and producers. With any language, practice will lead to improvement, so I invite you to explore some useful free datasets to improve your data literacy.

Here are a few to get started:

- **Kaggle**: `https://www.kaggle.com/datasets`
- **FiveThirtyEight**: `https://data.fivethirtyeight.com/`
- **The World Bank**: `https://data.worldbank.org/`

Let's begin with the *Kaggle* site, which was created to help companies to host data science competitions to solve complex problems using data. Improve your reading and working with data literacy skills by exploring these datasets and walking through the concepts learned in this chapter such as identifying the data type for each field and confirming a data dictionary exists.

Next is the supporting data from *FiveThirtyEight*, which is a data journalism site providing analytic content from sports to politics. What I like about their process is the offer of transparency behind the news stories published by exposing open GitHub links to their source data and discussions about their methodology behind the data.

Another important open source for data would be *The World Bank*, which offers a plethora of options to consume or produce data across the world to help to improve life through data. Most of the datasets are licensed under a **Creative Commons license**, which governs the terms of how and when data can be used, but making them freely available opens up opportunities to blend public and private data together with significant time savings.

Summary

Let's look back at what we learned in this chapter and the skills obtained before we move forward. First, we covered a brief history of data analysis and the technological evolution of data by paying homage to the people and milestone events that made working with data possible using modern tools and techniques. We walked through an example of how to summarize these events using a data visual trend chart that showed how recent technology innovations have transformed the data industry.

We focused on why data has become important to make decisions from both a consumer and producer perspective by discussing the concepts for identifying and classifying data using structured, semi-structured, and unstructured examples and the **3Vs** of big data: **Volume**, **Velocity**, and **Variety**.

We answered the question of what makes a good data analyst using the techniques of KYD, VOC, and ABA.

Then, we went deeper into understanding *data types* by walking through the differences between numbers (integer and float) versus strings (text, time, dates, and coordinates). This included breaking down data classifications (continuous, categorical, and discrete) and understanding data attribute types.

We wrapped up this chapter by introducing the concept of *data literacy* and its importance to the consumers and producers of data by improving communication between them.

In our next chapter, we will get more hands-on by installing and setting up an environment for data analysis and so begin the journey of applying the concepts learned about data.

Further reading

Here are some links that you can refer to for gathering more information about the following topics:

- America's Grow-a-Row: `https://www.americasgrowarow.org/wp-content/uploads/2019/09/AGAR-2018-Annual-Report.pdf`
- NIST Big Data Interoperability Framework: `https://bigdatawg.nist.gov/_uploadfiles/NIST.SP.1500-1.pdf`
- Google Drive FAQ: `https://support.google.com/drive/answer/37603?hl=en`
- Python Data Analysis for Beginners Guide GitHub repository: `https://github.com/mwintjen/Python_Data_Analysis_Beginners_Guide`
- *Dimensional Modeling Techniques* by Dr. Ralph Kimball from his book, *The Data Warehouse Toolkit*: `https://www.kimballgroup.com/data-warehouse-business-intelligence-resources/kimball-techniques/dimensional-modeling-techniques/`
- IBM Dictionary of Computing: `http://portal.acm.org/citation.cfm?id=541721`
- Kaggle datasets: `https://www.kaggle.com/datasets`
- FiveThirtyEight datasets: `https://data.fivethirtyeight.com/`
- The World Bank Data sources: `https://data.worldbank.org/`
- The Creative Commons license information: `https://creativecommons.org/`
- The Data Literacy Project site: `https://thedataliteracyproject.org/`

2
Overview of Python and Installing Jupyter Notebook

Now that you have a better understanding of concepts behind data literacy and the evolution of data analysis, let's set up our own environment to allow you to work with data. In this chapter, we are going to provide an introduction to the Python programming language along with a popular tool called Jupyter Notebook that's used to run commands for data analysis. We will walk through the installation process step by step and discuss key concepts to understand why they are required for data analysis. By the end of this chapter, you will have a workstation available to run a `hello world` program that will help in building your confidence to move forward into deeper concepts.

In this chapter, we will cover the following:

- Installing Python and using Jupyter Notebook
- Storing and retrieving data files
- Hello World! – running your first Python code
- Exploring Python packages

Technical requirements

Here's the GitHub repository of this book: `https://github.com/PacktPublishing/Practical-Data-Analysis-using-Jupyter-Notebook/tree/master/Chapter02`.

Further, you can download and install the required software from the following link: `https://www.anaconda.com/products/individual`.

Installing Python and using Jupyter Notebook

I'm going to start by admitting this chapter may become obsolete in the future because installing open source software on your workstation can be a painful process and, in some cases, is being replaced by preinstalled virtual machines or cloud versions. For example, Microsoft offers a free Azure subscription option for a cloud-hosted Jupyter Notebook.

Understanding all of the dependencies of software versions, hardware, **Operating System (OS)** differences, and library dependencies can be complex. Further, your IT department rules on software installations in enterprise environments may have security restrictions that prohibit access to your workstation filesystem. In all likelihood, with more innovation in cloud computing, most of the steps will already be done ahead of time, eliminating the need to install software altogether.

With that said, I'm going to walk you through the process of installing Python and Jupyter Notebook, pointing out tips and pitfalls to educate you on key concepts along the way. I would compare using these technology tools to work with data to driving a car. The ability to drive should not be dependent on your ability to repair the car engine! Just knowing that you need an engine should be sufficient to drive and move forward. So, my focus is on setting up your workstation for data analysis quickly without focusing on the layers of details behind these powerful technologies.

The open source project that created the Jupyter Notebook app evolved from iPython back in 2014. Many of the features that existed in iPython still exist today in Jupyter, for example, the interactive GUI to run Python commands and parallel processing. There is a kernel to control the input/output between your computer's CPU, memory, and filesystem. Finally, there's also the feature of a notebook that collects all of the commands, code, charts, and comments in a single shareable file with the .ipynb extension.

Just to give some context of how popular Jupyter notebooks have become for data analysis, I discovered a public GitHub repository by Peter Parente that collects a daily count of the number of public .pynb files found in GitHub since 2014. The growth is exponential, as the number grew from just over 65,000 to 5.7 million by November 2019, which means it has been doubling every year for the last five years!

The first prerequisite to using a Jupyter notebook is installing Python. We are going to use Python version 3.3 or greater and there are two methods you can use to install the software: a direct download or a package manager. A direct download will have more control over the installation on your workstation but then it requires additional time to manage dependent libraries. That said, using a package manager to install Python has become preferred method, hence, I cover this method in this chapter.

> Python is a powerful coding language with support on multiple OS platforms, including Windows, macOS, and Linux. I encourage you to read more about the history of this powerful software language and the creator, Guido van Rossum.

Python, at its core, is a command-line programming language, so you must be comfortable with running some commands from a prompt. When we have finished installation, you will have a Python command-line window, which will look like the following screenshot if your workstation has Windows OS:

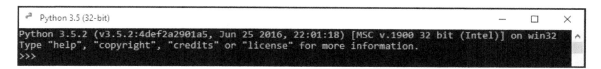

Think of the Python installation as a means to an end because what we really want to use as data analysts is a Jupyter notebook, which is also known as an **Integrated Development Environment** (IDE) used to run code and call libraries in a self-contained **Graphical User Interface** (**GUI**).

Since I recommend using a package manager for installation, the first decision you must make is which package manager to use for the installation on your computer. A package manager is designed to streamline the versions and layers of dependencies between the open source libraries, your OS, and software. The most common ones are `conda`, `pip`, or `docker`.

From researching the differences, I prefer `conda` over `pip` for someone just getting started, especially if you are unfamiliar with running command-line commands and managing software installs directly on your PC. For an app-store-like experience, where all you have to do is download, install with a few prompts, and then launch the software, I would recommend Anaconda especially since it includes Python, several popular libraries required for data analysis, and Jupyter all as part of the download package.

Remember, the goal is to get Jupyter Notebook up and running on your workstation, so feel free to choose installation alternatives, especially if you prefer a **Command-Line Interface (CLI)**.

Installing Anaconda

Follow these steps to install Anaconda. For this walkthrough, I have selected a Windows OS installer but the screenshots of installation will be similar regardless of which one is selected:

1. Download the software by choosing which installer is required based on your workstation's OS. To do this, navigate to the **Anaconda Distribution** page, which should look similar to the following screenshot and is found on `https://www.anaconda.com/`:

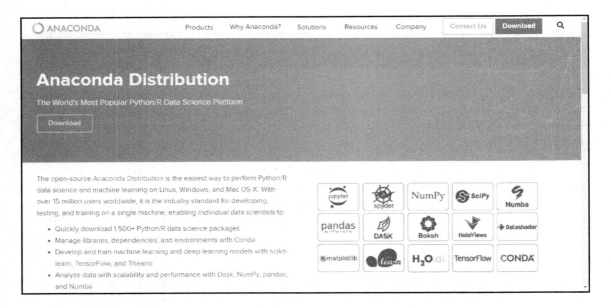

2. You should see the **Setup** wizard as shown in the following screenshot after you download the software and launch the installer on your PC:

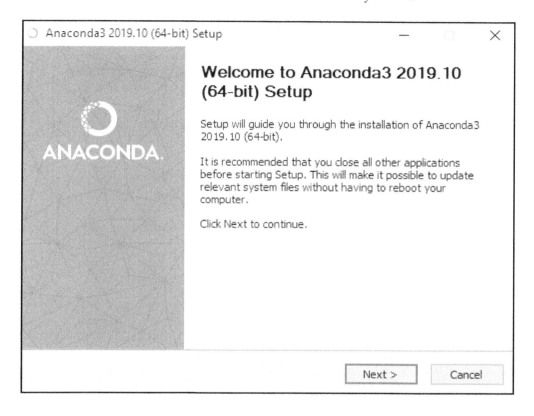

3. Select the default options in the install wizard and you should see a message similar to the following screenshot:

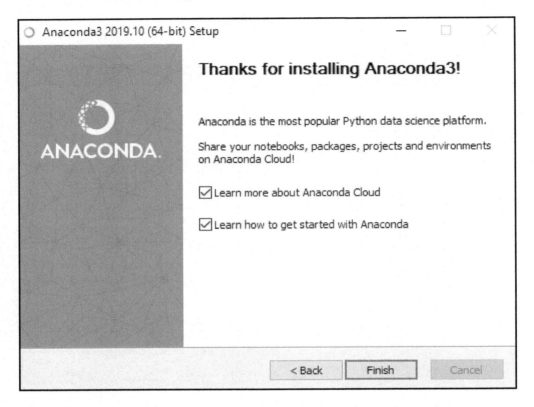

4. Now that Anaconda has completed the installation, you must launch the **Anaconda Navigator** application from your PC, which is shown in the following screenshot using a Windows OS. Since there are multiple OS options available such as Windows, macOS, or Ubuntu, your screen will vary from the following screenshot:

I think of the installation process as similar to why an artist would need to buy a canvas, easel, and supplies to begin painting. Now that we have a working Python environment installed and available to use called Anaconda, you are ready to launch Jupyter and create your first notebook.

Running Jupyter and installing Python packages for data analysis

Once the software is installed on your PC, launching your Jupyter notebook can be done in either of two ways. The first is via a command-line prompt with the `jupyter notebook` command from **Anaconda Prompt**, which will look similar to the following screenshot:

```
Anaconda Prompt - jupyter notebook                                    —    □    ×
Activating environment "C:\Program Files\Anaconda3"...

[Anaconda3] C:\Users\mwintjen>jupyter notebook
[I 07:48:06.541 NotebookApp] Serving notebooks from local directory: C:\Users\mwintjen
[I 07:48:06.541 NotebookApp] 0 active kernels
[I 07:48:06.541 NotebookApp] The Jupyter Notebook is running at: http://localhost:8888/
[I 07:48:06.542 NotebookApp] Use Control-C to stop this server and shut down all kernels (twice to skip confirmation).
```

You can also use the **Anaconda Navigator** software and click the **Launch** button from **My Applications** in Jupyter Notebook, which is shown in the following screenshot:

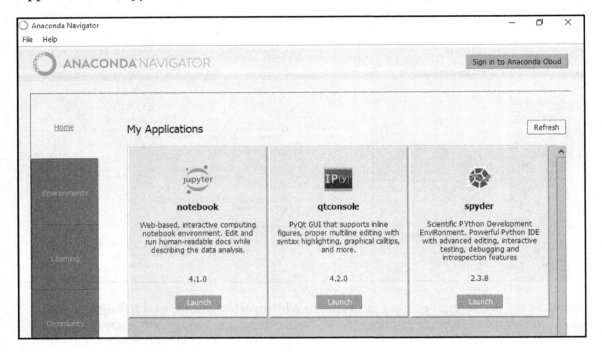

Either option will launch a new web browser session with the `http://localhost:8888/tree` URL, which is known as the Jupyter dashboard. If you do not see something similar to the following screenshot, you may need to reinstall the Anaconda software or check whether firewall ports are blocking commands or dependencies. In an enterprise setting, you may have to review your corporate policies or request IT support:

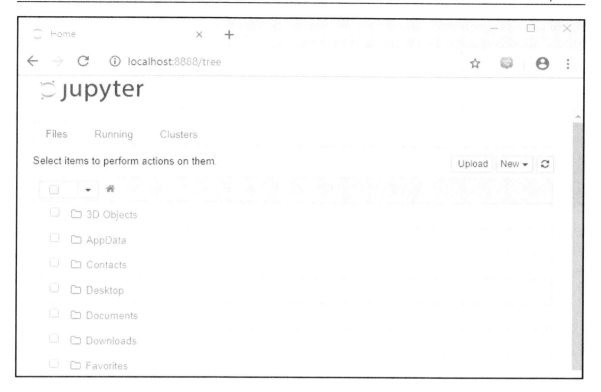

TIP

If you would like to try JupyterLab instead of Jupyter Notebook, either solution will work. JupyterLab uses the exact same Notebook server and file format as the classic Jupyter Notebook so that it is fully compatible with the existing notebooks and kernels. The classic Notebook and JupyterLab can run side to side on the same computer. You can easily switch between the two interfaces.

Notice that Jupyter defaults with access to your workstation's filesystem based on how it was installed. This should be sufficient in most cases but if you would like to change the default project home/root folder, you can easily change it using Anaconda Prompt. Just run the cd command to change directory before you type the jupyter notebook command.

For example, I created a project folder on my local c:\ drive path on my Windows PC first and then ran the Anaconda Prompt window with the following commands:

```
>cd \
>cd projects
>jupyter notebook
```

If you walk through this example, your Command Prompt window should look like the following screenshot if you're using Windows OS:

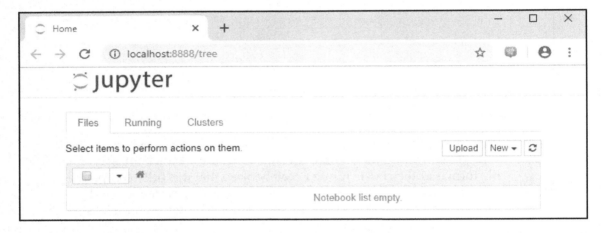

Once complete, the list of files and folders displayed in the Jupyter session will be blank and your session will look similar to the following screenshot:

You should now have the Jupyter software actively running on your workstation, ready to walk through all of the features available, which we will cover next.

Storing and retrieving data files

What I like about using Jupyter is that it is a self-contained solution for data analysis. What I mean by that statement is you can interact with the filesystem to add, update, and delete folders and files plus run Python commands all in one place. As you continue using this tool, I think you will find it much easier to navigate by staying in one ecosystem compared to hopping between multiple windows, apps, or systems on your workstation.

Let's begin with getting comfortable navigating the menu options to add, edit, or delete files. Jupyter defaults the dashboard by listing all files and folders that are accessible on your workstation from the directory paths it was installed. This is can be configured to change the starting folder but we will use the Windows default. In the following screenshot, I have highlighted the important sections of the Jupyter dashboard with letters for easy reference:

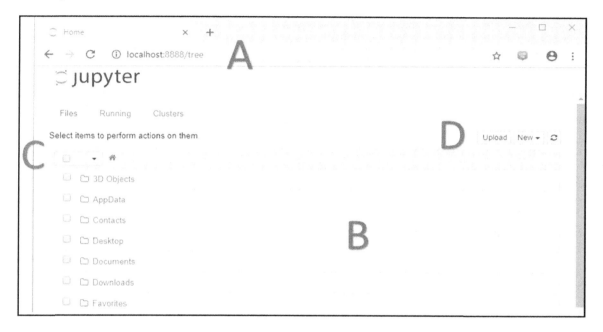

In the **A** section, the URL defaults to `http://localhost:888/tree` when running on your personal workstation. This URL will change if the notebook is hosted on a server or cloud. Notice, as you make selections to folders or files in the **B** section, the URL address will change to follow the location and path of your selections.

In the **B** section, you will find a hierarchy of accessible folders or files that are visible to the dashboard. If you click on any file, it will attempt to open it in the editor, whether or not the file is usable by Jupyter. Readable file extensions by the editor include images in formats such as `.jpeg`, `.png`, and `.svg`; semi-structured data files such as `.json`, `.csv`, and `.xml`; and code such as `.html`, `.py` (Python), and `.js` (JavaScript). Note that the URL path will change from the `tree` parameter word to `edit` as it opens the file.

If the editor does not recognize a file, it will provide an error in the first line and tell you why, similar to the following screenshot:

In the **C** section, you can select and filter one or more files or folders displayed on the dashboard. This can be used to organize your project workspace when creating multiple notebooks and organizing data files for analysis. Once any file or folder is selected, the title Select items to perform actions on them will change to the action buttons **Rename** and **Duplicate** and a red trashcan icon, which deletes the files or folder, as shown in the following screenshot:

In the dashboard, you will also notice the tabs labeled **Files**, **Running**, and **Clusters**. These are used by the Jupyter app to keep you oriented and track processes that are actively running. **Clusters** is an advanced feature and beyond the scope of this book. We have already covered the **Files** tab from section **B**.

Let's discuss the **Running** tab. It has two sections: **Terminals**, which would be system shell commands such as Powershell in the Windows OS, and **Notebooks**, which will show you all active notebooks that are in use. Once we create a few notebooks, I encourage you to refresh the browser to see which notebook files are active to better understand this feature. Use the **Shutdown** button if it becomes necessary to kill an active notebook that is unresponsive or taking up too much of your computer resources (CPU/RAM).

In the **D** section, you will see an **Upload** button that allows you to add files to the dashboard in any folder you have navigated. The **New** button includes a submenu to create a **Text File**, **Folder**, or **Python 3 Notebook**.

Hello World! – running your first Python code

Now that we have a better understanding of the dashboard and its navigation, let's create our first notebook and run some Python code. The easiest method is to click on the **New** button and select **Python 3** in the submenu. This will open a new tab or window in your browser that looks similar to the following screenshot:

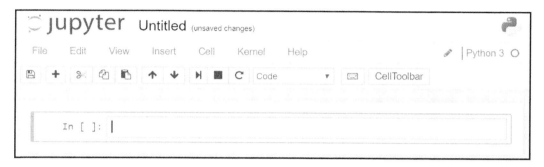

I recommend renaming the **Untitled** files of any notebook to make it easier to find them later. To do this, select **Rename** from the **File** menu, as shown in the following screenshot, and rename it `hello_world` or a relevant project name. Once you click on the **OK** button, the title bar at the top of the page will display the new name:

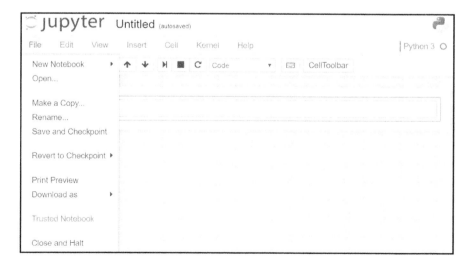

By renaming the notebook, a new file with the .ipynb extension will be created, which contains all of the contents in JSON format. This helps make the notebook file shareable to others and helps with version control, which is an audit trail of changes made in the file.

You can view the actual JSON metadata contents by selecting **Edit Notebook Metadata** from the **Edit** menu. The results will look similar to the following screenshot:

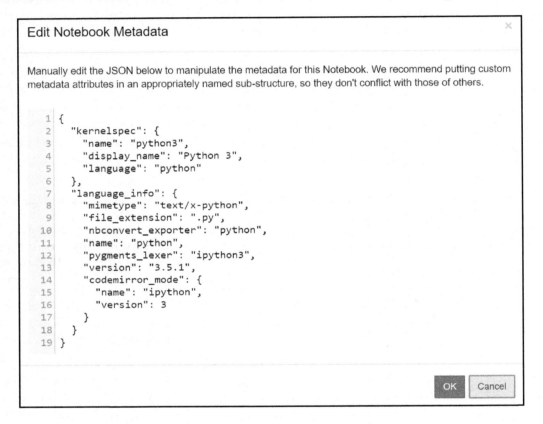

The UI for the notebook looks very similar to other modern web software used today as it was designed for easy navigation. The following menu options are easy to use icons that are collectively called the **Notebook Toolbar**, which supports keyboard shortcuts for optimal workflow as you get more comfortable using the tool. You can find the **User Interface Tour** and **Keyboard Shortcuts** in the **Help** menu, as shown in the following screenshot. I recommend going through them to take a look at all of the features available:

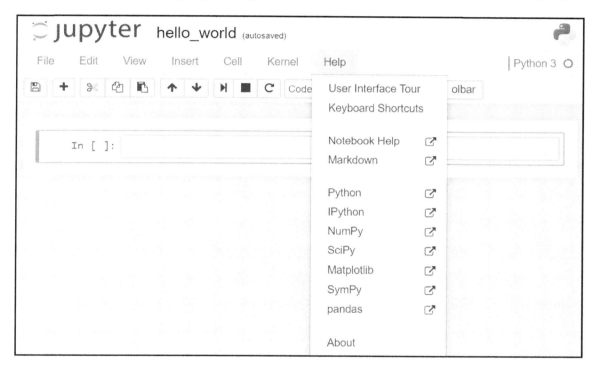

Once you feel comfortable with the **Help** menu options, let's write your first code by typing in the `print("hello world")` command in the notebook cell, which has a default of `In [] :`. Remember, if you are using a mouse to navigate the notebook, you must click on the cell to select it and have a cursor appear.

Pressing the *Enter* key after a command will only create a second line for more input. You must either use a keyboard shortcut, the **Cell** menu, or a Toolbar icon to execute any command.

Once you have entered the `print("hello world")` command in the cell and clicked on any one of the following options. The options to run the command in any cell are as follows:

- Click the [M] button from the toolbar.
- Select **Run Cells** from the **Cell** menu.
- Press the *Shift + Enter* or *Ctrl + Enter* keys.

The screen should look similar to the following screenshot:

Congratulations, you have created your first Jupyter notebook and run your first command! Click on the **Close and Halt** option from the **File** menu to return to the dashboard.

Creating a project folder hierarchy

Now that we have covered the basics, let's walk through a directory to find a particular file and create a project folder hierarchy to prepare for future data analysis learning modules. I recommend creating a starting `projects` folder on your workstation to keep all of your notebooks and data organized. A standard enterprise directory structure will vary by company but setting up a basic structure with subfolders makes the process portable and helps with sharing work with others. An example project folder template is shown in the following screenshot:

```
projectname
|
|--- README.md          <- About the data analysis project and summary information
|--- data
|    |--- source        <- Downloaded source raw data files as received
|    |--- wip           <- Work-In-Progress folder used for changes to the source data files
|    |--- target        <- Output data files after processed
|
|--- notebooks          <- Any Jupyter notebook files
|
|--- references         <- Data dictionary, detail project artifacts and supporting information
```

 Throughout this book, I will use chapter numbers as `projectname` to make each directory subfolder, such as `data` and `notebooks`, modular, independent, and easy to follow. Your workstation directory structure and tree should match with this book's GitHub repository to make it easier to synchronize your files and folders.

In the classic *do as I say, not as I do* fashion and because of limitations with relative paths across different OS versions, the examples use the same folder to prevent errors throughout this book. To proceed, you can either clone or download all of the files and subfolders from this book's GitHub repository, create all of the folders and files in the Jupyter dashboard, or create them on your workstation. Once completed, your project folder for this chapter should look like the following screenshot:

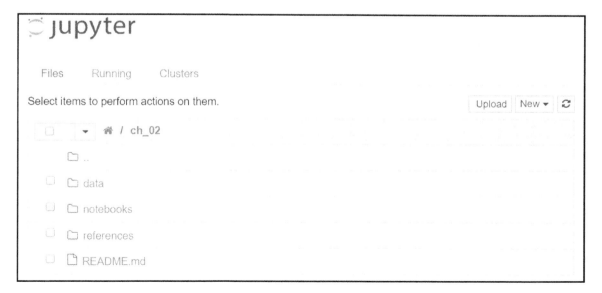

Uploading a file

Now that we have a project folder, let's walk through the following steps to upload a file for analysis. You must download the file ahead of time from the GitHub repository URL found in the *Technical requirements* section:

1. Click on the `data` folder name.
2. Click on the `source` subfolder name.
3. Click the **Upload** button at the top-right side of the screen.
4. Select `evolution_of_data_analysis.csv`.

5. Click the blue **Upload** button to proceed. Once done, you'll see a file in the dashboard, as shown in the following screenshot:

6. Navigate back to the `notebooks` folder and create a new notebook file by clicking on the **New** menu. Similar to the `hello_world` example, select **Python 3** in the submenu to create a default `Untitled` notebook.

   As mentioned earlier, I always rename the `Untitled` notebook before moving forward, so rename the notebook `evolution_of_data_analysis`.

7. To read data from a file in the notebook, you must run a few Python commands. These can be run all in one cell or as three separate cell entries. The commands to open the CSV file we uploaded earlier are as follows:

```
f = open("../data/source/evolution_of_data_analysis.csv","r")
print(f.read())
f.close()
```

Let's walk through the commands line by line. First, we assigned an open command value of the file to the f variable to shorten the length of additional commands in the next few lines. Notice the evolution_of_data_analysis.csv file includes the directory path of "../data/source/", which is required because the location of the active notebook, evolution_of_data_analysis, is in a different folder. The open command also includes a parameter of r, which means we only want to read the file and not edit the content.

The second line is to print the contents of the file by passing the f variable along with the read() function. This will display the results in the output cell, which will be similar to the following screenshot:

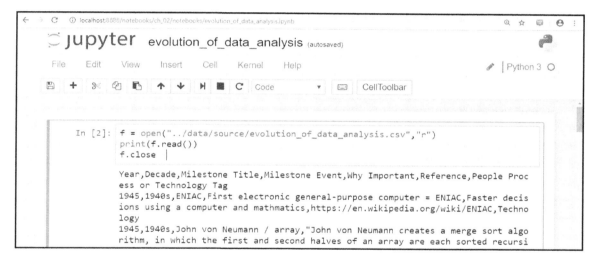

The last line is a best practice to close the file to avoid any conflicts using the file later or in the filesystem of your OS. Once you verify that you can see the contents of the CSV file in your notebook, click on the **Close and Halt** option from the **File** menu to return to the dashboard.

Exploring Python packages

Before wrapping up this chapter, let's explore the different Python packages required with data analysis and validate they are available to use in the Jupyter Notebook app. These packages have evolved over time and are open source so programmers can contribute and improve the source code.

The version of the Python packages will increment over time depending on when you install `conda` or `pip` (package manager) on your machine. If you receive errors running commands, validate they match the versions used in this book.

We will go into more depth about each individual package as we use their awesome features in future chapters. The focus in this chapter is to verify the specific libraries are available, and there are a few different approaches to use such as inspecting the installation folder for specific files on your workstation or running commands from a Python command line. I find the easiest method is to run a few simple commands in a new notebook.

Navigate back to the `notebooks` folder and create a new notebook file by clicking on the **New** menu and select **Python 3** in the submenu to create a default `Untitled` notebook. To stay consistent with best practices, be sure to rename the notebook `verify_python_packages` before moving forward.

Checking for pandas

The steps to verify whether each Python package is available are similar with slight variations to the code. The first one will be `pandas`, which will make it easier to complete common data analysis techniques such as pivoting, cleaning, merging and grouping datasets all in one place without going back to the source of record.

To verify whether the `pandas` library is available in Jupyter, follow these steps:

1. Type in `import pandas as pd` in the In []: cell.
2. Run the cell using the preferred method discussed earlier in the *Installing Python and using Jupyter Notebook* section:

   - Click the button from the toolbar.
   - Select **Run Cells** from the **Cell** menu.
   - Press the *Shift + Enter* or *Ctrl + Enter* keys.

3. Type in the `np.__version__` command in the next In []: cell.
4. Run the cell using the preferred method from *step 2*.
5. Verify the output cell displayed as Out [].

The version of `pandas` should be **0.18.0** or greater.

Now you will repeat these steps for each of the following required packages used in this book: numpy, sklearn, matplotlib, and scipy. Note that I have used the commonly known shortcut names for each library to make it consistent with best practices found in the industry.

For example, pandas has been shortened to pd, so as you call features from each library, you can just use the shortcut name.

Additional packages can and should be used depending on the type of analysis required, variations of the data input, and advancement of the Python ecosystem.

Checking for NumPy

NumPy is a powerful and common mathematical extension of Python created to perform fast numeric calculations against a list of values that is known as an array. We will learn more about the power of NumPy features in Chapter 3, *Getting Started with NumPy*.

To verify whether the numpy library is available in Jupyter, follow these steps:

1. Type in import numpy as np in the In []: cell.
2. Run the cell using the preferred method discussed earlier in the *Installing Python and using Jupyter Notebook* section:

    -   Click the button from the toolbar.
    -   Select **Run Cells** from the **Cell** menu.
    -   Press the *Shift + Enter* or *Ctrl + Enter* keys.

3. Type in the np.__version__ command in the next In []: cell.
4. Run the cell using the preferred method from *step 2*.
5. Verify the output cell displayed as Out [].

The version of NumPy should be **1.10.4** or greater.

Checking for sklearn

`sklearn` is an advanced open source data science library used for clustering and regression analysis. While we will not leverage all of the advanced capabilities of this library, having it installed will make it easier for future lessons.

To verify if the `sklearn` library is available in Jupyter, follow these steps:

1. Type in `import sklearn as sk` in the `In []:` cell.
2. Run the cell using the preferred method discussed earlier in the *Installing Python and using Jupyter Notebook* section:

    - Click the button from the toolbar.
    - Select **Run Cells** from the **Cell** menu.
    - Press the *Shift + Enter* or *Ctrl + Enter* keys.

3. Type in the `sk.__version__` command in the next `In []:` cell.
4. Run the cell using the preferred method from *step 2*.
5. Verify the output cell displayed as `Out []`.

 The version of `sklearn` should be **0.17.1** or greater.

Checking for Matplotlib

The **Matplotlib** Python library package is used for data visualization and plotting charts using Python.

To verify whether the `matplotlib` library is available in Jupyter, follow these steps:

1. Type in `import matplotlib as mp` in the `In []:` cell.
2. Run the cell using the preferred method discussed earlier in the *Installing Python and using Jupyter Notebook* section:

    - Click the button from the toolbar.
    - Select **Run Cells** from the **Cell** menu.
    - Press the *Shift + Enter* or *Ctrl + Enter* keys.

3. Type in the `mp.__version__` command in the next `In []:` cell.
4. Run the cell using the preferred method from *step 2*.
5. Verify the output cell displayed as `Out []`.

The version of `matplotlib` should be **1.5.1** or greater.

Checking for SciPy

SciPy is a library that's dependent on NumPy and includes additional mathematical functions used for the analysis of data.

To verify whether the `scipy` library is available in Jupyter, follow these steps:

1. Type in `import scipy as sc` in the `In []:` cell.
2. Run the cell using the preferred method discussed earlier in the *Installing Python and using Jupyter Notebook* section:

    * Click the button from the toolbar.
    * Select **Run Cells** from the **Cell** menu.
    * Press the *Shift + Enter* or *Ctrl + Enter* keys.

3. Type in the `sc.__version__` command in the next `In []:` cell.
4. Run the cell using the preferred method from *step 2*.
5. Verify the output cell displayed as `Out []`.

The version of `scipy` should be **0.17.0** or greater.

Once you have completed all of the steps, your notebook should look similar to the following screenshot:

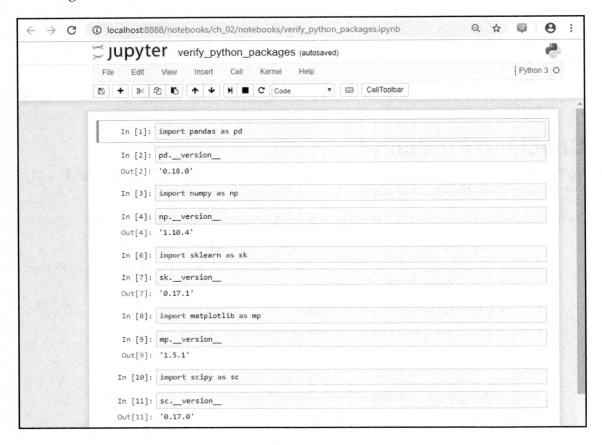

Summary

Congratulations, we have now set up an environment that's ready to work with data. We started by installing Python and the Jupyter Notebook app by using the `conda` package installer called Anaconda. Next, we launched the Jupyter app and discussed how to navigate all of the features of both the dashboard and a notebook. We created a working directory that can be used as a template for all data analysis projects.

We ran our first Python code by creating a `hello_world` notebook and walk through the core features available in Jupyter. Finally, we verified and explored different Python packages (NumPy, pandas, sklearn, Matplotlib, and SciPy) and their purposes in data analysis. You should now be comfortable and ready to run additional Python code commands in Jupyter Notebook.

In the next chapter, we will expand your data literacy skills with some hands-on lessons. We will discuss the foundational library of NumPy, which is used for the analysis of data structures called arrays.

Future reading

Here are some links that you can refer to gain more information about the topics related to this chapter:

- History of Python: `https://docs.python.org/3/license.html`
- Differences between the `pip` and `conda` Python package managers: `https://stackoverflow.com/questions/20994716/what-is-the-difference-between-pip-and-conda`
- Understanding `conda` and `pip`: `https://www.anaconda.com/understanding-conda-and-pip/`
- Jupyter Notebook tutorial: `https://www.dataquest.io/blog/jupyter-notebook-tutorial/`
- Comparison of cloud-based Jupyter Notebook services: `https://discourse.jupyter.org/t/in-depth-comparison-of-cloud-based-services-that-run-jupyter-notebook/460/7`
- Introduction to JupyterLab: `https://ipython-books.github.io/36-introducing-jupyterlab/`
- Reference information to change the starting folder in Jupyter: `https://stackoverflow.com/questions/35254852/how-to-change-the-jupyter-start-up-folder`
- History of the Jupyter project: `https://github.com/jupyter/design/wiki/Jupyter-Logo`
- Reference information about the location of files and directories after installing Jupyter: `https://jupyter.readthedocs.io/en/latest/projects/jupyter-directories.html`
- Handling different file types in Jupyter: `https://jupyterlab.readthedocs.io/en/stable/user/file_formats.html`
- Microsoft-hosted Jupyter Notebook site: `https://notebooks.azure.com/`
- Count of public Jupyter notebooks on GitHub: `https://github.com/parente/nbestimate`

Getting Started with NumPy 3

This chapter teaches one of the most powerful Python libraries for data analysis: NumPy. You will learn key functions used for analysis and we'll also discuss arrays and matrix data structures using NumPy. Finally, we'll walk through some practical examples that serve as a foundation for future learning modules.

In this chapter, we will cover the following:

- Understanding a Python NumPy array and its importance
- Differences between single and multiple dimensional arrays
- Making your first NumPy array
- Practical use cases of NumPy and arrays

Technical requirements

Here's the GitHub repository of this book: `https://github.com/PacktPublishing/Practical-Data-Analysis-using-Jupyter-Notebook/tree/master/Chapter03`.

You can download and install the required software from the following link: `https://www.anaconda.com/products/individual`.

Understanding a Python NumPy array and its importance

Several Python courses on NumPy focus on building programming or statistical examples intended to create a foundation for data science.

While this is important, I want to stay true to anyone who is just getting started working with data so the focus will be the practical usage of Python and NumPy for data analysis. This means not all of the features of NumPy will be covered, so I encourage you to learn more by looking at resources in the *Further reading* section. The history of the NumPy library has evolved from what was originally named **Numerical Python**. It was created as an open source project in 2001 by David Ascher, Paul Dubois, Konrad Hinsen, Jim Hugunin, and Travis Oliphant. According to the documentation, the purpose was to extend Python to allow the manipulation of large sets of objects organized in a grid-like fashion.

Python does not support arrays out of the box but does have a similar feature called **lists**, which has limitations in performance and scalability.

Additional research on the subject of why NumPy was created points to a need for efficiency in memory and storage when processing large volumes of data. Today, NumPy can be found as a dependent library for millions of Python projects in a public search of GitHub, including thousands of examples that handle image manipulation used for facial recognition.

The NumPy library is all about arrays, so let's walk through what an array is and why it is important. Any computer science or programming class I have taken has always included arrays. I was first introduced to an array before I even understood the concept thirty-seven years ago when I was introduced to a computer, the Apple IIe, in Mrs. Sherman's 4th-grade classroom.

One of the educational software available to run on the Apple IIe was called *Logo,* which was a programming language that allowed you to write simple commands to control the movement of a cursor on the computer monitor. To make the process more appealing to a younger audience, the commands allowed you to create geometric shapes and print values represented by a turtle. In *Logo,* arrays used the `list` command, which groups together one or more words or numbers as a single object that can be referenced during the same session. You can still find emulators available that allow you to run the *Logo* programming language, which was a fun walk down memory lane for me that I hope you will enjoy as well.

A more formal definition of an array is it is a container used to store a list of values or collections of values called elements. The elements must be defined with a data type that applies to all of the values in an array, and that data type cannot be changed during the creation of the array. This sounds like a rigid rule but does create consistency between all of the data values. There is some flexibility using the data types of arrays found in the NumPy library, which are known as dtype (data types). The most common dtype are Boolean for true/false values, char for words/string values, float for decimal numbers, and int for integers. A full list of supported data types could be found in the documentation found in the *Further reading* section.

Some examples of an array can be a list of numbers from 1 to 10 or a list of characters such as stock tickers, APPL, IBM, and AMZN. Even board games such as *Battleship* and chess are examples of arrays where pieces are placed on the board and identified with the interaction of letters and numbers. Arrays in NumPy support complex data types including sentences but remember, you must keep the data type defined and consistent to avoid errors. Arrays come in all shapes and sizes, so let's walk through a few examples.

Differences between single and multiple dimensional arrays

If the array only has one dimension, it would represent that list of values in a single row or column (but not both). The following example shows a one-dimensional array assigned to variable named 1d_array:

```
1d_array = ([1, 2, 3, 4, 5])
```

A two-dimensional array, also known as a matrix, would be any combination of multiple rows and columns. The following equation is an example of a two-dimensional array:

```
2d_array =
([1, 'a'],
 [2, 'b'],
 [3, 'c'],
 [4, 'e'],
 [5, 'f'])
```

You may have already realized from the examples that a structured data table that is made up of rows and columns is a two-dimensional array! Now you can see why understanding the array concept builds the foundation for data analysis against structured data.

Once an array is defined, it is available for use in calculations or manipulation by referencing it during the same session such as when changing the sequence of the values or even replacing values as needed. Arrays have a multitude of uses in programming so I want to stay focused on specific use cases related to data analysis.

Understanding arrays goes beyond just a simple table of rows and columns. The examples discussed have either one or two dimensions. If the array has more than one dimension, you can reference the values along the axis (*X*, *Y*, or *Z*).

With the `numpy` library package, the core feature is the `ndarray` object, which allows for any number of dimensions, which is called *n*-dimensional. This refers to the shape and size of the array across multiple axes. Hence, a 3D cube with an *X*, *Y*, and *Z* axis can also be created using NumPy arrays. A scatter plot visualization would be a useful way to analyze the type of data, which we will cover in `Chapter 9`, *Plotting, Visualization, and Storytelling*, with some examples.

Some other key features of NumPy include the following:

- The ability to perform mathematical calculations against big datasets
- Using operators to compare values such as greater than and less than
- Combining values in two or more arrays together
- Referencing individual elements in the sequence from how they are stored

Visual representations of the different types of arrays using blocks to represent the elements are shown in the following diagrams. The following diagram is a one-dimensional array with three elements, which is also known as a vector when dealing with ordinal numbers or a tuple when working with ordered pairs. The first element of any array is referenced with an index value of 0:

The following diagram is a two-dimensional array, which is also known as a matrix. This matrix builds from the first one-dimensional array but now has two rows with three columns for a total of six elements:

An *n*-dimensional array could be represented as a cube similar to the one in the following diagram. This *n*-dimensional array continues to build from the first two examples and now includes a third dimension or axis:

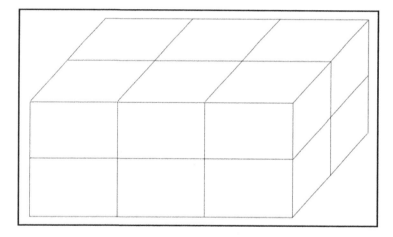

I find the best way to learn is to get hands-on and comfortable using the commands to work with the data, so let's launch a Jupyter notebook and walk through some simple examples.

Making your first NumPy array

The easiest example to create a one-dimensional array would be a straightforward command. After renaming your Jupyter notebook from `Untitled` to `array_basics`, the first thing to do is to import the `numpy` library into your active session by typing in `import numpy as np` in the `In []` command and running the cell.

I like to run this line first to ensure the library is installed properly so if you receive an error, double-check and ensure that conda or pip was set up correctly. See Chapter 2, *Overview of Python and Installing Jupyter Notebook*, for help.

Next, you want to assign the array object a variable name so you can reference it in future commands. It is common to use single character values such as a or x as a shortcut for your array but for just getting started, let's use something more descriptive, such as my_first_array for easier reference. To the right of the equals sign, we reference the numpy method using np.array followed by a parentheses and square brackets, which encapsulate the assigned values for each element. After running the command, to ensure the syntax is correct, the last command will be to print the array to ensure the output matches the input. Once completed, the results should look similar to the following screenshot:

```
In [1]:  import numpy as np

In [2]:  my_first_array = np.array([1,2,3])

In [3]:  print(my_first_array)
         [1 2 3]
```

Now that we have an array available, let's walk through how you can verify the contents.

Useful array functions

Some useful commands to run against any array in NumPy to give you metadata (data about the data) are included here. The commands are being run specifically against the variable named my_first_array:

- my_first_array.shape: It provides the array dimensions.
- my_first_array.size: This shows the number of array elements (similar to the number of cells in a table).
- len(my_first_array): This shows the length of the array.
- my_first_array.dtype.name: This provides the data type of the array elements.
- my_first_array.astype(int): This converts an array into a different data type—in this example, an integer that will display as int64.

If you run the preceding commands in Jupyter, your notebook should look similar to the following screenshot:

```
In [1]: import numpy as np

In [2]: my_first_array = np.array([1,2,3])

In [3]: print(my_first_array)
        [1 2 3]

In [4]: my_first_array.shape
Out[4]: (3,)

In [5]: my_first_array.size
Out[5]: 3

In [6]: len(my_first_array)
Out[6]: 3

In [7]: my_first_array.dtype.name
Out[7]: 'int64'

In [8]: my_first_array.astype(int)
Out[8]: array([1, 2, 3])
```

The shape, size, and length of a one-dimensional array will all output the same result.

To reference individual elements in the array, you use the square brackets along with an ordinal whole number, which is called the array index. If you are familiar with the Microsoft Excel function, vlookup, the behavior to reference the index of the data you want to retrieve has a similar concept. The first element in any array using NumPy would be 0 so if you wanted to just display the first value from the prior example, you would type in the print(my_first_array[0]) command, which will output 1 on the screen, as shown in the following screenshot:

```
In [9]: print(my_first_array[0])
        1
```

Since the array we are working with in this example has numeric values, we can also do some mathematical functions against the values.

 Note the default `dtype` of the array in NumPy is `float` but if you don't define a data type when you first create it, Python will assign one based on the values assigned or provide an error message.

Some useful statistical functions you can run against numeric arrays that have `dtype` of `int` or `float` include the following:

- `my_first_array.sum()`: Sums all of the element values
- `my_first_array.min()`: Provides the minimum element value in the entire array
- `my_first_array.max()`: Provides the maximum element value in the entire array
- `my_first_array.mean()`: Provides the mean or average, which is the sum of the elements divided by the count of the elements

If you run these statistical commands against `my_first_array` in your notebook, the output will look similar to the following screenshot:

```
In [11]: my_first_array.sum()
Out[11]: 6

In [12]: my_first_array.min()
Out[12]: 1

In [13]: my_first_array.max()
Out[13]: 3

In [14]: my_first_array.mean()
Out[14]: 2.0
```

As you can see from these few examples, there are plenty of useful functions built into the NumPy library that will help you with data validation and quality checks during the analysis process. In the *Further reading* section, I have placed a link to a printable one-page cheat sheet for easy reference.

Practical use cases of NumPy and arrays

Let's walk through a practical use case for working with a one-dimensional array in data analysis. Here's the scenario—you are a data analyst who wants to know what is the highest daily closing price for a stock ticker for the current **Year To Date (YTD)**. To do this, you can use an array to store each value as an element, sort the price element from high to low, and then print the first element, which would display the highest price as the output value.

Before loading the file into Jupyter, it is best to inspect the file contents, which supports our **Know Your Data (KYD)** concept discussed in Chapter 1, *Fundamentals of Data Analysis*. The following screenshot is a comma-delimited, structured dataset with two columns. The file includes a header row with a Date field in the format of YYYY-MM-DD and a field labeled Close, which represents the closing price of the stock by the end of the trading day for this stock ticker. This data was downloaded from Yahoo Business, manually changed to exclude some columns, and then stored as a file in the comma-delimited format. The file name represents the ticker of the stock, so AAPL represents the Apple Company, which is a publicly-traded company on the **National Association of Securities Dealers Automated Quotations (NASDAQ)** stock exchange:

```
Date,Close
2019-01-02,157.919998
2019-01-03,142.190002
2019-01-04,148.259995
2019-01-07,147.929993
2019-01-08,150.75
2019-01-09,153.309998
2019-01-10,153.800003
2019-01-11,152.289993
2019-01-14,150
2019-01-15,153.070007
2019-01-16,154.940002
2019-01-17,155.860001
2019-01-18,156.820007
2019-01-22,153.300003
2019-01-23,153.919998
2019-01-24,152.699997
2019-01-25,157.759995
2019-01-28,156.300003
2019-01-29,154.679993
```

The first step would be to load the file that contains the data. I have placed this file in this book's GitHub repository for convenience, so go ahead and set up a new project folder using the best practices covered in Chapter 2, *Overview of Python and Installing Jupyter Notebook*, by launching a new Jupyter Notebook.

Working with the syntax of Python is explicit and case sensitive so don't be discouraged if the expected output is wrong or you receive an error message. In most cases, a simple change in the code will resolve the issue and you can re-run the command.

For this scenario, there are a few options to load data in an array using NumPy.

Assigning values to arrays manually

The first option would be to explicitly assign the values to an array manually, as shown in the following screenshot:

```
In [1]:  import numpy as np

In [2]:  input_stock_price_array = np.array([142.19,148.26,147.93,150.75,153.31,153.8,152.28,150,153.07,154.94])

In [10]: sorted_stock_price_array = np.sort(input_stock_price_array)[::-1]

In [16]: print('Closing stock price in order of day traded:    ', input_stock_price_array)
         print('Closing stock price in order from high to low: ', sorted_stock_price_array)

         Closing stock price in order of day traded:     [142.19 148.26 147.93 150.75 153.31 153.8  152.28 150.   153.07 154.94]
         Closing stock price in order from high to low:  [154.94 153.8  153.31 153.07 152.28 150.75 150.   148.26 147.93 142.19]

In [17]: print('Highest closing stock price: ', sorted_stock_price_array[0])

         Highest closing stock price:  154.94
```

This option is fine for small datasets, testing syntax, or other specific use cases but will be impractical when working with big data or multiple data files. We took a few shortcuts using this option by only typing in a sampling of ten values from the source file. Since all of the stock prices are numeric and have a consistent data type, we can use a one-dimensional array that has a default dtype of float.

The steps to reproduce this option are as follows:

1. Launch Jupyter and create a new Python notebook.
2. To stay consistent with best practices, be sure to rename the notebook highest_daily_closing_stock_price_option_1 before moving forward.
3. Type in the following command to import the numpy library in the notebook, input In []:, and run the cell:

   ```
   In []: import numpy as np
   ```

4. In the next input cell, add the following command to assign a NumPy array of values using the shortcut of np and assigning it to a variable named input_stock_price_array. Proceed by running the cell, which will *not* produce an output, Out []:

```
input_stock_price_array =
np.array([142.19,148.26,147.93,150.75,153.31,153.8,152.28,150,153.0
7,154.94])
```

5. In the next input In [] : cell, add the following command to assign a NumPy array of values to a variable named sorted_stock_price_array and run the cell. Similar to before, the result will *not* produce an output, Out []:

```
sorted_stock_price_array = np.sort(input_stock_price_array)[::-1]
```

6. Type in the following commands, which use the print() function to display the results of each of the array variables:

```
print('Closing stock price in order of day traded: ',
input_stock_price_array)
print('Closing stock price in order from high to low: ',
sorted_stock_price_array)
```

Press the *Enter* key to create a new line so you can add the second line command before running the cell.

7. Verify that the output cell displays Out []:

   - There will be two rows of output with the first as the original array of values.
   - The second output row is a sorted list of the values from the array.

8. Type in the following command to use the print() function to display the result:

```
print('Highest closing stock price: ', sorted_stock_price_array[0])
```

9. Verify that the output cell displays Out []. The output should state Highest closing stock price: 154.94.

The key concepts to remember from these steps are that you load an initial array of stock price values and name it `input_stock_price_array`. This step was done after importing the NumPy library and assigning it to the `np` shortcut, which is a best practice. Next, you create a new array from the original, name it `sorted_stock_price_array`, and use the `sort()` function from NumPy. The benefit of the `sort()` function is that it will automatically order the elements of the original array from low to high. Since the goal of this scenario is to get the highest value, we add the `[::-1]` parameter to the function, which sorts the elements of values in descending order.

Creating a new array from the original array helps to make your analysis easier to repeat and reuse. The order of operation becomes critical in the process so you must walk through the steps in sequence to get the correct results.

To verify the results, we add an extra step to print both arrays together to visually compare the elements and confirm that the new array is sorted in descending order. Since the original task was to get the *highest* stock price, the final step is to print the first element in the sorted array, which has an index value of `0`. If the steps are performed without any errors, you'll see the highest closing stock price from the sampling of data, that is, `154.94`.

Assigning values to arrays directly

A more scalable option versus manually assigning values in the array is to use another NumPy command called the `genfromtxt()` function, which is available in the `numpy` library. Using this function, we can assign the array elements directly from reading in records from the file by row and column. The `genfromtxt()` function has a few parameters to support handling the structure of the data by isolating the specific column needed and its data type.

There are multiple required and optional parameters for the `genfromtxt()` function, which you can find in the *Further reading* section. For our example, let's walk through the ones required to answer our business question:

- The first parameter is the filename, which is assigned to the file we upload, named `AAPL_stock_price_example.csv`.
- The second parameter is the delimiter, which is a comma since that is how the input file is structured.
- The next parameter is to inform the function that our input data file has a header by assigning the `names=` parameter to `True`.

- The last parameter is `usecols=`, which defines the specific column to read the data from.

According to the `genformtxt()` function help, when passing a value to the `usecols=` parameter, the first column is always assigned to `0` by default. Since we need the `Close` column in our file, we change the parameter value to `1` to match the order that is found in our input file.

Once the `input_stock_price_array` is loaded using the `genfromtxt()` function, a quick *size* check will validate that the number of elements matches the number of rows in the source file. Note that the header row would be excluded from the size. In the following screenshot, you see a few modifications to the manual array option but once the array is populated with values, the remaining steps are very similar. I added `[:5]` to the `print()` function to displace the top five elements and make it easier to compare the source input array and the new sorted array:

```
In [1]:  import numpy as np

In [8]:  input_stock_price_array = np.genfromtxt('AAPL_stock_price_example.csv', delimiter=',', names=True, usecols = (1))

In [20]: input_stock_price_array.size
Out[20]: 229

In [10]: sorted_stock_price_array = np.sort(input_stock_price_array)[::-1]

In [18]: print('Closing stock price in order of day traded:    ', input_stock_price_array[:5])
         print('Closing stock price in order from high to low: ', sorted_stock_price_array[:5])

         Closing stock price in order of day traded:     [(157.919998,) (142.190002,) (148.259995,) (147.929993,) (150.75    ,)]
         Closing stock price in order from high to low:  [(267.100006,) (266.369995,) (266.290009,) (265.76001 ,) (264.470001,)]

In [19]: print('Highest closing stock price: ', sorted_stock_price_array[0])

         Highest closing stock price:  (267.100006,)
```

The steps to reproduce this option are as follows:

1. Launch Jupyter and create a new Python notebook.
2. To stay consistent with best practices, be sure to rename the notebook `highest_daily_closing_stock_price_option_2` before moving forward.
3. Upload the `AAPL_stock_price_example.csv` file to the Jupyter notebook.
4. Type in `import numpy as np` in the `In []:` cell.
5. Run the cell.

6. Type in `input_stock_price_array =`
   `np.genfromtxt('AAPL_stock_price_example.csv', delimiter=',',`
   `names=True, usecols = (1))` in the next `In []:` cell.

7. Run the cell.

8. Type in `input_stock_price_array.size` in the next `In []:` cell.

9. Verify that the output cell displays `Out []:`. The number of rows is `229` when excluding the header row.

10. Type in `sorted_stock_price_array =`
    `np.sort(input_stock_price_array)[::-1]` in the next `In []:` cell.

11. Run the cell.

12. Type in `print('Closing stock price in order of day traded: ',`
    `input_stock_price_array[:5])`
    `print('Closing stock price in order from high to low: ',`
    `sorted_stock_price_array[:5])` in the next `In []:` cell.

13. Run the cell.

14. Verify that the output cell displays `Out []:`

    - There will be two rows of output with the first as the original array of values.
    - The second output row is a sorted list of the values from the array.

15. Type in `print('Highest closing stock price: ',`
    `sorted_stock_price_array[0])` in the next `In []:` cell.

16. Run the cell.

17. Verify that the output cell displays `Out []:`. The output should state `Highest closing stock price: 267.100006`.

Assigning values to an array using a loop

Another approach that may use more code but has more flexibility to control data quality during the process of populating the array would be to use a loop. There are a few concepts to walk through using this approach but I think it will be useful to understand this and applicable to further learning exercises.

A summary of the process is as follows:

1. Read the file into memory
2. Loop through each individual record

3. Strip out a value from each record
4. Assign each value to a temporary array
5. Clean up the array
6. Sort the array in descending order
7. Print the first element in the array to display the highest price

The last few steps in this process should look familiar since they are a repeat from the previous option where we clean the array, sort it, and then print the first element. The complete steps to reproduce this option are as follows:

1. Launch Jupyter and create a new Python notebook.
2. To stay consistent with best practices, be sure to rename the notebook `highest_daily_closing_stock_price_option_3` before moving forward.
3. Upload the `AAPL_stock_price_example.csv` file to the Jupyter notebook.

 Be sure to upload the source CSV file in the correct file location so you can reference it in your Jupyter notebook.

4. Type in the following command to import the `numpy` library in the notebook input, `In []:`, and run the cell. There will be no output after running this command:

```
In []: import numpy as np
```

5. Initialize the array by cleaning out all of the values before we can populate it. There will be no output after running this command:

```
In []: temp_array = []
```

6. In the following block of code, we have to execute multiple consecutive commands in a loop. The sequence is important and Jupyter will auto-indent as you type in the `In []:` cell. I included comments to better understand the code. There will be no output after running this command:

```
#A. Read the file into memory
 with open('AAPL_stock_price_example.csv', 'r') as input_file:
    #B. load all the data into a variable
    all_lines_from_input_file = input_file.readlines()
    #C. Loop through each individual record
    for each_individual_line in all_lines_from_input_file:
```

```
#D. Strip out a value from each record
for value_from_line in \
   each_individual_line.rsplit(',')[1:]:
      #E. Remove the whitespaces from each value
      clean_value_from_line = \
                       value_from_line.replace("\n", "")
      #F. Assign each value to the new array by element
      temp_array.append(clean_value_from_line)
```

7. After `temp_array` is populated with elements, a quick `print()` function identifies another data cleanup step that is required to move forward. Type in the following command in the next `In []:` cell and run the cell:

   ```
   print(temp_array[:5])
   ```

8. Verify that the output cell displays `Out []`, which will look similar to the following screenshot. The array includes a header row value of `Close` and has single quotes around the price values:

   ```
   In [23]:   print(temp_array[:5])

              ['Close', '157.919998', '142.190002', '148.259995', '147.929993']
   ```

9. The header row from the source file has been included in our array, which is easy to remove by assigning the array to itself and using the `delete()` function to delete the first element. There will be no output after running this command:

   ```
   temp_array = np.delete(temp_array,0)
   ```

10. Use the `size()` function to confirm the size of the array matches the original source input file by adding the following commands running the cell:

    ```
    temp_array.size
    ```

11. Verify that the output cell displays `Out []`, which will look similar to the following screenshot. The number of rows is `229` when excluding the header row:

    ```
    In [26]:   temp_array.size
    Out[26]:   229
    ```

12. The data type of the array has single quotes around each element. This can be remedied using a simple command from the `astype()` method by converting `dtype` of the array into `float` since the stock prices are decimal numeric values. There will be no output after running this command:

```
input_stock_price_array = temp_array.astype(float)
```

13. Print the first few elements in the new array to verify the array has cleaned elements:

```
print(input_stock_price_array[:5])
```

14. Verify the array now has only numeric values in decimal format and the quotes have been removed, similar to the following screenshot:

```
In [32]: print(input_stock_price_array[:5])
         [ 157.919998  142.190002  148.259995  147.929993  150.75    ]
```

15. The last few steps are a repeat from the prior exercise. We start with sorting the array in descending order using the `sort()` function along with passing a parameter of `[::-1]` to sort from high to low. Type in the following command in the next `In []:` cell and run the cell. There will be no output after running this command:

```
sorted_stock_price_array = np.sort(input_stock_price_array)[::-1]
```

16. Print the first few elements in the array to display the highest price by referencing the first sorted element in `sorted_stock_price_array` using the `print()` function by typing in the commands and running the cell:

```
print('Closing stock price in order of day traded: ',
input_stock_price_array[:5])
print('Closing stock price in order from high to low: ',
sorted_stock_price_array[:5])
```

17. Verify that the output cell displays `Out []`:

- There will be two rows of output with the first as the original array of values.
- The second output row is a sorted list of the values from the array.

This will look similar to the following screenshot:

```
In [30]: print('Closing stock price in order of day traded:     ', input_stock_price_array[:5])
         print('Closing stock price in order from high to low: ', sorted_stock_price_array[:5])

         Closing stock price in order of day traded:     [ 157.919998  142.190002  148.259995  147.929993  150.75     ]
         Closing stock price in order from high to low: [ 267.100006  266.369995  266.290009  265.76001   264.470001]
```

18. To see the highest price, use the `print()` function and use the `[0]` command against the sorted array to display the first value:

```
print('Highest closing stock price: ', sorted_stock_price_array[0])
```

19. Verify that the output cell displays `Out []`, which will look similar to the following screenshot. The output should state `Highest closing stock price: 267.100006`:

```
In [31]: print('Highest closing stock price: ', sorted_stock_price_array[0])

         Highest closing stock price:  267.100006
```

Summary

Congratulations, we have now learned how to use key features of the numpy library along with some practical real-world examples. We started by learning about arrays and why they are important by providing examples of how they have been rooted in computer science and programming languages for decades. We also learned about the foundation of structured data, which uses the concepts of arrays, by explaining the differences between single and multiple dimensional arrays and how we commonly identify them as tables with columns and rows.

Once the history and theories were explained, we learned how to make a NumPy array and walked through some useful functions available. We ended this chapter with a practical real-world example by loading stock prices into an array to show how it can answer specific questions by using a few NumPy commands available for data analysis. Data literacy skills were re-enforced throughout this chapter by understanding why data types impact data analysis and why the concept of KYD from Chapter 1, *Fundamentals of Data Analysis*, is important.

In the next chapter, we will expand your data literacy skills with some hands-on lessons working with data structures called DataFrames using the pandas library.

Further reading

Here are some links that you can refer to, for more information on the relative topics of this chapter:

- Original NumPy user documentation: http://people.csail.mit.edu/jrennie/python/numeric/numeric-manual.pdf
- *Understanding Data Types in Python*: https://jakevdp.github.io/PythonDataScienceHandbook/02.01-understanding-data-types.html
- NumPy Cheat Sheet: Data Analysis in Python: https://www.datacamp.com/community/blog/python-numpy-cheat-sheet
- The NumPy genfromtxt() function help guide: https://docs.scipy.org/doc/numpy/reference/generated/numpy.genfromtxt.html
- Image Processing with NumPy: http://www.degeneratestate.org/posts/2016/Oct/23/image-processing-with-numpy/
- History of the Logo programming language: http://www.sydlexia.com/logo.htm
- Logo emulator: https://www.calormen.com/jslogo/#
- Difference between Python lists and NumPy arrays: https://webcourses.ucf.edu/courses/1249560/pages/python-lists-vs-numpy-arrays-what-is-the-difference
- Yahoo Finance Stock Ticker data: https://finance.yahoo.com/quote/AAPL/history?period1=1546318800period2=1574744400interval=1dfilter=historyfrequency=1d

4

Creating Your First pandas DataFrame

In this chapter, we will go through the core data analysis skills of using filesystems and formats. We will explore different file formats for text data using the Python OS and string libraries to manipulate textual and numerical data from source files, such as **Comma-Separated Values (CSV)**, **Extensible Markup Language (XML)**, and **JavaScript Object Notation (JSON)**. You will learn what a pandas DataFrame is and how to create DataFrames from file sources for data analysis.

We will cover the following topics in this chapter:

- Techniques for manipulating tabular data
- Understanding pandas and DataFrames
- Handling essential data formats
- Data dictionaries and data types
- Creating your first DataFrame

Technical requirements

Here's the GitHub repository for this book: https://github.com/PacktPublishing/Practical-Data-Analysis-using-Jupyter-Notebook/tree/master/Chapter04.

You can download and install the required software from the following link: https://www.anaconda.com/distribution/

Techniques for manipulating tabular data

Now that we have a better understanding of array data structures from using the NumPy library in Chapter 3, *Getting Started with NumPy*, we can now expand our data analysis expertise. We will do this by working with tabular data and focusing on a powerful library available in Python named pandas, which is available to use in our Jupyter notebooks.

The pandas library extends our ability to analyze structured data and was introduced as a Python library back in 2008 by Wes McKinney. McKinney recognized the power of extending the Python language by using libraries and the need to fill the gap that existed between data preparation and data insights by *carrying out the entire data analysis workflow in Python without having to switch to a more domain-specific language such as R.*

The pandas Python library name was taken from the term **panel data** (by McKinney) by shortening and combining the terms to get pan and da. Panel data is defined as observations that can be measured over a period of time with multiple dimensional values and is very common in statistical studies and research papers. I have also seen panel data referred to as longitudinal data, facts panel data, or cross-sectional time-series data. Panel data is presented in tabular form with rows and columns and comes in a few different types, such as balanced, unbalanced, long, short, fixed, and rotating.

Each of these panel data types are based on how precisely the quantity of the dataset is represented. The total number of observations (rows of data) is commonly identified using the letter N. The unit of the time element used, such as year, month, quarter, or date is typically identified using the letter T in either upper or lowercase. The dimensions or variables (columns of data) can be represented with specific letters for each entity, such as x or z. What is measured can be represented as one or more variables and is commonly assigned to y. You should be able to summarize any panel data as a representative sample in descriptive terms for the consumer to understand before viewing or working with it in tabular form.

Depending on the dataset, the dimensions may or may not change over time, so different letters, such as k, may be assigned to represent that distinction.

An example of panel data is a daily closing price over 3 days for three publicly traded companies, as in the following table:

Date	Stock Ticker	Closing Price
12/2/2019	ABC	$50.21
12/3/2019	ABC	$52.22
12/4/2019	ABC	$51.01
12/2/2019	DEF	$24.22
12/3/2019	DEF	$26.22
12/4/2019	DEF	$29.50
12/2/2019	GHI	$61.22
12/3/2019	GHI	$65.33
12/4/2019	GHI	$75.00

Another example is the minimum, maximum, and average temperatures, in Fahrenheit, by ZIP code for the last three months (by month), as in the following table:

Month	ZIP Code	Minimum Temperature	Maximum Temperature	Average Temperature
June	19901	75	88	82
July	19901	77	90	84
August	19901	68	85	77
June	08618	76	89	83
July	08618	78	91	85
August	08618	69	86	78
June	18940	74	87	81
July	18940	76	89	83
August	18940	67	84	76

An unbalanced panel would be one where one or more values are missing for any one of the dimensional values. A balanced panel would be an inclusive dataset where all the elements from each dimension are included across all periods of time.

We know from Chapter 1, *Fundamentals of Data Analysis*, that data comes in all shapes and sizes, so having data structured in tabular form will be the first step in the analysis process, but in many cases, not the final one. For example, in the following table, we have a summary pivot table of total sales by city over the last 3 years.

This summary data can be identified as a cross table, which makes it easier for the consumer of this data to quickly identify the highest and lowest sales by **City** and by **Year**. In this case, this would be New York in 2019 with $120,000 and Boston in 2017 with $25,000:

City	2017	2018	2019
Philadelphia	$50,000	$75,000	$100,000
New York	$35,000	$65,000	$120,000
Boston	$25,000	$40,000	$ 90,000

If this tabular form of data had a limited number of rows and columns, this would be the final step in your analysis because you can quickly answer most business questions without additional manipulation, such as which city has the highest sales. However, what if the number of records increased to display over 100 cities and we increased the number of years to the last 10? What if you wanted to get more details to better understand the sales, breaking down the amount by increasing the number of dimensions, such as the product, store number, date of the transaction, time of the day, and method of payment?

Increasing the number of columns would make it challenging and time-consuming to answer a simple business question, such as what is the average sales across all cities across all years? Therefore, the ability to scale your analysis is dependent on your ability to manipulate the data beyond how the source is received.

A best practice in data analysis is *to begin with the end in mind*. So, for this example, the output table we want to produce will look similar to the following table, where we have transposed the columns into rows to make it easier for additional analysis to be carried out and so that we are prepared to handle a larger volume of data:

 A large scale of data volume is a subjective term but the techniques used should support analyzing millions or billions of rows of data. You will need additional infrastructure beyond the limits of your personal workstation's available RAM and CPU.

City	Year	Sales
Philadelphia	2017	$50,000
	2018	$75,000
	2019	$100,000
New York	2017	$35,000
	2018	$65,000
	2019	$120,000
Boston	2017	$25,000

	2018	$40,000
	2019	$90,000

From the preceding output, we can see that:

- The first advantage of having data structured similar to the way it is in the preceding output table is that there is a single conformed data type for each column, which is also known as a dimension or axis.
- The second advantage is that it becomes much easier for statistical analysis to be carried out because each dimension can be treated as an independent array of values of the same data type where calculations can be performed using NumPy, as covered in Chapter 3, *Getting Started with NumPy*.
- The third advantage is the ability to sort by any field in the table without worrying about the data values in each row/tuple becoming misaligned or inconsistent.
- Keeping the integrity of your data builds trust in your process and ensures your analysis will be accurate.

It is recommended that you break down each step during the manipulation of data to allow the repeatability of the process—for example, if you were asked to go through the process after a few months had passed or if you had to troubleshoot anomalies that exist in the underlining source data, which is very common.

Understanding pandas and DataFrames

Now that we have a better understanding of tabular data and we have provided some background about panel data and the origins of why the pandas library was created, let's dive into some examples using pandas and explain how DataFrames are used.

The pandas library is a powerful Python library used for changing and analyzing data. A pandas DataFrame is a feature available in the library and is defined as a two-dimensional, size-mutable, potentially heterogeneous tabular data structure with labeled axes (rows and columns). A DataFrame is a two-dimensional data structure—that is, data is aligned in a tabular fashion in rows and columns. It is commonly known that pandas DataFrame consists of three principal components: the data, the rows, and the columns. Being a visual learner myself, I created an example of this with the following diagram, which we can go through now:

DataFrames can be compared to a spreadsheet, such as Microsoft Excel or Google Sheets, a single database SQL table found in any **Relational Database Management System (RDBMS)**, or even a **QlikView Data (QVD)** file. The previous examples all include a common element of a **header row** that defines a label and alignment for your data, **rows** (with each one identified as a single record), **columns** that categorize the structure of each field value, and **data** that contains numeric and/or text values.

In our example, each row includes an identity record of the ID field, but that is not a requirement in a pandas DataFrame. DataFrames are treated as objects in Python and support loading data from files or SQL sources directly into memory for additional manipulation and analysis. Some key benefits of using DataFrames include the following:

- It allows you to convert all source files into readable data objects for easier merging and analysis.
- It provides auto- or defined indexing to help with looking up a value or selecting a cross selection from your DataFrame, which is also known as a data slice.
- Each column can be treated as a single NumPy array, which can collectively have multiple data types.
- It really excels at fixing data alignment and missing data elements, which are displayed and referenced as **Not a Number (NaN)**.
- It allows pivoting and reshaping data without going back to the source of record for each dataset.
- It is easy to add, remove, or change data using single Python commands to expedite the analysis of one or more data sources.
- Allows aggregations, such as Group By, and other calculations against metrics, such as sum, min, max, can all be performed against the DataFrame.
- Allows merging, sorting, joining, and filtering against one or more DataFrames.
- It is scalable to support a repeatable workflow of analysis. For example, the following pseudo-code steps are easy to replicate in a Jupyter notebook:

  1. Import the pandas library.
  2. Load the source file into a new DataFrame.
  3. Create a second DataFrame that drops duplicate rows or columns from the original.
  4. Create summary metrics.
  5. Save the second DataFrame as a new file.

What I enjoy about using pandas and DataFrames is the flexibility of the built-in commands that are provided to you as a data analyst. Let's walk through a few examples. To create a DataFrame from scratch on a limited number of records, you can simply add them with a few commands:

1. To load pandas, you just need to add the following command to your Jupyter notebook and run the cell. Feel free to follow along by creating your own notebook; I have added a copy to GitHub for reference:

   ```
   In[]: import pandas as pd
   ```

2. Next, we have a few products—a, b, and c—along with the quantity sold, and we assign this input data to a variable named product_data:

   ```
   product_data = {
       'product a': [13, 20, 0, 10],
       'project b': [10, 30, 17, 20],
       'project c': [6, 9, 10, 0]
   }
   ```

   When loading data manually, note the placement of square brackets to encapsulate the values for each column label and how the arrays must all be of the same length.

3. Then, we want to load the DataFrame by calling the command using the pd shortcut to reference the pandas library, along with the DataFrame() command. We assign the DataFrame input data as a second variable for easier reference, called purchase_data. The In[] cell will look like this:

   ```
   purchase_data = pd.DataFrame(product_data)
   ```

4. To validate the results, you can run the head() function to display the first five rows of data using the following command:

   ```
   purchase_data.head()
   ```

After executing the preceding code, we can see that:

- The output would look as in the following screenshot, where the individual arrays' by-products have been converted into a DataFrame with a labeled header row, and each of the quantity sold values are aligned for easy reference.
- Notice that a new index column has been created to the left of product a with assigned sequential values, starting at 0:

	product a	project b	project c
0	13	10	6
1	20	30	9
2	0	17	10
3	10	20	0

5. Having the indexed values are useful for reference, but if we want to define them as we create the DataFrame, we can include a relevant command during its creation, as follows:

```
purchase_data = pd.DataFrame(product_data, index=['Ronny,' 'Bobby,'
'Ricky,' 'Mike'])
```

6. Now, if you run the `head()` command to display the results, you will see specific values assigned to each indexed number, which will display as in the following screenshot:

	product a	project b	project c
Ronny	13	10	6
Bobby	20	30	9
Ricky	0	17	10
Mike	10	20	0

7. To select a specific row from the DataFrame, you use the `loc` function to retrieve the results by index, as follows:

```
purchase_data.loc['Ronny']
```

This will have an output, as in the following screenshot, where the individual values from the row assigned to `Ronny` are displayed in summary format, with each column and value presented by a row with a final description that includes the name of the index with a data type of the values (`dtype:   int64`):

```
product a      13
project b      10
project c       6
Name: Ronny, dtype: int64
```

Once the index is labeled, you must access the `loc[]` function with the name in single quotes; however, you can use the `iloc[]` or `ix[]` functions to reference the row index by a number, with the first row starting with 0. So, `purchase_data.iloc[0]` or `purchase_data.ix[0]` will both return the same results as in the preceding screenshot.

Handling essential data formats

With a better understanding of the power of using the `pandas` library and the DataFrames feature, let's explore working with multiple data formats, including from source files such as CSV, JSON, and XML. We briefly covered these different file formats as part of understanding structured data in Chapter 1, *Fundamentals of Data Analysis*, so let's dive deep into each source file type and learn some essential skills when working with them.

CSV

First, we have CSV, which has been an industry standard for most of my career. The way to identify CSV files is typically by the `.csv` file extension; however, you will learn, over time, that this is not always the case, nor is the delimiter used to separate values always a comma within data records. CSV files are popular because they are portable and technologically agnostic from the source system that created them.

This means a CSV file could have been created with any coding language, such as Python, C++, or Java. Also, the same OS used to create the CSV file, such as Windows, Unix, Linux, or macOS, is not required to read the file. This has helped with its adoption for many different use cases by IT professionals because it helps move data between systems in and out of the organization as needed.

Because of its longevity, you will find that many different variations and standards have been adopted over the years. For example, records may or may not include a header row and the delimiter between each field/column could be a tab, a pipe (|), or any other ASCII or UTF-8 character value.

American Standard Code for Information Interchange (ASCII) is a common character-encoding standard used by computers to interpret keyboard values digitally. **Unicode Transformation Format (UTF-8)** is the universal character-encoding standard and is backward-compatible with ASCII. Both standards are popular and commonly used.

There are some rules defined for proper CSV format, but the more you continue to work with them, the more you will probably find exceptions. Some of the rules that were published by Y. Shafranovich in *The Internet Society* (2005) include the following:

- Each record in the CSV file should be independent and include a line break (CRLF) to identify each row.
- It is optional to have a line break with the last record, but some kind of **End of File (EOF)** signifier would help with reading data between systems.
- A header row is optional but should include the same number of fields/columns as the corresponding record level data.
- Each record should have a consistent delimiter, such as a comma (,), a semicolon (;), a pipe (|), or a tab.
- The inclusion of double quotes between each field value is optional but is recommended to avoid misalignment or confusion, especially when reading in large, descriptive text data that includes a comma in the field value itself, such as Also, Stacy enjoys watching movies.
- Leading and trailing spaces between each field are optional as well but should be used consistently throughout the entire file.
- The size of a CSV file will vary but can be quite large and is dependent on the density of the data (the number of distinct values, the number of rows, and the number of fields).

TIP

Depending on the OS, such as Linux, a CSV would only include a **line feed (LF)** and not a **carriage return (CR)** for each row.

In the following screenshot, I have included a few examples of samples rows within a CSV file that all include the exact same information but using different formats to delimit the fields within the file:

| ```
1  Year,Decade,Milestone Title
2  1945,1940s,ENIAC,First elec
3  1945,1940s,John von Neumann
4  1956,1950s,First Hard Disk,
5  1958,1950s,Modem,The modem
6  1961,1960s,John Tukey / dat
7  1970,1970s,Dr. EF Codd / no
8  1972,1970s,FORTRAN supports
9  1982,1980s,Mike Bloomberg /
10 1983,1980s,Edward Tufty / D
``` | **Comma Delimited** |
| ```
1  Year       Decade   Milestone Title
2  1945       1940s    ENIAC    First e
3  1945       1940s    John von Neuman
4  1956       1950s    First Hard Disk
5  1958       1950s    Modem    The mod
6  1961       1960s    John Tukey / da
7  1970       1970s    Dr. EF Codd / n
8  1972       1970s    FORTRAN support
9  1982       1980s    Mike Bloomberg
10 1983       1980s    Edward Tufty /
``` | **Tab Delimited** |
| ```
1  Year|Decade|Milestone Title
2  1945|1940s|ENIAC|First elec
3  1945|1940s|John von Neumann
4  1956|1950s|First Hard Disk|
5  1958|1950s|Modem|The modem
6  1961|1960s|John Tukey / dat
7  1970|1970s|Dr. EF Codd / no
8  1972|1970s|FORTRAN supports
9  1982|1980s|Mike Bloomberg /
10 1983|1980s|Edward Tufty / D
``` | **Pipe Delimited** |

One big advantage of consuming or producing CSV over any other format is the capability to share between other tools used for data analysis. For example, spreadsheet solutions such as Excel can easily read a CSV file without the need to convert the file or use a third-party extension. However, a disadvantage is the loss of defined data types for each column, which could lead to misrepresenting values in your analysis. For example, a value in a column of 1 or 0 could represent a Boolean flag or a user hit count from a website.

XML

The XML file format was introduced as a standard format in the 1990s. I still remember how early on in my career XML was proposed as a replacement to CSV or even to the use of databases as a data repository. XML is flexible as a solution for developers to create web applications and, similar to CSV, is used to move data between systems in and out of the organization. XML is open source and has a defined standard that is maintained by the **World Wide Web Consortium (WC3)** organization. Some key characteristics of XML file format are as follows:

- It is most commonly identified with a file extension of .xml.
- The first line should include a declaration with encoding details and the .xml version, such as <?xml version = "1.0" encoding="UTF-8" ?>.
```

- It uses tags around each element that are similar to HTML tag code, using a beginning tag of < and > or />.

- It contains elements, which are the defined fields or columns of the structured data.

- It contains attributes, which are the data values within each defined element.

- It is optional but recommended to include a **Document Type Definition** (DTD), which provides details and helps define how the elements should be used, along with the data types

A sample XML file is shown in the following screenshot. Here, I converted `evolution_of_data_analysis.csv` into XML format and displayed a few sample records:

```xml
1   <?xml version="1.0" encoding="UTF-8" ?>
2   <Evolution_of_Data_Milestone="ENIAC">
3       <Year>1945</Year>
4       <Decade>1940s</Decade>
5       <Milestone_Title>ENIAC</Milestone_Title>
6       <Milestone_Event>First electronic general-purpose computer = ENIAC</Mil
7       <Why_Important>Faster decisions using a computer and mathmatics</Why_Im
8       <Reference>https://en.wikipedia.org/wiki/ENIAC</Reference>
9       <People_Process_or_Technology_Tag>Technology</People_Process_or_Technol
10  </Evolution_of_Data_Milestone>
11  <Evolution_of_Data_Milestone="John von Neumann / array">
12      <Year>1945</Year>
13      <Decade>1940s</Decade>
14      <Milestone_Title>John von Neumann / array</Milestone_Title>
15      <Milestone_Event>John von Neumann creates a merge sort algorithm, in wh
16      <Why_Important>Arrays allow mathmatics, grouping and sorting of data</W
17      <Reference>https://en.wikipedia.org/wiki/John_von_Neumann</Reference>
18      <People_Process_or_Technology_Tag>People</People_Process_or_Technology_
19  </Evolution_of_Data_Milestone>
```

While a disadvantage of XML is a larger file size, due to adding tags and definitions to each element, an advantage of using the XML format is the ability to support data hierarchies and a defined schema. Let's break down those two points.

Data hierarchy

Data hierarchies are defined and consistent groupings of data fields or records. The hierarchy can be obvious—for example, a son has a father and a mother—but from a data perspective, that relationship must be defined. In XML file format, you use a concept called an XML tree. The tree is defined by elements within the XML file that have a defined relationship. In the case of the `Evolution of Data Analysis.xml` file, each milestone has the details grouped together. Now, we can easily identify that the milestone event of `John von Neumann / array` was created in 1945, along with the rest of the supporting elements that are tagged, such as `<Decade>`, `<Milestone Title>`, `<Milestone Event>`, `<Why Important>`, `<Reference>`, and `<People Process or Technology Tag>`. This hierarchy relationship is commonly known as a **parent-child** relationship, where each indented element is a child to the *parent* element, `Evolution_of_Data_Milestone`.

Defined schema

A defined schema means the data elements will also include metadata (data about the data) to help with the conformity of each element and attribute. This concept was required in most RDBMSes, but XML offers the concept of a DTD file to be included with one or more XML files. The file extension is `.xsd`, and it should complement each XML file.

The contents of the XSD file can be complex and very dense, depending on the complexity of records found in the XML file and the need to define a rigid structure when consuming the XML data. For example, a defined data type for each element would help you to better understand how to use the data during analysis. For example, say with `type="xs:decimal"` you know the attribute value in each element *must* contain numeric values and any text values should *not* exist. Another useful schema definition would be the definition for an element of `use="required"`, which means specific elements must always have a value and should *not* contain any null/empty attributes.

There are more details on this topic available on the W3C website, which you can find in the *Further reading* section of this chapter.

JSON

JSON is another open source file standard for the communication of data between systems. It was created by Douglas Crockford around 2001 to improve communication between computers and web browsers using a concept called **stateless**. This means your computer's web browser, which is known as the **client**, doesn't have to wait for the **server** to respond, and vice versa. This is also known as **Representational State Transfer (REST)** architecture and is very common in web, API, and modern technologies because it scales to support millions of concurrent users.

Once REST became a popular web architecture, the need to find a faster and more efficient communication protocol drove the adoption of JSON data, which can either be streamed or persisted as a file. Having many websites that use JavaScript and a JavaScript-friendly notation also increased JSON's popularity.

Similar to XML and CSV, JSON is readable by humans as well as many different types of computer systems and languages, such as Python. This also means JSON is not a binary file format, which means it does not require the file to be compiled for use by a computer. I included JSON as a milestone in the *"The evolution of data analysis and why it is important"* section in `Chapter 1`, *Fundamentals of Data Analysis*, because of its contributions to advancing how we communicate using data. A sample JSON format is shown in the following screenshot, which is very similar to the XML format sample from the previous *XML* section because you now see the data organized and grouped by record using curly brackets ({ and }) to encapsulate each row from the original CSV file. Each grouping using curly brackets is identified as an object:

```
 1   [
 2     {
 3       "Year": 1945,
 4       "Decade": "1940s",
 5       "Milestone Title": "ENIAC",
 6       "Milestone Event": "First electronic general-purpose computer = ENIAC",
 7       "Why Important": "Faster decisions using a computer and mathmatics",
 8       "Reference": "https://en.wikipedia.org/wiki/ENIAC",
 9       "People Process or Technology Tag": "Technology"
10     },
11     {
12       "Year": 1945,
13       "Decade": "1940s",
14       "Milestone Title": "John von Neumann / array",
15       "Milestone Event": "John von Neumann creates a merge sort algorithm, in which th
16       "Why Important": "Arrays allow mathmatics, grouping and sorting of data",
17       "Reference": "https://en.wikipedia.org/wiki/John_von_Neumann",
18       "People Process or Technology Tag": "People"
19     },
```

One important concept to understand with JSON data is that it evolved from XML but streamlines many of the complexities that could exist in XML formats. Like XML, it benefits from the ability to define a data hierarchy and includes a defined schema that supports a concept called **schema on read**.

In traditional solutions that have a defined schema, the producer was forced to establish a schema before any data is loaded or transferred between systems. This process required expertise and extra steps during data ingestion and delayed the delivery of data to the consumer. With JSON and the concept of schema on read, the producer can send over the data along with all the metadata at the same time. All the details, such as field names, data types (dtype) for each field, and, in some cases, a full data dictionary, will be included. Providing this level of detail helps the consumer of the data to better understand the relationships within each element and attribute.

You will find, in a lot of JSON-formatted data, the concept of name: value pairs, which are also used in the example in the previous screenshot. This concept allows values to be assigned within the identification of the field within each record while still maintaining the hierarchy, rather than breaking out the records across multiple rows. Each field name is identified to the left of the colon (:) and the value is found to the right.

Each name: value relationship is separated by a comma and many examples will have a unique record identity, which helps with carrying out analysis on one-to-many relationships. So, you can nest many different relationships deep within a JSON structure and still have a way to identify which record the name: value pair belongs. If an array of values are required to be stored in a JSON file, they use square brackets ([and]) to define the list of values.

Defining a schema forces the data to have controls and context beyond what is observed. It removes assumptions about the data attributes and helps with interpreting how the data values should be used for analysis. For example, a value of 20191219 could be easily understood to be an integer value or could be the representation of the 12/19/2019 date with the format stored as YYYYMMDD. Without having a defined schema to reference, along with details about how and why that field is supposed to be used, your analysis of the data could be flawed.

Data dictionaries and data types

Throughout the book, I will continue to re-enforce the need to have a data dictionary to help with the analysis of data. As with any data we have uncovered so far, a data dictionary will come in all shapes and sizes. This means it could be documented outside the source file, which is common on a help page, a wiki, or a blog or within the source data, as we discussed with XML and JSON files.

Having the data defined and documented will aid you in the journey to understand it but will not be the only method required to become a domain expert for a dataset. Domain expertise comes from experience with understanding how the data is used, along with the business or purpose behind the underlining source data. We covered some of these concepts in `Chapter 1`, *Fundamentals of Data Analysis*, looking at how **Know Your Data (KYD)** and having a data dictionary available aids in the effort to learn more about the underlying dataset.

 The analysis of data and the KYD concept should be applied throughout the process of analyzing data, so be sure to check the numbers and verify that the results match up to how the data is defined to build trust and confidence in your insights.

Data dictionaries are common for legacy systems, RDBMS, and traditional **Enterprise Data Warehouses (EDW)**. It is common to have a data catalog available and, in many cases, they are required to build communication data pipelines between different systems. In some cases, a data dictionary is required as part of regulatory requirements or as part of a governed corporate policy.

In modern systems, **Application Programming Interfaces (APIs)** have become the central repository for metadata and the de facto data dictionary because JSON is a popular communication vehicle where the schema is defined and should be well documented. However, in practice, I find that documentation is written for programmers by programmers, so it may not meet all the needs to fully understand the data and answer all the business questions during analysis.

It is also common to version a data dictionary as part of a **Master Data Management (MDM)** or data governance solution. Within these versions, you will uncover details behind the *what* and the *why* for the data. For example, a field may be defined as inactive but still available, so it becomes sparsely populated because the application/system used to populate it changed.

Having that level of detail may help to identify data gaps or to better understand how to build a data bridge by combining values from two different fields at different periods of time for accurate historical analysis. I worked with a client once who was replacing a large enterprise legacy system, which cost millions of dollars, with consulting hardware and software. The consulting time was calculated by the hour, with dozens of specialists traveling every week to the client site.

There was a pivotal moment in the project where it was determined infeasible and too costly to migrate all the legacy supply chain, accounting, and HR details from the old system to the new one. To avoid delays, we proposed an analytics solution where both the legacy system data and the new system data were merged together daily. A rolling window of time logic was built in so that after 7 years, the legacy data would no longer be used for analysis, but during that timeframe, a blend of both systems, which included different fields and records, would be presented for analysis.

Having a data dictionary was a must for this type of solution, and providing additional documentation was required to ensure the audience understood where the source of the data came from depending on the time period of the reporting and analysis. Part of that documentation required details behind the different fields and variations in the data types. Some systems will allow a mix of different data types or, as in Python, will default to specific data types.

Just remember that you may need to convert a data type between multiple sources, especially when blending between different systems and file formats. For example, in JSON, a number defined as `real` would be called `float` in Python. If you run into issues with converting data types during the loading of data, you may need to go back to the data source provider and request it to be resent in a format that would be easier to consume.

As you continue increasing your data literacy, you need to understand that different technologies and data formats will lead to different data types, which will require translation to ensure accurate analysis of the data, especially from multiple sources.

Creating our first DataFrame

Before we begin with some hands-on examples, some useful commands to run in `pandas` are as follows:

- `pd.read_csv('inport_filename.csv', header=1)`: Reads data from a CSV file directly into a `pandas` DataFrame
- `my_df.to_csv('export_filename')`: Directly exports the DataFrame to a CSV file to your workstation
- `my_df.shape`: Provides the number of rows and columns of your DataFrame
- `my_df.info()`: Provides metadata about your DataFrame, including data types for each column
- `my_df.describe()`: Includes statistical details with a column that includes the count, mean, **standard deviation (std)**, minimum, maximum, and percentiles (25th, 50th, and 75th) for any numeric column
- `my_df.head(2)`: Displays the first two records from the DataFrame
- `my_df.tail(2)`: Displays the last two records from the DataFrame
- `my_df.sort_index(1)`: Sorts by the labels along an axis—in this example, by the column label headers alphabetically from left to right
- `my_df.isnull()`: Displays a list of all rows with a `True`/`False` indicator if any of the values by column are null

Our first example will load data from a CSV file into a `pandas` DataFrame that has a pipe (|) delimiter and will run some of the preceding commands:

1. Launch Jupyter and create a new Python notebook.
2. To stay consistent with the best practices, be sure to rename the notebook `exploring_the_pandas_library` before moving forward.
3. Type `import pandas as pd` into the `In []:` cell.
4. Run the cell. No output will be displayed after you run the cell.
5. Type `my_df = pd.read_csv('evolution_of_data_analysis.csv', header=0, sep="|")` into the next `In []:` cell.
6. Run the cell. No output will be displayed after you run the cell.
7. Type `my_df.shape` into the next `In []:` cell.

8. Verify that the output cell displays Out []. (42, 7) will be displayed, which tells you that there are 42 rows and 7 columns, as in the following screenshot:

```
In [1]:  import pandas as pd

In [15]: my_df = pd.read_csv('evolution_of_data_analysis.csv', header=0, sep="|")

In [16]: my_df.shape

Out[16]: (42, 7)
```

9. Type my_df.info() into the next In []: cell.
10. Run the cell.
11. Verify that the output cell displays Out []. There will be multiple rows, including data types for all seven columns, as in the following screenshot:

```
In [17]: my_df.info()

<class 'pandas.core.frame.DataFrame'>
RangeIndex: 42 entries, 0 to 41
Data columns (total 7 columns):
Year                             42 non-null int64
Decade                           42 non-null object
Milestone Title                  42 non-null object
Milestone Event                  42 non-null object
Why Important                    42 non-null object
Reference                        39 non-null object
People Process or Technology Tag 42 non-null object
dtypes: int64(1), object(6)
memory usage: 2.4+ KB
```

12. Type my_df.describe() into the next In []: cell.
13. Run the cell.
14. Verify that the output cell displays Out []. There will be multiple rows of output, with one column with a header of Year, as in the following screenshot. Statistical values from the Year field will be displayed, including count, mean, and max:

```
In [20]: my_df.describe()
Out[20]:
```

	Year
count	42.000000
mean	1993.833333
std	18.876901
min	1945.000000
25%	1987.500000
50%	1999.000000
75%	2006.750000
max	2018.000000

15. Type `my_df.head(2)` into the next `In []:` cell and run the cell.

16. Verify that the output cell displays `Out []:`

    - The output should include an index in the first column with a starting row of 0, as in the following screenshot.
    - All seven columns will be displayed, along with the first two rows from the source file:

```
In [23]: my_df.head(2)
Out[23]:
```

	Year	Decade	Milestone Title	Milestone Event	Why Important	Reference	People Process or Technology Tag
0	1945	1940s	ENIAC	First electronic general-purpose computer = ENIAC	Faster decisions using a computer and mathmatics	https://en.wikipedia.org/wiki/ENIAC	Technology
1	1945	1940s	John von Neumann / array	John von Neumann creates a merge sort algorith...	Arrays allow mathmatics| grouping and sorting...	https://en.wikipedia.org/wiki/John_von_Neumann	People

17. Type `my_df.tail(2)` into the next `In []:` cell and run the cell.

18. Verify that the output cell displays `Out []`. The output should include an index in the first column with a starting row of `40`, as in the following screenshot. All seven columns will be displayed, along with the last two rows from the source file:

```
In [7]: my_df.tail(2)
```

	Year	Decade	Milestone Title	Milestone Event	Why Important	Reference	People Process or Technology Tag
40	2015	2010s	Alexa	Amazon Alexa Ecosystem	Making voice to data mainstream and allowing A...	https://www.zdnet.com/article/technology-that-...	Technology
41	2018	2010s	The Data Literacy Project	The Data Literacy Project launches	Building a data driven culture where anyone ca...	https://www.businesswire.com/news/home/2018101...	Process

19. Type `my_df.sort_index(1)` into the next `In []:` cell and run the cell.

20. Verify that the output cell displays `Out []`. The output should include an index in the first column with a starting row of `0`, as in the following screenshot. All seven columns will be displayed, but the order of the columns has changed to alphabetically sort from left to right, starting with `Decade` and ending with `Year`:

```
In [8]: my_df.sort_index(1)
```

	Decade	Milestone Event	Milestone Title	People Process or Technology Tag	Reference	Why Important	Year
0	1940s	First electronic general-purpose computer = ENIAC	ENIAC	Technology	https://en.wikipedia.org/wiki/ENIAC	Faster decisions using a computer and mathmatics	1945
1	1940s	John von Neumann creates a merge sort algorith...	John von Neumann / array	People	https://en.wikipedia.org/wiki/John_von_Neumann	Arrays allow mathmatics| grouping and sorting ...	1945
2	1950s	The first computer hard disk used	First Hard Disk	Technology	https://fiftiesweb.com/pop/inventions/	Storing data for reuse = reduces time to recre...	1956

In the next example, let's answer a few business questions from the data by exploring some of the features available in `pandas`. The first question is *how many milestone events occurred by decade?* To answer this question, we need to use the `groupby` feature, so let's go through the steps to provide the answer.

The steps to reproduce this example are as follows:

1. Launch Jupyter and create a new Python notebook.
2. To stay consistent with the best practices, be sure to rename the notebook `exploring_the_pandas_library_example_2` before moving forward.
3. Type `import pandas as pd` into the `In []:` cell and run the cell.
4. Type `my_df = pd.read_csv('evolution_of_data_analysis.csv', header=0, sep="|")` into the next `In []:` cell and run the cell.
5. Type `my_df.head(2)` into the next `In []:` cell and run the cell.
6. Verify that the output cell displays `Out []:`

   - The output should include an index in the first column with a starting row of `0`.
   - All seven columns will be displayed, along with the first two rows from the source file.

7. Type `my_df.groupby(['Decade']).agg({'Year':'count'})` into the `In []:` cell and run the cell.
8. Verify that the output cell displays `Out []:`

   - The output will display 10 rows of data with 2 columns.
   - The header row in the first column will be `Decade` and will be `Year` for the second column.

- The results will match the following screenshot:

```
In [9]:   import pandas as pd

In [10]:  my_df = pd.read_csv('evolution_of_data_analysis.csv', header=0, sep="|")

In [11]:  my_df.head(2)
```

Out[11]:

	Year	Decade	Milestone Title	Milestone Event	Why Important	Reference	People Process or Technology Tag
0	1945	1940s	ENIAC	First electronic general-purpose computer = ENIAC	Faster decisions using a computer and mathmatics	https://en.wikipedia.org/wiki/ENIAC	Technology
1	1945	1940s	John von Neumann / array	John von Neumann creates a merge sort algorith...	Arrays allow mathmatics| grouping and sorting ...	https://en.wikipedia.org/wiki/John_von_Neumann	People

```
In [12]:  my_df.groupby(['Decade']).agg({'Milestone Event':'count'})
```

Out[12]:

	Milestone Event
Decade	
1940s	2
1950s	2
1960s	1
1970s	2
1980s	5
1990s	9
2000s	14
2010s	7

In the preceding screenshot, we followed the previous steps to load the CSV file as a DataFrame named `my_df`. To verify that the DataFrame loaded correctly, we ran the `head()` function and included the parameter of `2` to limit the number of rows displayed in the notebook. The last command is to run `groupby` against the `Decade` column and combine it with an aggregation to count the values from the `Milestone Event` field/column. We can now answer some questions about this dataset, such as that 14 milestone events occurred during the 2000s or that the first decade to have any milestone events was the 1940s because that is the first row that has any values.

Summary

Congratulations, you have now created your first DataFrame using the `pandas` library! We started the chapter by introducing you to the concepts of structured tabular data and the different techniques available to manipulate it by transposing and pivoting the data. More importantly, we discussed the importance of why data should be in tabular form. We then introduced the `pandas` library and defined a DataFrame, and demonstrated the many benefits of this powerful feature that are available for you during data analysis. In the handling of essential data formats, we went through the different data formats available by going through the details of the CSV, XML, and JSON file formats. Before we ended the chapter by creating our first DataFrame, we discussed the importance of data dictionaries and how different data types improve your data literacy, as well as why they are important before, during, and after the data analysis workflow has completed.

In the next chapter, `Chapter 5`, *Gathering and Loading Data in Python*, we will introduce you to how to load data from databases using SQL and continue working with the features available in `pandas` and DataFrames.

Further reading

- McKinney, W., *Data Structures for Statistical Computing in Python, Proceedings of the 9th Python in Science Conference*, Vol. 445 (2010)
- Torres-Reyna, O., *Panel Data Analysis Fixed and Random Effects using Stata* (v. 4.2), *Princeton.edu*, (2007), available at `https://www.princeton.edu/~otorres/Panel101.pdf` [accessed 23 Dec. 2019]
- **National Longitudinal Surveys (NLSes)** for examples of panel data: `https://www.bls.gov/nls/home.htm`
- A definition of a `pandas` DataFrame: `https://www.geeksforgeeks.org/python-pandas-dataframe`
- **Quick details about the QVD file format:** `https://help.qlik.com/en-US/sense/June2019/Subsystems/Hub/Content/Sense_Hub/Scripting/work-with-QVD-files.htm`
- **ASCII stands:** `https://www.ansi.org/about_ansi/overview/overview?menuid=1`
- **Unicode format and encoding standards:** `https://home.unicode.org/`
- **CSV rules and standards:** `https://tools.ietf.org/html/rfc4180`
- **The W3C organization standards:** `https://www.w3.org/`
- **The REST standards:** `https://www.ics.uci.edu/~fielding/pubs/dissertation/rest_arch_style.htm#sec_5_1_3`
- **History of Unicode:** `https://docs.python.org/3.4/howto/unicode.html`

Gathering and Loading Data in Python

5

This chapter will explain what SQL is and why it is important for data analysis by teaching you how to use and access databases using SQLite for our examples. An overview of relational database technology will be provided along with insightful information on database systems to help to improve your data literacy when communicating with experts. You will also learn how to run SQL `SELECT` queries from the Jupyter Notebook and how to load them into DataFrames. Basic statistics, data lineage, and metadata (data about data) will be explained using the `pandas` library.

We will cover the following topics in this chapter:

- Introduction to SQL and relational databases
- From SQL to pandas DataFrames
- Data about your data explained
- The importance of data lineage

Technical requirements

Here's the GitHub repository of this book: `https://github.com/PacktPublishing/Practical-Data-Analysis-using-Jupyter-Notebook/tree/master/Chapter05`.

You can download and install the required software from the following link: `https://www.anaconda.com/products/individual`.

Introduction to SQL and relational databases

We are now at a point in this book where my professional career started, working with databases and SQL. **Structured Query Language (SQL)** was created decades ago as a means to communicate with structured data stored in tables. Over the years, SQL has evolved from multiple variations that were specific to the underlining database technology. For example, IBM, Oracle, and Sybase all had variations in their SQL commands, which built loyalty in their customers but required changes when switching vendors. The adoption of the **International Organization for Standardization (ISO)** and **American National Standards Institute (ANSI)** standards helped to define what is commonly used today.

So far in this book, all of the examples of structured data focused on one table or file. Relational databases solve the problem of storing data together in multiple tables while keeping consistency across them using the concept of a primary and foreign key:

- A primary key is the unique value (typically an integer) used to represent a single distinct record or tuple in each table.
- A foreign key would be a field in one table that references the primary key from another.

This relationship defines integrity between one or more tables for consistency for all of the data. Since the concept of storing and joining the data is abstract, this allows it to be applied to many different data subjects. For example, you can create a database to store sales from a manufacturing company, user hits from a website, or stock purchases in a financial services company. Because of this versatility, SQL remains a top programming language and a must-have skill for data analysis.

SQL was created to communicate with data stored in database tables that have a defined schema. A database schema is like a blueprint that defines a structure for storing data before the data is loaded. This definition includes rules, conditions, and specific data types for each field in a table. The foundation for the database technology was created by Dr. EF Codd back in 1970 and was a milestone of the *Evolution of Data Analysis*, which I defined in Chapter 1, *Fundamentals of Data Analysis*. The concept of persisting data in defined columns and rows as tables in a structured relationship showcases the legacy of Dr. Codd's contribution to this technology and data. His contributions to the technology along with others such as Ralph Kimball and Bill Inmon has created new industries and careers over the years. If you come across an **Enterprise Data Warehouse (EDW)**, you can bet money it uses the Kimball or Inmon methods as a standard. Their influence, which defined new skills to work with data, cannot be understated. I have immense gratitude for the people who have evolved technologies and concepts supporting all things data.

What is defined as a relational database is a vast subject so I'm going to focus on what is relevant for building your data literacy and the analysis of data from consuming data using SQL. The key concepts to focus on behind working with any **Relational Database Management System (RDBMS)** begin with how to communicate with the system or servers that host the database. Most of them support using an ODBC driver, which handles authentication and communication over a network. **Open Database Connectivity (ODBC)** is a common standard used to send and receive data between your analysis tool, for example, the Jupyter Notebook, and where the data is stored. Most large-scale, enterprise relational database systems support ODBC connections to communicate with the database.

Traditionally, this would be known as a client-server architecture, where your local computer is known as the client and the location of the database would be managed by one or more servers. When I was a consultant, the most common enterprise RDBMSes I worked with were Microsoft SQL Server, Oracle, IBM DB2, MySQL, and PostgreSQL.

 An ODBC driver may need to be installed and configured on your workstation to communicate with a client-server architecture.

Today, other flavors of both open source and vendor database products exist but many do and should support SQL or a variation of it. For example, Apache's HiveQL is very similar to ASCI SQL but runs on top of the **Hadoop Distributed File System (HDFS)** instead of a database. For our examples, we will be using SQLite, which is a file-based database you can install locally or connect with via ODBC. SQLite is open source and cross-platform, which means we can install it on any operating system, and it is touted as the *most widely deployed and used database engine in the world* according to their download page, which you can find in the *Further reading* section.

Once a connection has been established, a user ID and password are commonly required, which control what actions you can perform and which tables you can access. If you installed the database yourself, you are the owner of the database and probably have system administrator rights, which gives you full access to create, delete, and read any table. If you are a client, the **Database Administrator (DBA)** would be responsible for setting up access and permission for your user ID.

I find what makes the SQL a popular language even today is the learning curve required to use it. In my experience, many business users and data analysts find the syntax intuitively obvious even without a background in computer science. SQL code is easy to read and it's quickly understood what the expected results are. It also supports instant gratification where a few commands can produce results in less than one second even with large volumes of data once it's been optimized for performance.

For example, let's say I want to know the highest closing stock price of Apple stock in all of 2018. Even without really understanding all of the details behind how or where that data is stored, the syntax for this one line of code is easy to interpret:

```
SELECT max(closing_price) FROM tbl_stock_price WHERE year = 2018
```

Let's walk through this code and break out the key components:

- First, I capitalized the reserved words, which are universal across any RDBMS that supports ISO standard/ASCI SQL.
- The SELECT command instructs the code to retrieve data in the form of rows and columns from a table defined after the FROM statement.
- Between the SELECT and the FROM reserved words is the max(closing_price) command. This is using the max() function that is available in SQL to retrieve the maximum or largest value from the closing_price field. The max function will only return one row and one value regardless of whether duplicate values exist in the data.
- The FROM section of the code lets the SQL interpreter know a table or object is being referenced immediately afterward. For this example, we are looking for records from the tbl_stock_price table.
- The WHERE clause from the SELECT SQL statement restricts the data by reducing the number of rows to a specific condition, which is defined by a specific field of year and value to the right of the equals sign of 2018.

SELECT is the most common SQL command and has many different use cases and levels of complexity. We are just scratching the surface but you can find more resources in the *Further reading* section.

SQL is not case sensitive but the tables and fields referenced might be, depending on which RDBMS is being used. Spaces are important between reserve words but you typically won't find spaces in the table or field names. Rather, underscores or dashes are common.

From SQL to pandas DataFrames

Now that we have some background on SQL and relational databases, let's download a local copy of an SQLite database file, set up a connection, and load some data into a pandas DataFrame. For this example, I have provided the database file named customer_sales.db so be sure to download it from the GitHub repository beforehand.

To give you some context about this database file and support the **Know Your Data (KYD)** concept that we learned in Chapter 1, *Fundamentals of Data Analysis*, we have three tables named tbl_customers, tbl_products, and tbl_sales. This would be a simple example of any company that has customers who purchase products that generate sales over any period of time. A visual representation of how the data is stored and joined together, which is commonly known as an **ERD** (short for **Entity Relationship Diagram**), is shown in the following diagram:

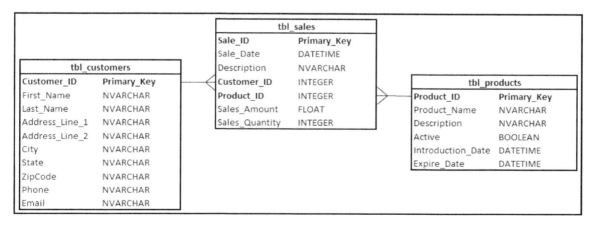

In the preceding diagram, we have a visual of three tables with the column name defined on the left side of each box and the data type of each column immediately to the right. The primary key for each table is identified with a suffix in the name of _ID, along with bolding the text in the first row of each table. The primary key commonly has a data type of integer, which is also the case here.

The `tbl_sales` table includes two of those fields, `Customer_ID` and `Product_ID`, which means they are classified as foreign keys. The lines between the tables reinforce the relationship between them, which also indicates how to join them together. The small lines that look like *crow's feet* tell the consumer these tables are defined with a one-to-many relationship. In this example, `tbl_sales` will have many customers and many products but a record in `tbl_customers` will only have one value assigned per `Customer_ID` and `tbl_products` will only have one value assigned per `Product_ID`.

Now that we have more information about the data, let's launch a new Jupyter notebook and name it `retrieve_sql_and_create_dataframe`. To create a connection and use SQLite, we have to import a new library using code:

1. To load an SQLite database connection, you just need to add the following command in your Jupyter notebook and run the cell. Feel free to follow along by creating your own notebook (I have placed a copy in GitHub for reference):

   ```
   In[]: import sqlite3
   ```

The `sqlite3` module comes with the Anaconda distribution installed. Refer to `Chapter 2`, *Overview of Python and Installing Jupyter Notebook*, for help with setting up your environment.

2. Next, we need to assign a connection to a variable named `conn` and point to the location of the database file, which is named `customer_sales.db`. Since we already imported the `sqlite3` library in the prior `In[]` line, we can use this built-in function to communicate with the database:

   ```
   In[]: conn = sqlite3.connect('customer_sales.db')
   ```

Be sure to copy the `customer_sales.db` file to the correct Jupyter folder directory to avoid errors with the connection.

3. The next library to import should be very familiar, which allows us to use `pandas` so the code will be as follows:

```
In[]: import pandas as pd
```

4. To run a SQL statement and assign the results to a DataFrame, we have to run this one line of code. The `pandas` library includes a `read_sql_query()` function to make it easier to communicate with databases using SQL. It requires a connection parameter, which we named `conn` in the previous steps. We assign the results to a new DataFrame as `df_sales` to make it easier to identify:

```
In[]: df_sales = pd.read_sql_query("SELECT * FROM tbl_sales;",
conn)
```

5. Now that we have the results in a DataFrame, we can use all of the available `pandas` library commands against this data without going back to the database. To view the results, we can just run the `head()` command against this DataFrame using this code:

```
In[]: df_sales.head()
```

The output will look like the following screenshot where the `tbl_sales` table has been loaded into a DataFrame with a labeled header row with the index column to the left starting with a value of `0`:

In [13]:	df_sales.head							
Out[13]:		Sale_ID	Sale_Date	Description	Customer_ID	Product_ID	Sales_Amount	Sales_Quantity
	0	1	12/31/2014	Purchased from Store	2	2	20	1
	1	2	1/15/2015	Phone Purchase	1	1	30	2
	2	3	6/14/2015	Internet Purchase	3	3	5	1
	3	4	11/11/2015	Sales Convention Purchase	3	3	500	100
	4	5	4/18/2016	Internet Purchase	4	1	20	2

6. To sort the values in the DataFrame, we can use the `sort_values()` function and include a parameter of the field name, which will default to ascending order. Let's begin by sorting the results by date to see when the first sale was recorded in the database by using this command:

```
In[]: df_sales.sort_values(by='Sale_Date')
```

The output would look like the following screenshot where the DataFrame output is now sorted by the `Sale_Date` field from `1/15/2015` to `6/9/2019`. Notice the difference in `Sale_ID`, which is out of sequence:

```
In [14]: df_sales.sort_values(by='Sale_Date')
```

	Sale_ID	Sale_Date	Description	Customer_ID	Product_ID	Sales_Amount	Sales_Quantity
1	2	1/15/2015	Phone Purchase	1	1	30	2
5	6	10/15/2016	Purchased from Store	5	1	20	1
3	4	11/11/2015	Sales Convention Purchase	3	3	500	100
0	1	12/31/2014	Purchased from Store	2	2	20	1
6	7	3/17/2017	Internet Purchase	4	1	20	1
4	5	4/18/2016	Internet Purchase	4	1	20	2
8	9	5/25/2019	Internet Purchase	1	3	10	2
2	3	6/14/2015	Internet Purchase	3	3	5	1
7	8	6/15/2018	Purchased from Store	3	3	5	1
9	10	6/9/2019	Internet Purchase	2	3	10	2

7. To limit the data displayed, we can use the `DataFrame.loc` command to isolate specific rows or columns based on how it is labeled by the header row. To retrieve the first row available, we simply run this command against our DataFrame and reference the index value, which begins with 0:

```
In[]: df_sales.loc[0]
```

The output would look like the following screenshot where a single record is displayed as a series with the rows transposed from multiple columns to multiple rows:

```
In [61]: df_sales.loc[0]

Out[61]: Sale_ID                            1
         Sale_Date                 12/31/2014
         Description       Purchased from Store
         Customer_ID                        2
         Product_ID                         2
         Sales_Amount                      20
         Sales_Quantity                     1
         Name: 0, dtype: object
```

Using this method, you must know which specific record you are looking for by index, which reflects how the data was loaded from the SQL statement. To ensure consistency between the database tables, you may want to include an ORDER BY command when loading the data into the DataFrame.

8. To restrict the data displayed, we can use a nested command to isolate specific rows based on a condition. A business task you could address using this data would be to *identify customers with high sales so we can thank them personally*. To do this, we can filter the sales by a specific value and display only the rows that meet or exceed that condition. For this example, we assigned high to an arbitrary number so any Sales_Amount over 100 will be displayed using this command:

```
In[]: df_sales[(df_sales['Sales_Amount'] > 100)]
```

The output would look like the following screenshot where a single record is displayed based on the condition because there is only one record where Sales_Amount is greater than 100, which is Sale_ID equal to 4:

In [52]: df_sales[(df_sales['Sales_Amount'] > 100)]

Out[52]:

	Sale_ID	Sale_Date	Description	Customer_ID	Product_ID	Sales_Amount	Sales_Quantity
3	4	11/11/2015	Sales Convention Purchase	3	3	500	100

9. Another example of how to restrict results would be looking for a specific value assigned to a specific field in the DataFrame. If we wanted to better understand this data, we could do so by looking at the Sales_Quantity field and seeing which records only had one product purchased:

```
In[]: df_sales[(df_sales['Sales_Quantity'] == 1)]
```

The output would look like the following screenshot, where multiple records are displayed based on the condition where `Sales_Quantity` is equal to `1`:

```
In [57]: df_sales[(df_sales['Sales_Quantity'] == 1)]
```

Out[57]:

	Sale_ID	Sale_Date	Description	Customer_ID	Product_ID	Sales_Amount	Sales_Quantity
0	1	12/31/2014	Purchased from Store	2	2	20	1
2	3	6/14/2015	Internet Purchase	3	3	5	1
5	6	10/15/2016	Purchased from Store	5	1	20	1
6	7	3/17/2017	Internet Purchase	4	1	20	1
7	8	6/15/2018	Purchased from Store	3	3	5	1

The steps define a best practice for an analysis workflow. Retrieving SQL results, storing them in one or more DataFrames, and then performing analysis in your notebook is common and encouraged. Migrating data between sources (from database to Jupyter Notebook) can take high compute resources depending on the volume of data, so be conscious of how much memory you have available and how large the databases you are working with are.

Data about your data explained

Now that we have a better understanding of how to work with SQL sourced data using Python and pandas, let's explore some fundamental statistics along with practical usage for data analysis. So far, we have focused on descriptive statistics versus predictive statistics. However, I recommend not proceeding with any data science predictive analytics without a firm understanding of descriptive analytics first.

Fundamental statistics

Descriptive analytics is based on what has already happened in the past by analyzing the digital footprint of data to gain insights, analyze trends, and identify patterns. Using SQL to read data from one or more tables supports this effort, which should include basic statistics and arithmetic. Having the data structured and conformed, which includes defined data types per column, makes this type of analysis easier once you understand some key concepts and commands.There are many statistical functions available in both SQL and Python.

I have summarized a few that are fundamental to your data analysis in this table:

Statistical Measure	Description	Best For/Use Case	SQL Syntax	pandas Function
Count	The number of occurrences of a value regardless of data type	Finding out the size of a table/number of records	`SELECT Count(*) FROM table_name`	`df.count()`
Count Distinct	The number of distinct occurrences of a value regardless of data type	Removing duplicate values/verify distinct values used for categories of data	`SELECT Count(distinct field_name) FROM table_name`	`df.nunique()`
Sum	The aggregation of values as a whole or total against numeric data types	Finding the total population or measuring the amount of money	`SELECT Sum(field_name) FROM table_name`	`df.sum()`
Mean	The arithmetic average from a set of two or more numeric data types	Sum of values divided by the count of values	`SELECT AVG(field_name) FROM table_name`	`df.mean()`
Min	The lowest numeric value of a value in a field	Finding the lowest value	`SELECT MIN(field_name) FROM table_name`	`df.min()`
Max	The highest numeric value of a value in a field	Finding the highest value	`SELECT MAX(field_name) FROM table_name`	`df.max()`

The most common statistical measure I use in SQL is *Count* where you are counting the number of records per table. Using this function helps to validate that the volume of data you are working with is in line with the source system, producers of data, and business sponsors. For example, you are told by the business sponsor that they use a database to store customers, products, and sales and they have over 30,000 customers. Let's say you run the following SQL query:

```
SELECT count(*) from customers
```

There are 90,000 results. Why is there such a dramatic difference? The first question would be: are you using the correct table? Any database is flexible so it can be organized by the DBA to manage relationships based on application and business needs, so active customers (customers who purchased a product and created sales data) could be stored in a different table, such as `active_customers`. Another question would be: is there a field used to identify whether the record is active or not? If so, that field should be included in the `WHERE` section of your `SELECT` statement, for example, `SELECT count(*) from customers where active_flag = true`.

A second advantage of using the `count()` function for analysis is to set expectations for yourself as to how much time it takes for each query to return results. If you run a `count(*)` on products, customers, and sales tables, the amount of time taken to retrieve the results will vary depending on the volume of data and how the DBA has optimized the performance. Tables have shapes, which means the number of rows and columns will vary between them. They also can grow or shrink depending on their intended use. A table such as `sales` is transactional so the number of rows will dramatically increase over time. We can classify transaction tables as deep because the number of columns is minimal, but the number of rows will grow. Tables such as `customers` and `products` are known as reference tables, which are wide in shape because they could have dozens of columns with significantly fewer rows compared to transaction tables.

Tables with high numbers of rows and columns and densely-populated distinct values take up more disk space and require more memory and CPU to process. If the `sales` table has billons of rows, counting the number of rows could take hours waiting for the response from `SELECT count(*) from sales` and would be discouraged by the administrators/IT support team. I worked with a data engineering team that was able to retrieve SQL results in less than 10 seconds against a 100 billion record table. That kind of response time requires developer expertise and administrative access to configure the table to support a super-fast response time.

Another valid point when dealing with the `count()` function is knowing the difference between frequency versus distinct values. Depending on which table you are performing a counting function against, you may be just counting the number of occurrences, or frequency of records. For the 30,000 customers example, if there is a difference in the results between `count(customer_id)` and `count(distinct customer_id)`, we know counting the records includes duplicate customers. This may not be an issue depending on the analysis you are performing. If you wanted to know how often a customer buys any product, then `counting(customer_id)` will answer that question. If you wanted to know how many customers are buying each product, using `distinct` would provide more accurate information.

The sum() function, which is short for summation, is another common measure used for statistical analysis in descriptive analytics. One key difference between counting versus summing would be that sum requires a number value to calculate accurate results whereas counting can be done against any data type. For example, you cannot and should not sum the customer_name field in the customers table because the data type is defined as a string. You can technically sum the customer_id field if it's defined as an integer, however, that would give you misleading information because that is not the intended use of the field. Like count, sum is an aggregate measure used to add together all of the values found in a specific field such as sales_amount or quantity from a sales table.

To use the sum() function in SQL is easy. If you want to know the sum for all time with no constraints or conditions, use the following:

```
SELECT sum(field_name) from table_name
```

You can then add a condition such as only active customers by including the WHERE clause with the flag field, which has the following syntax: SELECT sum(field_name) from table_name WHERE active_flg = TRUE.

We will uncover more advanced features such as aggregation using SQL in Chapter 8, *Understanding Joins, Relationships, and Aggregates*.

The mean or average function is another common statistical function very useful for data analysis, and it's easy to write the command using SQL. average is the sum of all values divided by the count with the syntax of SELECT avg(field_name) from table_name.

The denominator of counting values is using the frequency/number of occurrences versus distinct values so you should understand how the table is populated before running the SQL command. For example, a sales table is transaction-based with many customers and products so the average would be different from the average against the product or customer table because each record would be distinct.

The min and max functions are also useful and easy to interpret using SQL. The built-in functions are min() and max(), which return the minimum numeric value from a population of data along with the maximum or highest value. A good business question to understand from your table would be what is the lowest and highest sales amount for 2018? The syntax in SQL would be as follows:

```
SELECT min(sales_amount), max(sales_amount) from sales_table where year = 2018
```

This information would be useful to know to understand the range of sales per customer and product across all periods of time.

An important factor to recognize when running these statistical functions against your data is to understand when values are blank or what is commonly known as null. In SQL, NULL represents nothing and the nonexistence of a value. In RDBMS, null values are a rule when a DBA defines the schema for each table. During that process of creating columns by defining the data type for each field, there is an option to allow null values. The reasons vary by use case whether to allow nulls during the design of a database table, but what's important to understand for analysis is whether they exist in your data and how they should be treated.

Let's start with an example from our `customers` table where one of the fields such as the second address line allows NULL, which is common. Why is this common? Because a second address field is optional and is not even used in many cases, but what if you are a company that needs to physically mail marketing materials or invoices to customers? If the data entry always required a value, it would unnecessarily populate a value in that second address field in the database, which is inefficient because it takes more time to enter a value for each customer and takes more storage space. In most cases, forcing a value in large-scale enterprise systems creates poor data quality, which then requires time to fix the data or creates confusion working with the data, especially working with millions of customers.

Metadata explained

Metadata is commonly known as descriptive information about the data source. A key concept exposed in metadata analysis is related to understanding that nulls exist in databases. From a data analysis perspective, we need to make sure we understand how it impacts our analysis. In Python and other coding languages such as Java, you may see the word NaN returned. This is an acronym for *Not a Number* and helps you to understand that you may not be able to perform statistical calculations or functions against those values. In other cases such as Python, NaN values will have special functions to handle them, such as the following:

- In NumPy, use the `nansum()` function
- Use pandas with the `isnull()` function
- In SQL, use `is null` or `isnull` depending on the RDBMS you are working with

Since you are testing for a condition to exist, you can also include the keyword of `NOT` to test for the opposite, for example, `Select * from customer_table where customer_name is NOT null`.

Understanding nulls and `NaN` boils down to KYD and metadata about the source datasets you are working with. If you don't have access to the database system to see the metadata and underlining schema, we can use pandas and DataFrames to gain some insights about SQL data. Let's walk through an example, by loading a single table from the database into a DataFrame in a notebook and run some metadata functions to gain more information.

To begin, create a new Jupyter notebook and name it `test_for_nulls_using_sql_and_pandas`:

1. Similar to the prior example, to load an SQLite database connection, you just need to add the following command in your Jupyter notebook and run the cell:

   ```
   In[]: import sqlite3
   ```

2. Next, we need to assign a connection to a variable named `conn` and point to the location of the database file, which is named `customer_sales.db`. Since we already imported the `sqlite3` library in the prior `In[]` line, we can use this built-in function to communicate with the database:

   ```
   In[]: conn = sqlite3.connect('customer_sales.db')
   ```

3. Import the `pandas` library as shown in the following code:

   ```
   In[]: import pandas as pd
   ```

4. Using the `read_sql_query()` function, we assign the results to a new DataFrame as `df_customers` to make it easier to identify:

   ```
   In[]: df_customers = pd.read_sql_query("SELECT * from
   tbl_customers;", conn)
   ```

5. To view the results, we can just run the `head()` command against this DataFrame using this code:

   ```
   In[]: df_customers.head()
   ```

The output would look like the following screenshot where the `tbl_customers` table has been loaded into a DataFrame with a labeled header row with the index column to the left starting with a value of `0`:

	Customer_ID	First_Name	Last_Name	Address_Line_1	Address_Line_2	City	State	ZipCode	Phone	Email
0	1	Johnny	Smith	123 Main Street	None	Miami	FL	12345	302-555-1212	jsmith@email.com
1	2	Debbie	Winner	31 Roundtree Lane	None	Dover	NJ	18888	None	debbie_winner@email.com
2	3	Seth	Winer	310 Roundtree Lane	None	Dover	NJ	18888	None	sw@email.com
3	4	Anthony	Leedessa	Dallas Drive	Unit 806	El Paso	TX	99928	None	alligator@email.com
4	5	Pete	Einstein	Morton Street	None	Philadelphia	PA	28373	215-555-1212	peter_einstein@email.com

6. We can profile the DataFrame and easily identify any NULL values using the following command. The `isnull()` pandas function tests for null values across the entire DataFrame:

```
In[]: pd.isnull(df_customers)
```

The output would look like the following screenshot where the DataFrame will return a `True` or `False` value rather than the actual value by the cell for each row and column:

```
In [12]: pd.isnull(df_customers)
```

	Customer_ID	First_Name	Last_Name	Address_Line_1	Address_Line_2	City	State	ZipCode	Phone	Email
0	False	False	False	False	True	False	False	False	False	False
1	False	False	False	False	True	False	False	False	True	False
2	False	False	False	False	True	False	False	False	True	False
3	False	False	False	False	False	False	False	False	True	False
4	False	False	False	False	True	False	False	False	False	False

With a few commands, we learned how to communicate with databases and identify some important metadata about the data stored in tables. To continue improving our data literacy, let's understand how the data was populated into the database by understanding data lineage.

The importance of data lineage

Data lineage is the ability to trace back the source of a dataset to how it was created. It is a fun topic for me because it typically requires investigating the history of how systems generate data, identifying how it was processed, and working with the people who produce and consume the data. This process helps to improve your data literacy, which is the ability to read, write, analyze, and argue with data because you can learn how the data impacts the organization. Is the data critical to business functions such as generating sales or was it created for compliance purposes? These types of questions should be answered by learning more about the lineage of the data.

From experience, this process of tracing data lineage involves working sessions directly with the people who are responsible for the data and uncovering any documentation like an ERD demonstrated in the *From SQL to pandas DataFrames* section or help guides. In many cases, the documentation available for enterprise systems that have matured over time will not reflect the nuances that you will see when analyzing the data. For example, if a new field was created on an existing table that is populated from a web form that did not exist before, historical data will have NULL or NaN values until the point in time when the data entry started.

Data lineage can quickly become complex, which takes time to unwind and multiple resources to expose the details when not properly documented. When multiple systems are involved, working with **Subject Matter Experts (SMEs)** will fast track the process so you don't have to reverse engineer all of the steps in the data flow.

Data flow

Data flow is a subset of data lineage that is typically part of a larger data governance strategy within large organizations so there may be existing tools or systems already in place that visually represent how the data is processed, which is commonly known as data flow. A hypothetical example of a data flow diagram would be the following diagram where we look at some of the data we have been working with in our exercises so far. In this diagram, we have a logical representation of how the `tbl_customers` table is populated from our SQLite database. I have documented the inputs and outputs as stages one to four:

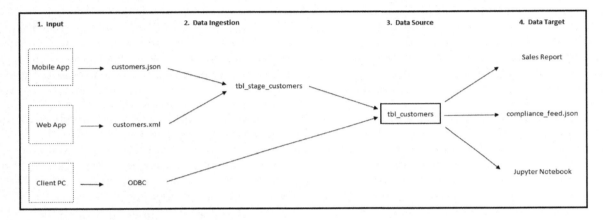

The input stage

First, we have the **Input** stage, which is identified as the **Mobile App**, **Web App,** and **Client PC** systems. These systems have created feeds out into multiple file formats. In our example, this data is batch processed, where the data files are saved and sent out for the next stage.

The data ingestion stage

The **Data Ingestion** stage is where multiple files such as `customers.json` and `customers.xml` are processed. Because this is a logical diagram rather than a highly technical one, the details behind what technologies are used to process the data ingestion are omitted. Data ingestion is also known as **ETL**, which is an acronym for **Extract, Transform, and Load**, which is automated and maintained by data engineering teams or developers.

We can see an intermediary step called `tbl_stage_customers` during this ETL, which is a landing table for processing the data between the source files and the target table in the database. Also included in this stage is an ODBC connection where the **Client PC** system has direct access to insert, update, and delete records from the `tbl_customers` table.

 During the process of learning more about the data flow, be sure to ask whether the tables are defined with logical delete versus the physical deleting of rows. In most cases, the direct removal of rows in a table is not supported, so Boolean data type columns are used to indicate whether the record is active or flagged for deletion by the system or user.

The data source stage

The third stage is named **Data Source**, which is defined as the `tbl_customers` table. Some questions to ask the developer or DBA are as follows:

- What is your retention policy for this data/how long is the data preserved?
- What is the average daily volume of records being populated in this table?
- Can they provide some metadata such as how many rows, columns, and data types for each field?
- What are the dependencies/joins to this table including primary and foreign keys?
- How often is this table backed up and is there system downtime we should be aware of that would impact analysis?
- Does a data dictionary exist for this table/database?

The data target stage

The fourth stage, named **Data Target**, helps a data analyst to understand downstream dependencies from the source table. In this example, we have a **Sales Report**, the `compliance_feed.json` file, and **Jupyter Notebook**. Some useful information to uncover would be the frequency of how often that compliance feed is sent and who the consumers of that data are.

This may become important if the timing of your analysis is not in line with data feeds from the **Data Source** stage. Trust in your analysis and the ability to argue that your analysis is complete and accurate comes from understanding timing issues and your ability to reconcile and match counts between multiple data-target outputs.

Business rules

Another important point about data lineage is to uncover business rules, lookup values, or mapping reference sources. A business rule is an abstract concept that helps you to understand software code that is applied during data processing. An example would be when the user of the **Mobile App** clicks a **Submit** button, a new `customers.json` file is created. Business rules can also be more complex, such as `tbl_stage_customers` table does not populate records in the `tbl_customers` until all source files are received and a batch process runs at 12 A.M. EST daily. Business rules may be explicitly defined in the database during the creation of a database table such as the rule to define a primary key on a column, coded on a web form or mobile application.

Documenting these business rules should be included in your methodology to support your analysis. This helps you to argue insights from your data analysis by either verifying the existence of the business rule or identifying outliers that contradict assumptions made about the source data. For example, if you were told a database table was created to not allow NULL in specific fields but you end up finding it, you can review your findings with the DBA to uncover how this occurred. It could have easily been a business exception that was created or that the enforcement of the business rule was implemented after the table was already populated.

Understanding business rules helps to identify data gaps and verifies accuracy during analysis. If the average daily volume of records for this table drops to zero records for multiple consecutive days, there might be an issue in stage 2 during the **Data Ingestion** or it just might be a holiday where no customer records were received and processed.

In either case, learning how to ask these questions of the subject matter experts and verifying the data lineage will build confidence in your analysis and trust with both producers and consumers of the data.

Now that you understand all of the concepts, let's walk through the data lineage of the data we are working with in this chapter—`customer_sales.db`:

1. In the **Input** stage for this database, three source CSV files were manually created for example purposes. Each source table has a one-for-one match with a CSV file named `tbl_customers`, `tbl_products`, and `tbl_sales`.

2. In the **Data Ingestion** stage, each file was imported using a few SQL commands, which created the schema for each table (the field names, defined data types, and join relationships). This process is commonly known as an ETL where the source data is ingested and persisted as tables in the database. If any changes between the source files and the target database table are required, a business rule should be documented to help to provide transparency between the producers and consumers of the data. For this example, the source and target match.

3. The **Data Source** stage in this example would be `customer_sales.db`. This now becomes the golden copy for data flowing out of the database for analysis and any reporting.

4. The **Target** stage in our example would be the Jupyter notebook and the creation of DataFrames for analysis.

While this is a small example with only a few steps, the concepts apply to large-scale enterprise solutions with many more data sources and technologies used to automate the data flow. I commonly sketch out the stages for data lineage before doing any data analysis to ensure I understand the complete process. This helps to communicate with stakeholders and SMEs to ensure accuracy in the insights you gain from data sources.

Summary

We have covered a few key topics in this chapter to help you to improve your data literacy by learning about working with databases and using SQL. We learned about the history of SQL and the people who created the foundation for storing structured data in databases. We walked through some examples and how to insert records from a SQL `SELECT` statement into a `pandas` DataFrame for analysis.

By using the `pandas` library, we learned about how to sort, limit, and restrict data along with fundamental statistical functions such as counting, summing, and average. We covered how to identify and work with `NaN` (that is, nulls) in datasets along with the importance of data lineage during analysis.

In our next chapter, we will explore time series data and learn how to visualize your data using additional Python libraries to help to improve your data literacy skills.

Further reading

Here are some links that you can refer to for more information on the relative topics of this chapter:

- Historical details about how SQL was created: `http://www.contrib.andrew.cmu.edu/~shadow/sql/sql1992.txt`
- Handling NULL values: `https://codeburst.io/understanding-null-undefined-and-nan-b603cb74b44c`
- Handling duplicate values with pandas: `https://www.python-course.eu/dealing_with_NaN_in_python.php`
- About SQLite databases: `https://www.sqlite.org/about.html`
- Data modeling techniques: `https://www.kimballgroup.com/data-warehouse-business-intelligence-resources/kimball-techniques/dimensional-modeling-techniques/`
- pandas DataFrame functions: `https://pandas.pydata.org/pandas-docs/stable/reference/api/pandas.DataFrame.html`

Section 2: Solutions for Data Discovery 2

In this section, we'll learn how to visualize data for analysis by working with time series data. Then, we'll learn how to clean and join multiple datasets together using both SQL and DataFrames with Python. After that, we'll go back to data visualization and learn about the best practices when it comes to data storytelling. By the end of this section, you will understand the foundations of descriptive analytics.

This section includes the following chapters:

- Chapter 6, *Visualizing and Working with Time Series Data*
- Chapter 7, *Exploring, Cleaning, Refining, and Blending Datasets*
- Chapter 8, *Understanding Joins, Relationships, and Aggregates*
- Chapter 9, *Plotting, Visualization, and Storytelling*

6
Visualizing and Working with Time Series Data

Regardless of whether the data source is from a file or database, we have now defined a repeatable analysis workflow. This is used to load the data into either an array or DataFrame and then answer business questions by running a few Python commands using their respective libraries.

This process has served us well so far and is a necessary step to *up-skill* our learning of how to work with data, which ultimately improves data literacy. Now, we are going to take yet another exciting step to help you communicate analysis by visualizing your data. In this chapter, we will learn how to create visual artifacts that can support structured data. We will break down the anatomy of a chart by uncovering the fundamentals of how data visualizations are created. Using the plotting features available in Python, you will create your first time series chart using the `matplotlib` library.

We will cover the following topics in the chapter:

- Data modeling for results
- Anatomy of a chart and data viz best practices
- Comparative analysis
- The shape of the curve

Let's get started.

Technical requirements

You can find the GitHub repository for this book at `https://github.com/PacktPublishing/Practical-Data-Analysis-using-Jupyter-Notebook/tree/master/Chapter06`.

You can download and install the required software from `https://www.anaconda.com/products/individual`.

Data modeling for results

The introduction to data modeling we provided in `Chapter 5`, *Gathering and Loading Data in Python*, gave us an understanding of relational databases and fundamental statistics that can be performed against structured data. In those examples, we learned about the relationships of data and how data can be modeled from the perspective of the data producer. **Data producers** are responsible for storing data in a structure to ensure the data's integrity is consistent. In the previous chapter, we also learned how an **Entity Relationship Diagram (ERD)** can be used to define the relationships between tables. In this chapter, we will apply these same concepts with the *data consumer* in mind. As a result, we will focus on creating new relationships with data, making it easier for analysis. This concept was an evolution in reporting and spawned a new industry commonly known as **Business Intelligence (BI)** and **Analytics**.

Introducing dimensions and measures

Data modeling for analysis means we are building new relationships from the source tables with the intention of answering business questions for the consumer. Creating a new data model with this focus scales up your analysis beyond single SQL `SELECT` statements that are run one at a time to answer one question. On the contrary, using a newly derived data model for analysis will provide answers to dozens of questions using only a few or even one table. How is this possible? It's all about why the new analysis tables are needed and how those relationships are defined. For example, the database tables required to support a mobile application used for social media would not be the same data model that's used for a sales analysis.

In some cases, the data model that is created from the data producer may be reused for a consumer so that you don't have to make any changes, such as in our example in the previous chapter. In other cases, you will simply extend the existing data model with the addition of new fields, which could be from new data sources or derived from the existing data rows and columns. In either case, from a data analyst perspective, we are changing how we look at an existing data model by looking at how we could use columns as either dimensions or measures.

Dimensions in data models are values with descriptive attributes that are commonly used to identify a person, place, or thing. The easiest way to remember dimensional fields is that they can be classified as a *noun*. A good example would be a date dimension where any given date value, such as `12/03/1975`, would have multiple attributes that can be derived from this one value, as shown in the following table:

Field Name	Field Value
Date	`12/03/1975`
Year	`1975`
Month Number	`12`
Month Name	`December`
WeekDay	`Wednesday`
Quarter	`Q4`
Is_Weekend_Flag	`FALSE`

A **measure** in a data model is any field that has values that can be aggregated using statistical calculations such as `sum`, `min`, `max`, or `average`. An easy way to identify a measure field is to question whether the values are in action so you could classify them as verbs. In many cases, measure values repeat with high frequency in a table source. Common fields that can be identified as a measure include a sales amount, sales quantity, or stock closing price. Measure fields are typically stored in tables that you can abstract to a `fact` table. A `fact` table will already be defined by the producer or could be derived during analysis. A fact table represents an event, transaction, or entity defined by a single row in a database table. A primary key, which we defined in `Chapter 5`, *Gathering and Loading Data in Python*, is used to uniquely identify each row to ensure consistency for reporting and analysis. If multiple fields are required to uniquely identify a record, a surrogate key field would be created.

Joined to the fact table will be one or more dimensional tables organized in a way that they answer business questions in a repeatable manner. Unlike a relational data model, which is used to support systems and applications, a dimensional data model should be built for analysis and reporting.

These concepts were introduced to me over 10 years ago by my mentor and former colleague Rich Hunter while we worked at Axis Group, LLC in Berkley Heights, NJ. I would define the people who worked at this boutique BI consulting company as *data marines* because of their ability to understand, adapt, and overcome problems using data. Solving problems and creating data solutions were part of their standard operating procedures. It was during this time that Rich changed my perspective on how to work with data by introducing me to a new way to look at data that changed my career. I am excited to share the same foundational data analysis concepts with you now. I will forever be grateful for working with my former colleagues at Axis Group.

It begins with learning about the data modeling methods created by Ralph Kimball and Bill Inmon, who are commonly known as the founding fathers of data warehousing. Both men defined approaches that can be used to structure data that scales with any size of company and subject area, with a focus on the analysis of data and creating reports against it. Their contributions to the data technology industry were so monumental that I identified them as part of the *Evolution of Data Analysis*, which I discussed in `Chapter 1`, *Fundamentals of Data Analysis*.

A data warehouse, which is commonly known as an **Enterprise Data Warehouse (EDW)**, is a centralized location of data from multiple sources with the purpose of providing, reporting, and analyzing data. Traditional data warehouses are organized by subjects such as human resources, sales, or accounting. Depending on the complexity of the Vs of data (**Variety**, **Volume**, and **Velocity**), a data warehouse may be centrally located in one technology solution or distributed across different technologies.

Why would an organization create a centralized data warehouse? Because the consistency and accuracy of reporting against the data source are worth the cost. In some cases, the importance of quality is so high that companies invest in the creation of one or more data warehouses. Once an organization has defined a need for a centralized location for all data, it would be commonly known as a *single version of the truth* for all reporting and analysis. Ideally, this is where different datasets from different technology sources could be collected and conformed with defined and consistent business rules. A sales manager and **human resources (HR)** manager can individually look at data from different reports but have the same accuracy so that data-driven decisions can be made.

Now that you understand why a data warehouse is an important concept, let's briefly review the two common approaches that are used to build them. First, they are not defined to a specific technology, so when a data architect is creating them, the focus is on defining the structure, which is known as the database schema, to support the different subject areas. Data subject areas are typically organized by lines of business or organizational structures. For example, the HR warehouse will have a focus on employee attributes such as hire date, manager, and job title. Once the tables and relationships have been defined, a unique employee identifier can be shared across the organization and other downstream systems such as employee benefits and compensation.

The approach we use to build the warehouse design up and out across the company follows two different approaches. Bill Inmon suggests a top-down approach where the organization makes a strategic solution to define a common standard before implementation. Ralph Kimball recommends a bottom-up approach, where each subject area is built to support management decision needs with less enforcement to a rigid standard.

For example, I was with a client where the sales teams did geographic hierarchal reporting with defined regions to organize the counties they did business with. So, a region was defined in the warehouse with the precise short abbreviations to represent the values and provide consistency between any reports or analytic applications. **EMEA** represented all countries in Europe, the Middle East, and Africa, for example.

This approach worked fine until the HR team decided they wanted to break out the counties in EMEA for better reporting and analysis. To solve this, they had a few options, including creating a second level in the hierarchy in between the country and the region so that reporting would need a drill-down; for example, EMEA to the Middle East to Israel.

Another option was to create an HR region field that was independent of how the sales regions were defined. This allowed us to send reporting and analysis details to executives without impacting anything related to sales analysis. This option worked as a solution because the engineering team was able to please business users across multiple departments while still creating the value of consistency across all downstream reporting solutions.

Dimensionally modeling your data for reporting and analysis is technology-agnostic. While the concept and techniques are commonly found in SQL solutions, you are not restricted to using only database technologies to model your data for analysis. The first step is to understand what questions you are *trying* to answer with the data. Then, you can decide which model will best answer the questions at hand. Some common questions you can apply to almost any data model are as follows:

- **Who?** Identifying the who in data should be straightforward. For employee data, the who is the actual employee unique identifier, along with all the attributes that make up that individual, including their first name, last name, date of birth, email, hire date, and so on. For sales-related data, the customer would be the *who*, so this would be the customer's name, mailing address, email, and so on.

- **What?** What product or server is being purchased? This would also include all the attributes (columns) unique to each product. So, if I purchased a cup of coffee, the size, flavor, and unit cost should be included.

- **When?** When is a very common question and with it, it's easy to identify the different fields associated with answering this question. All date, time, and timestamp fields are used to answer the question of when. For example, if a web user accesses a website, the *when* is the specific date and time that was recorded for that event. This becomes more complicated if the date/time data type is not standardized or doesn't account for time zones such as **Coordinated Universal Time. (UTC)**. Once you have the specific grain of detail behind all associated values, *Year*, *Month*, *Week*, and *Weekday* can be determined.

- **Where?** Where did the sale of the product or service occur? Do we have geographic location details or was it a store located with a street address?

- **How?** How does the event occur and how did it happen? Was the *how* of an activity, event, or outcome like a user clicking on a button to add an item to their shopping cart?

- **Why?** I think *why* is usually the most important question in data analysis and the one that's requested the most often by business users. Was the *why* a promotion or marketing campaign such as a flash sale for a specific product or service?

A visual representation of this can be seen in the following diagram, which shows all these key questions as dimensions, with an **Event Fact** in the center. This is commonly known as a **star schema** relationship, where high-volume transactions with many rows are stored in the **Event Fact** and distinct and unique values are stored in dimensional tables that address the questions of **Who, What, When, Where, How**, and **Why**:

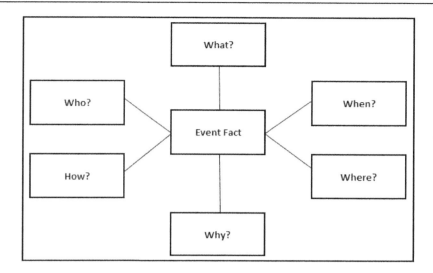

The rule of thumb is that the Event Fact table is narrow (a low number of fields with multiple join key fields) with a high number of rows. Dimensional tables will have district records with wide attributes (a high number of fields with a single join key).

In the process of asking and answering these questions, you end up grouping one or more fields together from the source data into defined relationships. For example, for all the customer attributes, you could create a table, CSV file, or DataFrame with all the different fields using a single unique key to identify each customer. Creating a data model is the foundation of building out charts and data visualizations.

Anatomy of a chart and data viz best practices

So, what makes a good chart or visualization? The answer depends on a few factors, most of which boils down to the dataset you are working with. Think of a dataset as a table of rows and columns that has consistency for each column or field available. For example, **Year** should have values of 2013, 2014, and 2015 all in the same consistent format. If your dataset has inconsistent formats or a mix of values, then cleansing your dataset before creating the chart is recommended. Data cleansing, or scrubbing, is the process of fixing or removing inaccurate records from your dataset. Charts need uniformity for reasons such as sorting the year values in ascending order to present a trend accurately.

Let's go with a simple example, as shown in the following diagram. Here, on the left-hand side of this dataset, we have a uniform table of data with four rows, two columns, and a header row. To ensure that you understand this concept, a table is a type of chart where you can define dimensions and measures. The header of this chart makes it easy for us to understand what the values should represent for each row because each column has consistent formats. As we covered in `Chapter 1`, *Fundamentals of Data Analysis*, we call this a *data type*, where every value in the same column will help to create a chart that will be much faster:

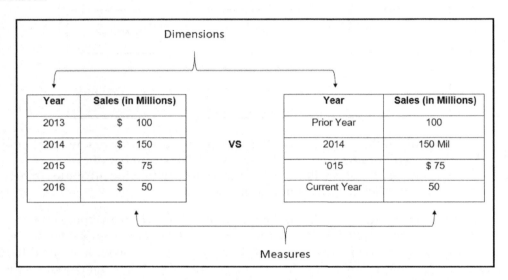

For the preceding chart, we have some obvious cleanup work to do before creating any visualization. The **Year** column in this chart has a mixture of values that will make it difficult for us to create a visual trend because of all the inconsistencies. Also, for the **Sales (in Millions)** column, it will be hard to create any aggregation, such as the sum of the total sales, because the values are a blend of numbers and characters. Regardless of the tool that's used to create a chart, having the data cleansed will ensure its quality and accuracy.

Analyzing your data

Once we have a clean dataset, we are ready to classify the fields of the dataset by the fundamentals of a chart – a dimension and a measure. As we discussed earlier, the easiest way to explain this difference is that a dimension is a noun, which is classified as a person, place, or thing. The most common dimensional field that can be applied to many different datasets is date/time, which allows you to create trends over time.

Measures are verbs, which are action columns from your data that allow aggregation (sum, count, average, min, max, and so on). In the following diagram, we have a bar chart labeled **Sales (in Millions)** where I have identified the distinction between them:

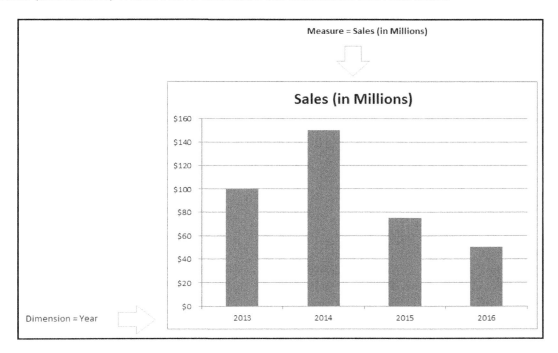

Any field with any data type can be used as either a dimension or measure in a chart, so be sure the visual you choose answers the business question or provides the required insights.

So, why are these concepts important when it comes to creating a chart? They are common across almost all the different chart types, regardless of the technology used to create it. A bar chart that shows trends over time must have a date dimension (day, month, or year) and something to measure – sales, average price, or count of users.

So, now that we understand the basics, let's walk through a few examples. The bar trend chart shown in the following diagram has a dimension of **year** and a measure of **Sales by Product**:

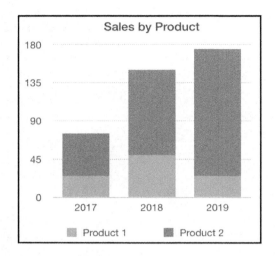

To mix it up, the chart has multiple dimensions. In this case, we have two dimensions—the year and the product. The year is displayed in a series on the *x* axis and is not labeled. The **Product** values are represented as stacked bars with consistent colors for each value corresponding to the legend measured on the *y* axis.

Charts can be visualized in different types, including the most common: bar, line, and pie. The line chart shown in the following screenshot visually offers us an easy way to identify the accelerated growth over time:

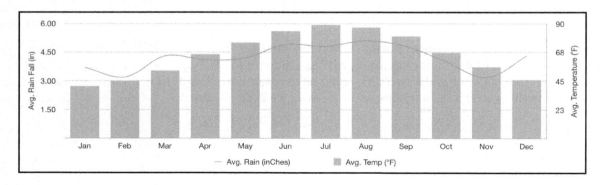

The **Combo** chart in the preceding screenshot has both a line and bars in the same chart, with two different measures on the two different axes. In this example, the bars represent the measure of **Avg. Temperature (F)**. These can be seen on the right axis and are using Fahrenheit as a scale. The line shows the **Avg. Rain Fall (in)** measure, which is labeled on the left-hand side axis from **1.50** to **6.00** inches.

Having two measures allows us to perform a comparative analysis against different measures using a common dimension, which is a date in the prior example. Depending on the charting technology used in this example, different date dimensions such as timestamp, date, or numeric month values can be used on the x axis as a month represented in **MMM** format. The end result of this chart tells a dramatic story of how these two measures compare throughout time by highlighting the low and high outliers without scanning or searching for them in a table.

Why pie charts have lost ground

Pie charts have lost favor as the go-to chart, but were widely used in the past. In fact, an entire book written by Stephen Few covers the *dos and don'ts of dashboarding*, where he points out why pie charts should be replaced by alternatives, such as the horizontal bar chart provided here. I have provided a reference to the book in the *Further reading* section if you want to find out more.

Some key advantages of horizontal bar charts over a pie chart are as follows:

- **Ease of consumption**: I don't have to look at a legend to look up the dimension's values.
- **Sort ability**: You can sort by the highest or lowest values to emphasize importance within your dataset.
- **Best of both worlds**: They have distribution and relative value, just like a pie chart. If you look at the following chart, you'll see that **Product 1** is twice as large as **Product 5**. Here, you can quickly see by how much because the same x axis is used for easy reference to the bar width.

The following is an example of a horizontal bar chart:

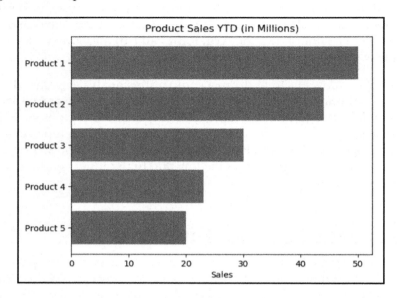

If you still find a need to use pie charts, they work best if you only have two distinct values. In the following example, you can easily see the distribution between the **Yes** and **No** values. The use of a primary color for emphasis, as well as using a muted grey color for the negative, helps communicate a positive message in this chart:

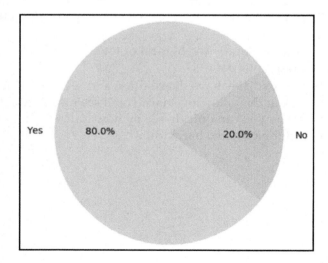

Choosing the right chart is a balance between what story the author wants to tell using the data and the number of dimensions and measures available from the data. I find it to be an *art and science* approach where practice improves how you create good visualizations. There are numerous resources available regarding which chart helps you tell the best story. Now that you know the ingredients of any chart type that use dimensions and measures, you have a common framework that you can apply across any technology and subject area. Choosing the right visual chart that helps you convey the right message also takes time, experience, and even trial and error.

Since I classify data visualization as *an art and a science*, it does take time to go through the profile and understand the business questions you are trying to answer. Feel free to use the chart options outlined in the *Further reading* section for guidance. Be sure to remember a few of these tips:

- **Reusing code is highly encouraged**: Don't reinvent the wheel by creating a new chart from scratch. Find a good example and attempt to fit your data into the dimensions and measures.
- **Less is more**: Avoid distractions and let the data tell the story – use visual cues for emphasis and highlighting outliers. Overusing multiple colors is distracting to the consumer, so only use one color to highlight what you want the audience of the chart to focus on.
- **There are plenty of experts out there**: Use them! I have placed a few URL links in the *Further reading* section to help.

Art versus science

For me, data visualization is *an art and a science*. For me, it started in fourth grade with my teacher, Mr. Segar, who inspired creativity and introduced me to master craftsmen such as Van Gogh, Chaggal, and Cezzane. Art is creating and inspiring free thought through visual imagery. How art is defined is subjective, but it commonly includes the *elements of art*, which are shape, form, value, line, color, space, and texture. Let's break down each one:

- **Shape** as an element of art is defined as the *area defined by edges*. Shape provides visual context and boundaries outside the work of art to the consumer of it.
- **Form** is defined as the *perceived volume or dimensionality* of an artwork. So, form would control the boundaries inside the shape.
- **Value** is the use of lightness and darkness within the artwork. Light is obviously an important element for any work of art and includes the full spectrum of light and lack thereof.

- **Line** as an element of art, which can be straight or curved, spans the distance between two points, which allows the artist to define intensity in the form.
- **Color** is probably the most well-known elements of art and is from when light impacts an object. This helps the consumer of the work of art to visually interpret pieces individually or in their totality. The properties of color include hue, which is what we commonly identify with colors such as *red*, *yellow*, and *blue*. Color also includes intensity, which is controlled by the full spectrum of colors available, along with value, which controls the brightness.
- **Space** is the area defined by the artist when they include the background and foreground. The distance in or around the space is another important factor to consider.
- **Texture** for the consumer of the artwork is the visual feeling portrayed in two-dimensional art.

Science is all about empirical evidence, which can be defined as data that's acquired by observation or experimentation. Data has always been part of the scientific method and is critical to collecting evidence to prove a theory or hypothesis.

When these two concepts come together, they allow you to tell a story with information using data visualizations that provide insights and give us the ability to understand trends instantly.

What makes great data visualizations?

For me, it has been a subjective question with my answer evolving over time, which means it can be a challenge to provide a straightforward answer.

What I find beautiful and intuitive might not be as insightful to others. This is similar to works of art where different styles, periods, and artists will have lovers and critics. Over the last few years, I have witnessed how data visualizations have evolved into an art form where technology and coding have allowed creativity to flourish. This movement from creating simple charts, plots, and graphics has evolved to what is commonly known as **data viz**.

Data viz can be anything from an infographic to an animated visual that can tell a story with data. When I see something that is aesthetically pleasing and inspires me to take action, I would classify that as a great data visualization. These actions can vary based on the information provided, but common responses include sharing the data viz with others with the intention of sparking a dialog about it. Also, a great data viz should reveal patterns and trends. This helps the consumer easily separate the actionable information from the noise. Noise in data means the audience is confused by the chart or no recognizable visual patterns are evident. The graphic that's displayed should be intuitive to the audience and not require additional context or force the consumer to look up additional information just to understand the chart.

There are experts in the field of data viz that I've included in the *Evolution of data analysis* section of `Chapter 1`, *Fundamentals of Data Analysis*. They include Stephen Few, Edward Tufte, and Alberto Cairo. I would encourage you to research their many different books and writings about this subject – I have also added some of their works in the *Further reading* section.

Another champion in the world of data viz is Naomi B Robinson, who is the founder of the **Data Visualization New York** chapter on `Meetup.com`. This public community brings together professional experts across any industry with spectrum specialty skills including journalism, software development, data architects, UI/UX experts, graphic designers, and data scientists. With members from around the world, their mission is to share best practices, expertise, and create an open forum to promote data as a craft. Membership is open to anyone, so I would encourage you to join as a member and hope you enjoy the events as much as I do.

Some of the insights I have gained over the years about data viz include the following:

- *Data viz is a craft* that will take time to master but will have rewards as a career because the more techniques you learn, the better you will get at creating them.
- Technology alone will not make a great data visualization. Technology enables the author of a chart, dashboard, or app to create data solutions, but there is a learning curve when it comes to mastering each tool.
- A *great data viz will inspire people to promote and evangelize the story* about data without the context of how it was created.

An example of a great data viz can be found in the documentary *The Inconvenient Truth*, where a single line chart was the focal point of why people should pay attention to climate change. The inclusion of this one graph, which was shaped like a hockey stick, sparked both controversy and conversation. More importantly, this data visualization conveyed a story using data to an audience beyond the scientific community.

Comparative analysis

Now that we have a better understanding of the anatomy of a chart, we can start looking at time series charts in depth by explaining some of the differences between the date and time trends in charts.

Date and time trends explained

We'll begin with the example shown in the following graph, where we have a line chart with each data point represented by a single value. The first great thing about visualizing data is how easy it is to interpret the results without having all the context of how it was generated:

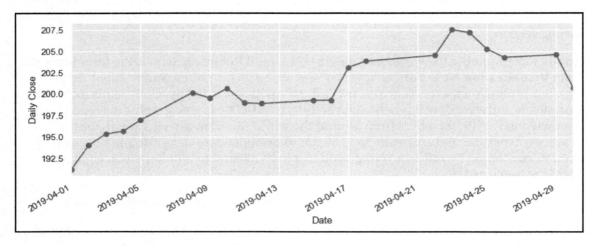

A best practice to emphasize in the preceding chart is the date values that are presented are in the standard and consistent format of **YYYY-MM-DD**. There are multiple reasons why this is important. For the producer of the chart, having a consistent data type ensures all the values are accurate for sorting and completion, which means the data visual matches the source data. Another factor to consider as the producer of the chart is regarding what the lowest available date value available is in the source data across all the values. This concept is known as the *grain of data*, which determines which date can be used as the dimension for the chart. If a mix of daily and monthly data values exists in the same field, you should not display them in the same chart *as is* as this may confuse the consumer.

My colleague Mike Ursitti is fond of saying good dashboard design is when you have created a solution where the consumer does not have to think, so interpretation by any audience becomes natural. He's right, of course – it's easy to create distractions where the date values that are displayed are inconsistent or overuse color leads, which leads to more questions about what the producer of the chart was attempting to portray. So, as a data analyst, spend time thinking about which layout and design will present your analysis in a logical fashion that is easy to consume by any audience.

In the following chart, we have the same data source as in the previous example but now the data has been aggregated by month, represented as an integer value from 1 to 12. The labels used in this case are important to help the consumer understand which aggregation is used to represent the values displayed for each period of time. The ability to look at data from different date formats is a crucial skill to learn for data analysis and improves your data literacy:

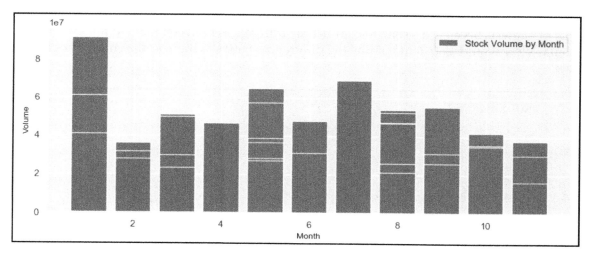

To *argue* about the insights from this chart requires that you understand whether the correct aggregation is used appropriately. In many cases, that requires both the consumer and producer to have an understanding of the data subject and how it should be used. For this example, summing the values in the *Daily Close Stock price* per month would not be relevant for this data domain and a subject matter expert would call this type of measure inaccurate.

However, offering a different date format provides us with an opportunity to look at the data in a way that may not have been originally considered. You also can provide insights faster because you don't have to hunt to find a specific value at the individual date value. For example, looking at a 12-month trend shows 12 data points on a line chart versus displaying dozens or even hundreds of individual days.

Comparing results over periods of time in a chart allows you to quickly spot outliers or identify trends in the data. For example, if you plot a chart of Apple's closing stock prices for each day, you will see upward or downward trends visually based on the skew of the line. This allows the consumer to identify patterns in the data faster and may not be as evident if you looked at each value individually.

Another popular and useful data analysis is **year over year**. If you are looking at the current year, this analysis is commonly known as **year to date (YTD)** versus **prior year to date (PYTD)**. In this case, you have to define a fixed point in the current year, such as the current day or month, and then only include the days or months from last year that align to the prior year.

The following chart is an example of this useful analysis where we compare the volume of Apple shares traded over every month from January to April in the current year, which was identified as **2019**, and then compared the results with the same months during the prior year, which was identified as **2018**. I find using a line chart is a useful way to visualize this type of analysis because it's easy to contrast the differences between the two lines. A simple tabular view would also demonstrate the differences between them to the consumer of this data:

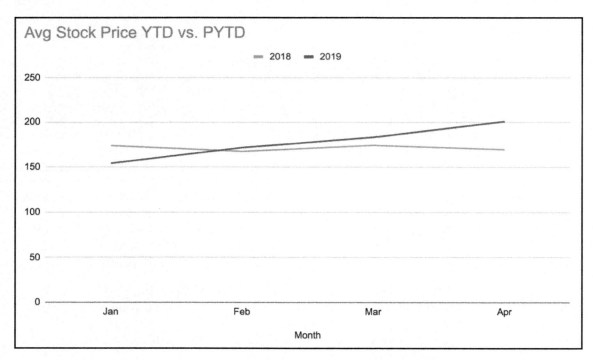

The following table shows an example of the same data but displayed in a different chart type. The preference of how to present this data visually can vary and you should be able to produce either option for your audience:

Month	2018	2019
Jan	174.01	154.00
Feb	167.64	171.73
Mar	174.50	183.29
Apr	169.83	200.52

The shape of the curve

We will now dive into creating visualizations from data using a new library named `matplotlib`, which was installed when you used Anaconda for the first time. According to the history page from `matplotlib.org`, this library evolved from MATLAB graphics and was created by John D. Hunter with the philosophy that *you should be able to create simple plots with just a few commands, or just one!*

Like many of the libraries we've introduced, there is a multitude of features and capabilities available to help you create charts and data visualizations. The `matplotlib` library has an ecosystem that you can apply to different use cases that nicely compliment the libraries of `pandas` and `numpy`.

There are many tutorials and additional resources available to help you learn the library. I have added the necessary links in the *Further reading* section for your reference.

In this example, we are going to load a CSV file that contains stock price details for a publicly-traded company on the **National Association of Securities Dealers Automated Quotations Exchange (NASDAQ)**. We are going to visualize one dimension and one measure using a line chart to see if we can identify any trends in the data.

To dive in, let's create a new Jupyter Notebook and name it `create_chart_with_matplotlib`. For this example, we will use a few libraries and commands we learned in prior chapters. I'll walk you through each step in the code, so feel free to follow along. I have placed a copy on GitHub for reference.

Creating your first time series chart

Follow these steps to create your first time series chart:

1. To load the `pandas` library, use the following command in your Jupyter Notebook and run the cell:

   ```
   In[]: import pandas as pd
   ```

   This library should already be available using Anaconda. Refer to `Chapter 2`, *Overview of Python and Installing Jupyter Notebook*, for help with setting up your environment.

2. Next, we can load the CSV file in a new DataFrame as `df_stock_price` to make it easier to identify. To reduce the number of steps to prepare the data for analysis, we are passing some parameter commands to the `pd.read_csv` function to index the first column in the file. We will also include the `parse_dates` parameter to define the data type of the `Date` field as `datetime64`:

   ```
   In[]: df_stock_price=pd.read_csv('AAPL.csv',
   index_col=0,parse_dates=True)
   ```

   Be sure you have copied the `AAPL.csv` file to the correct Jupyter folder directory to avoid errors when importing the data file.

3. As a good best practice before visualizing the data, let's ensure the DataFrame can be read using the `head()` command:

   ```
   In[]: df_stock_price.head(3)
   ```

4. The output will look as follows, where the source CSV file has been loaded into a DataFrame with a labeled header row with the index column defined as `Date`:

```
[ ]:  df_stock_price.head(3)

[ ]:              Open         High          Low         Close      Adj Close      Volume

     Date

     2019-01-02  154.889999  158.850006   154.229996   157.919998  155.582367   37039700

     2019-01-03  143.979996  145.720001   142.000000   142.190002  140.085220   91312200

     2019-01-04  144.529999  148.550003   143.800003   148.259995  146.065353   58607100
```

5. To validate that the data type of the index field is accurate, you can run the following command:

   ```
   In[]: df_stock_price.index
   ```

6. The output will look as follows, where the data type (**dtype**) of the index that was defined for this DataFrame is assigned to the Date field:

```
[4]:  df_stock_price.index

[4]:  DatetimeIndex(['2019-01-02', '2019-01-03', '2019-01-04', '2019-01-07',
                    '2019-01-08', '2019-01-09', '2019-01-10', '2019-01-11',
                    '2019-01-14', '2019-01-15',
                    ...
                    '2019-11-13', '2019-11-14', '2019-11-15', '2019-11-18',
                    '2019-11-19', '2019-11-20', '2019-11-21', '2019-11-22',
                    '2019-11-25', '2019-11-26'],
                   dtype='datetime64[ns]', name='Date', length=229, freq=None)
```

Having the index defined as a datetime data type field series will make the plot features much easier to work with. The more data preparation that's done before visualizing will ensure faster creation of charts.

7. Now, we can import the matplotlib library so that we can reference functions to visualize data. Matplotlib is a powerful library with multiple modules. We will explicitly focus on the pyplot module for this example. We'll use the common plt shortcut for easy reference and adoption of the best practice standards:

   ```
   In[]: import matplotlib.pyplot as plt
   ```

8. Let's create a quick line chart using the `plot()` function against our DataFrame. To avoid confusion when it comes to interpreting the visualization or an error processing the chart, let's include the specific `Close` field. Be sure to include a semicolon at the end of the line when using this library:

```
In[]: df_stock_price['Close'].plot()
```

You may need to include an additional line of `%matplotlib inline` to display results in your Jupyter Notebook. This extra line is known as a magic function.

9. The output will look as follows, where a line chart is displayed, which is the default option. This displays a trend line with the *x* axis using the `Date` field, which is also the dimension, and the *y* axis using the `Close` price field values, which is our measure:

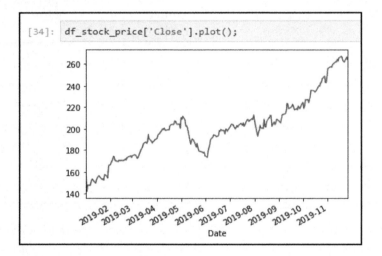

10. The `plot()` function has many different parameters that can be used to customize the visualization. Let's explore a few easy changes by adjusting the line width, color, and line style using the following command:

```
In[]: df_stock_price['Close'].plot(linewidth=.5,
color='green',linestyle='dotted')
```

11. The output will look as follows, where the same line chart is displayed, except the color has changed, the line width has been reduced, and the style of the line is dotted:

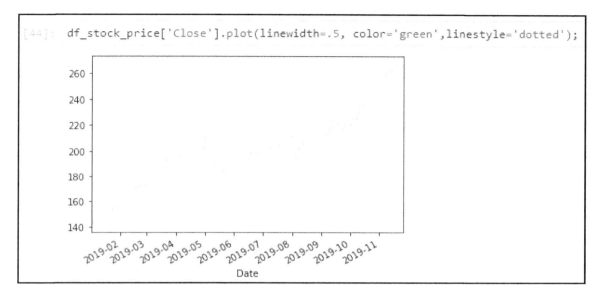

```
[44]: df_stock_price['Close'].plot(linewidth=.5, color='green',linestyle='dotted');
```

There are many different parameters that allow you to change the style of the visualization with some minor adjustments. I've put a reference to the library for you to explore in the *Further reading* section.

12. Next, let's enrich the chart features by including more details for the consumer by adding labels:

```
In[]: df_stock_price['Close'].plot(linewidth=.5,
color='green',linestyle='dotted')
plt.xlabel('Close Date')
plt.ylabel('Close Price')
plt.suptitle('AAPL Stock Price Trend');
```

13. The output will look as follows, where the same line chart is displayed before, except now we include context details such as dimension and measure labels, along with the header of the chart:

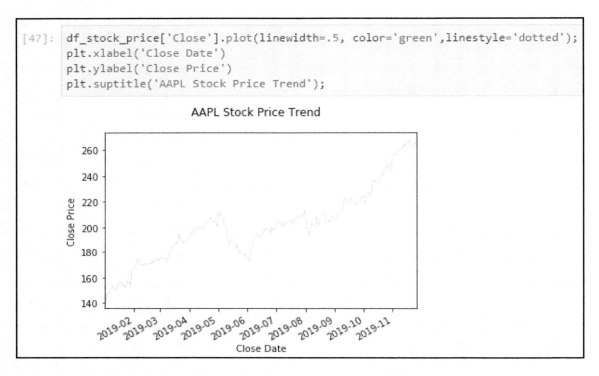

```
[47]: df_stock_price['Close'].plot(linewidth=.5, color='green',linestyle='dotted');
      plt.xlabel('Close Date')
      plt.ylabel('Close Price')
      plt.suptitle('AAPL Stock Price Trend');
```

14. Another data visualization feature available in this library is a bar chart. To use this feature, we have to make a few adjustments to the commands. To answer the question, *What is the stock volume trend?*, we can use this command. Note the use of .index to pass the Date field values:

```
In[]: plt.bar(df_stock_price.index,df_stock_price['Volume']);
```

The output will look as follows, where the chart displays values as a bar chart:

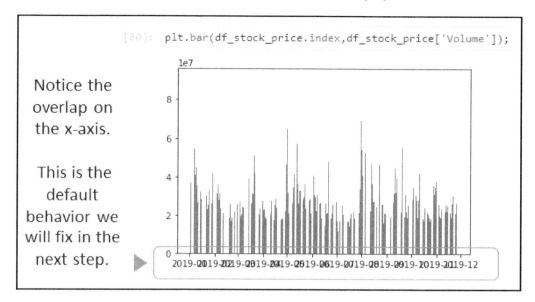

15. However, I see some issues with how this chart is presented to the consumer. The labels are overlapping, so it's difficult to understand the visualization. Let's add a few minor adjustments to make the chart more aesthetically pleasing:

```
In[]: plt.bar(df_stock_price.index,df_stock_price['Volume'],
color='blue')
plt.xticks(rotation = 90)
plt.yticks(fontsize = 10)
plt.xlabel('Date')
plt.ylabel('Volume')
plt.suptitle('AAPL Stock Volume Trend');
```

The output will look as follows, where the chart displays values as a bar chart. Note, however, that the labels have been added to make the chart easier to consume and understand:

```
[86]: plt.bar(df_stock_price.index,df_stock_price['Volume'], color='blue')
      plt.xticks(rotation = 90)
      plt.yticks(fontsize = 10)
      plt.xlabel('Date')
      plt.ylabel('Volume')
      plt.suptitle('AAPL Stock Volume Trend');
```

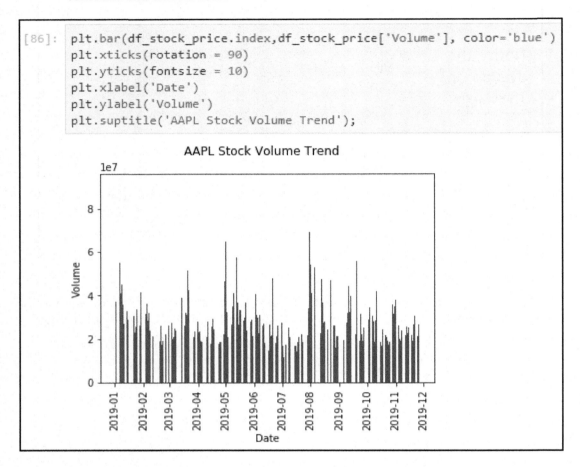

These steps define the best practice for producing an analysis workflow to visualize your data. Once you store data in a DataFrame and load the `matplotlib` library, visualizing your data becomes much faster. A little trial and error as you make adjustments to the parameters during this process is common. Always save your work and examples so that you can easily recreate the data visualizations that provide insights quickly without you having to sift through rows of data.

Summary

Congratulations – you have now learned some exciting new ways to visualize data and interpret various chart types to help expand your data literacy skills! In this chapter, you learned some best practices to find the right chart for the right type of analysis. You also learned the difference between a dimension and a measure, along with how to model data for analysis to answer questions.

Next, you learned some essential skills for making various plots, such as line graphs and bar charts, by exploring the various time series and date functionality in pandas. We highlighted leaders such as Alberto Cairo and Naomi B. Robbins in the world of data visualization and discussed how they have influenced the evolution of data analysis. Finally, you used the .plot() method to create time series charts using the matplotlib library.

In the next chapter, we will explore techniques we can use to clean, refine, and blend multiple datasets together.

Further reading

- Reference to all the Matplotlib library features: https://matplotlib.org/index.html
- Data visualization pitfalls to avoid: https://www.ometis.co.uk/data-visualisation-pitfalls/
- Nice writeup to help you choose the right chart: http://extremepresentation.typepad.com/blog/2006/09/choosing_a_good.html
- A great website to help you find the right chart for the right type of analysis: http://labs.juiceanalytics.com/chartchooser/index.html
- A nice cheat sheet to improve data viz: http://billiondollargraphics.com/wp-content/uploads/2015/09/Billion-Dollar-Graphics-Graphic-Cheat-Sheet.pdf
- Data visualization guide: http://www.excelcharts.com/blog/god-and-moses-the-differences-between-edward-tufte-and-stephen-few/
- The Functional Art blog: http://www.thefunctionalart.com/

- The NYC Data Visualization Meetup chapter, which is open to members from around the world: `https://www.meetup.com/DataVisualization/`
- The Kimball Group Dimensional Modeling Techniques: `https://www.kimballgroup.com/data-warehouse-business-intelligence-resources/kimball-techniques/dimensional-modeling-techniques/`

7

Exploring, Cleaning, Refining, and Blending Datasets

In the previous chapter, we learned about the power of data visualizations, and the importance of having good-quality, consistent data defined with dimensions and measures.

Now that we understand *why* that's important, we are going to focus on the *how* throughout this chapter by working hands-on with data. Most of the examples provided so far included data that was already *prepped* (prepared) ahead of time for easier consumption. We are now switching gears by learning the skills that are necessary to be comfortable working with data to increase your data literacy.

A key concept of this chapter is cleaning, filtering, and refining data. In many cases, the reason why you need to perform these actions is the source data does not provide high-quality analytics *as is*. Throughout my career, high-quality data is not the norm and data gaps are common. As good data analysts, we need to work with what we have available. We will cover some techniques to enrich the quality of the data so you can provide quality insights and answer questions from the data even when the source does not include all of the information required.

In my experience, highlighting the poor quality of the source data is the insight because not enough transparency exists and key stakeholders are unaware of the challenges of using the data. The bottom line is poor quality should not stop you from proceeding with working with data. My goal is to demonstrate a repeatable technique and workflow to improve data quality for analysis.

We will cover the following topics in this chapter:

- Retrieving, viewing, and storing tabular data
- Learning how to restrict, sort, and sift through data
- Cleaning, refining, and purifying data using Python
- Combining and binning data

Technical requirements

Here's the GitHub repository of this book: `https://github.com/PacktPublishing/Practical-Data-Analysis-using-Jupyter-Notebook/tree/master/Chapter07`.

You can download and install the required software from the following link: `https://www.anaconda.com/products/individual`.

Retrieving, viewing, and storing tabular data

The ability to retrieve and view tabular data has been covered multiple times in prior chapters; however, those examples were focused on the perspective of the consumer. We learned the skills necessary to understand what structured data is in, the many different forms it can take, and how to answer some questions from data. Our data literacy has increased during this time but we have relied on the producers of data sources to make it easier to read using a few Python commands or SQL commands. In this chapter, we are switching gears from being exclusively a **consumer** to now a **producer** of data by learning skills to manipulate data for analysis.

As a good data analyst, you will need both sides of the consumer and producer spectrum of skills to solve more complicated questions with data. For example, a common measure requested by businesses with web or mobile users is called **usage analytics**. This means counting the number of users over snapshots of time, such as by day, week, month, and year. More importantly, you want to better understand whether those users are new, returning, or lost.

Common questions related to usage analytics are as follows:

- How many new users have hit the website this day, week, or month?
- How many returning users have accessed the website this day, week, or month?
- How many users have we lost (inactive for more than 60 days) this week, month, or year?

To answer these types of questions, your data source must have, at a minimum, `timestamp` and unique `user_id` fields available. In many cases, this data will have high volume and velocity, so analyzing this information will require the right combination of people, processes, and technology, which I have had the pleasure of working with. Data engineering teams build out ingestion pipelines to make this data accessible for reporting and analytics.

You may need to work with the data engineering team to apply the business rules and summary levels (also known as aggregates) to the data that include additional fields required to answer the user analytics questions. For our examples, I have provided a much smaller sample of data and we are going to derive new data fields from the existing source data file provided.

I find the best way to learn is to walk through the steps together, so let's create a new Jupyter notebook named `user_churn_prep`. We will begin with retrieving data from SQL against a database and loading it into a DataFrame, similar to the steps outlined in `Chapter 5`, *Gathering and Loading Data in Python*. To keep it simple, we are using another SQLite database to retrieve the source data.

> If you would like more details about connecting to SQL data sources, please refer to `Chapter 5`, *Gathering and Loading Data in Python*.

Retrieving

To create a connection and use SQLite, we have to import a new library using the code. For this example, I have provided the database file named `user_hits.db`, so be sure to download it from my GitHub repository beforehand:

1. To load a SQLite database connection, you just need to add the following command in your Jupyter notebook and run the cell. I have placed a copy on GitHub for reference:

   ```
   In[]: import sqlite3
   ```

2. Next, we need to assign a connection to a variable named `conn` and point to the location of the database file, which is named `user_hits.db`:

   ```
   In[]: conn = sqlite3.connect('user_hits.db')
   ```

Be sure that you have copied the `user_hits.db` file to the correct Jupyter folder directory to avoid errors with the connection.

3. Import the `pandas` library so you can create a DataFrame:

   ```
   In[]: import pandas as pd
   ```

4. Run a SQL statement and assign the results to a DataFrame:

   ```
   In[]: df_user_churn = pd.read_sql_query("SELECT * FROM
   tbl_user_hits;", conn)
   ```

5. Now that we have the results in a DataFrame, we can use all of the available `pandas` library commands against this data without going back to the database. Your code should look similar to the following screenshot:

   ```
   In [8]:  import sqlite3

   In [9]:  conn = sqlite3.connect('user_hits.db')

   In [10]: import pandas as pd

   In [11]: df_user_churn = pd.read_sql_query("SELECT * FROM tbl_user_hits;", conn)
   ```

Viewing

Perform the following steps to view the results of the retrieved data:

1. To view the results, we can just run the `head()` command against this DataFrame using this code:

   ```
   In[]: df_user_churn.head()
   ```

   The output will look like the following table, where the `tbl_user_hits` table has been loaded into a DataFrame with a labeled header row with the index column to the left starting with a value of `0`:

```
In [7]:  df_user_churn.head()

Out[7]:
           userid  date
     0   1         1/1/2017
     1   2         1/2/2017
     2   3         1/3/2017
     3   4         1/1/2018
     4   5         1/2/2018
```

Before we move on to the next step, let's verify the data we loaded with a few metadata commands.

2. Type in `df_user_churn.info()` in the next `In[]:` cell and run the cell:

```
In[]: df_user_churn.info()
```

Verify that the output cell displays `Out []`. There will be multiple rows, including data types for all columns, similar to the following screenshot:

```
In [13]:  df_user_churn.info

          <class 'pandas.core.frame.DataFrame'>
          RangeIndex: 9 entries, 0 to 8
          Data columns (total 2 columns):
          userid   9 non-null int64
          date     9 non-null object
          dtypes: int64(1), object(1)
          memory usage: 224.0+ bytes
```

Storing

Now that we have the data available to work with as a DataFrame in Jupyter, let's run a few commands to store it as a file for reference. Storing data as a snapshot for analysis is a useful technique to learn, and while our example is simplistic, the concept will help in future data analysis projects.

To store your DataFrame into a CSV file, you just have to run the following command:

```
In[]: df_user_churn.to_csv('user_hits_export.csv')
```

The results will look similar to the following screenshot, where a new CSV file is created in the same project folder as your current Jupyter notebook. Based on the OS you are using on your workstation, the results will vary:

Name	Date modified	Type	Size
ch_07_retrieve_sql_and_create_dataframe.ipynb	2/20/2020 4:39 PM	IPYNB File	4 KB
user_hits_export.csv	2/20/2020 4:38 PM	Microsoft Excel Comma Separated Values File	1 KB

There are other formats you can export your DataFrame to, including Excel. You should also note the file path from which you are exporting the data file. Check out the *Further reading* section for more information.

Learning how to restrict, sort, and sift through data

Now that we have the data available in a DataFrame, we can walk through how to restrict, sort, and sift through data with a few Python commands. The concepts we are going to walk through using pandas are also common using SQL, so I will also include the equivalent SQL commands for reference.

Restricting

The concept of restricting data, which is also known as filtering data, is all about isolating one or more records based on conditions. Simple examples are when you are only retrieving results based on matching a specific field and value. For example, you only want to see results for one user or a specific point in time. Other requirements for restricting data can be more complicated, including explicit conditions that require elaborate logic, business rules, and multiple steps. I will not be covering complex examples that require complex logic but will add some references in the *Further reading* section. However, the concepts covered will teach you essential skills to satisfy many common use cases.

For our first example, let's isolate one specific user from our DataFrame. Using `pandas` commands, that is pretty easy, so let's start up a new Jupyter notebook named `user_churn_restricting`:

1. Import the `pandas` library so you can create a DataFrame:

   ```
   In[]: import pandas as pd
   ```

2. Create a new DataFrame by loading the data from the CSV file we created in the prior example:

   ```
   In[]: df_user_churn = pd.read_csv('user_hits_export.csv');
   ```

The file path and filename must be the same as those you used in the prior example.

Now that we have all user data loaded into a single DataFrame, we can easily reference the source dataset to restrict results. It is a best practice to keep this source DataFrame intact so you can reference it for other purposes and analysis. It is also common during analysis to need to make adjustments based on changing requirements, or that you will only gain insights by making adjustments.

In my career, I follow a common practice of *you don't know what you don't know* while working with data, so having the flexibility to easily reference the source data without undoing your changes is important. This is commonly known as snapshotting your analysis and having the ability to roll back changes as needed.

When working with big data sources where the sources are larger than a billion rows, snapshots will require a large number of resources where RAM and CPU will be impacted. You may be required to snapshot incrementally for a specific date or create a rolling window of time to limit the amount of data you can work with at one time.

To restrict our data to a specific user, we will be creating a new DataFrame from the source DataFrame. That way, if we need to make adjustments to the filters used to create the new DataFrame, we don't have to rerun all of the steps from the beginning.

3. Create a new DataFrame by loading the data from the source DataFrame. The syntax is nested so you are actually calling the same `df_user_churn` DataFrame within itself and filtering results only for the explicit value where `userid` is equal to 1:

```
In[]: df_user_restricted =
df_user_churn[df_user_churn['userid']==1]
```

4. To view and verify the results, you can run a simple `head()` command:

```
In[]: df_user_restricted.head()
```

The results will look similar to the following screenshot, where the only two rows in the new `df_user_restricted` DataFrame have a value where `userid` is 1:

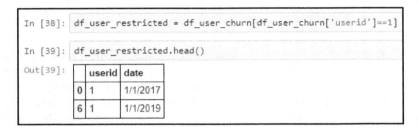

Restricting data helps to isolate records for specific types of analysis to help to answer additional questions. In the next step, we can start answering questions related to usage patterns.

Sorting

Now that we have isolated a specific user by creating a new DataFrame, which is now available for reference, we can enhance our analysis by asking questions such as the following:

- When did a specific user start using our website?
- How frequently does this user access our website?
- When was the last time this user accessed our website?

All of these questions can be answered with a few simple Python commands focused on sorting commands. Sorting data is a skill that computer programmers of any programming language are familiar with. It's easily done with SQL by adding an `order by` command. Many third-party software, such as Microsoft Excel, Google Sheets, or Qlik Sense, has a sorting feature built in. The concept of sorting data is well known, so I will not go into a detailed definition; rather, I will focus on important features and best practices when performing data analysis.

With structured data, sorting is commonly understood to be row-level by specific columns, which will be defined by ordering the sequence of the values from either low to high or high to low. The default is low to high unless you explicitly change it. If the values have a data type that is numeric, such as integer or float, the sort order sequence will be easy to identify. For textual data, the values are sorted alphabetically, and, depending on the technology used, mixed case text will be handled differently. In Python and pandas, we have specific functions available along with parameters to handle many different use cases and needs.

Let's start answering some of the questions we outlined previously using the `sort()` function:

1. To answer the question *When did a specific user start using our website?*, we just need to run the following command:

   ```
   In[]: df_user_restricted.sort_values(by='date')
   ```

   The results will look similar to the following screenshot, where the results are sorted in ascending order by the `date` field:

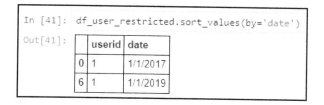

2. To answer the question "*When is the last time this user accessed our website?*", we just need to run the following command:

   ```
   In[]: df_user_restricted.sort_values(by='date', ascending=False)
   ```

The results will look similar to the following screenshot, where the same records are displayed as the previous one; however, the values are sorted in descending order by last date available for this specific `userid`:

```
In [42]:   df_user_restricted.sort_values by='date', ascending=False

Out[42]:
```

	userid	date
6	1	1/1/2019
0	1	1/1/2017

Sifting

The concept of sifting through data means we are isolating specific columns and/or rows from a dataset based on one or more conditions. There are nuanced differences between sifting versus restricting, so I would distinguish sifting as the need to include additional business rules or conditions applied to a population of data to isolate a subset of that data. Sifting data usually requires creating new derived columns from the source data to answer more complex questions. For our next example, a good question about usage would be: *Do the same users who hit our website on Monday also return during the same week?*

To answer this question, we need to isolate the usage patterns for a specific day of the week. This process requires a few steps, which we will outline together from the original DataFrame we created previously:

1. Create a new DataFrame by loading the data from the source file:

   ```
   In[]: df_user_churn_cleaned =
   pd.read_csv('user_hits_binning_import.csv', parse_dates=['date'])
   ```

   Next, we need to extend the DataFrame by adding new derived columns to help to make the analysis easier. Since we have a `Timestamp` field available, the pandas library has some very useful functions available to help the process. Standard SQL has built-in features as well and will vary depending on which RDMS is used, so you will have to reference the date/time functions available. For example, a Postgres database uses the syntax of `select to_char(current_date, 'Day');` to convert a date field into the current day of the week.

2. Import a new `datetime` library for easy reference to date and time functions:

   ```
   In[]: import datetime
   ```

3. Assign a variable to the current `datetime` for easier calculation of the `age` from today:

```
In[]: now = pd.to_datetime('now')
```

4. Add a new derived column called `age` that is calculated from the current date minus the date value per user:

```
In[]: df_user_churn_cleaned['age'] = now -
df_user_churn_cleaned['date']
```

If you receive `datetime` errors in your notebook, you may need to upgrade your `pandas` library.

Cleaning, refining, and purifying data using Python

Data quality is highly important for any data analysis and analytics. In many cases, you will not understand how good or bad the data quality is until you start working with it. I would define good-quality data as information that is well structured, defined, and consistent, where almost all of the values in each field are defined as expected. In my experience, data warehouses will have high-quality data because it has been reported on across the organization. In my experience, bad data quality occurs where a lack of transparency exists against the data source. Bad data quality examples are a lack of conformity and inconsistency in the expected data type or any consistent pattern of values in delimited datasets. To help to solve these data quality issues, you can begin to understand your data with the concepts and questions we covered in Chapter 1, *Fundamentals of Data Analysis*, with **Know Your Data (KYD)**. Since the quality of data will vary by source, some specific questions you can ask to understand data quality are as follows:

- Is the data structured or unstructured?
- Does the data lineage trace back to a system or application?
- Does the data get transformed and stored in a warehouse?
- Does the data have a schema with each field having a defined data type?
- Do you have a data dictionary available with business rules documented?

Receiving answers to these questions ahead of time would be a luxury; uncovering them as you go is more common for a data analyst. During this process, you will still find the need to clean, refine, and purify your data for analysis purposes. How much time you need to spend will vary on many different factors, and the true cost of quality will be the time and effort required to improve data quality.

Cleaning data can take on many different forms and has been a common practice for decades for data engineers and analytic practitioners. There are many different technologies and skillsets required for enterprise and big data cleansing. Data cleaning is an industry within **Information Technology** (**IT**) because good-quality data is worth the price of outsourcing.

A common definition of data cleansing is the process of removing or resolving poor-quality data records from the source, which can vary based on the technology used to persist the data, such as a database table or encoded file. Poor-quality data can be identified as any data that does not match the producers' intended and defined requirements. This can include the following:

- Missing or null (NaN) values from the fields of one or more rows
- Orphan records where the primary or foreign keys cannot be found in any referenced source tables
- Corrupted records where one or more records cannot be read by any reporting or analysis technology

For our example, let's look at our usage data again and see whether we can find any issues by profiling it to see whether we can find any anomalies:

1. Import the CSV file and run the `info()` command to confirm the data types and row counts and profile the DataFrame for more information:

   ```
   In[]: df_usage_patterns = pd.read_csv('user_hits_import.csv')
   df_usage_patterns.info()
   ```

   The results will look similar to the following screenshot, where metadata of the DataFrame is presented:

   ```
   <class 'pandas.core.frame.DataFrame'>
   RangeIndex: 12 entries, 0 to 11
   Data columns (total 2 columns):
   userid    9 non-null float64
   date      12 non-null object
   dtypes: float64(1), object(1)
   memory usage: 272.0+ bytes
   ```

One anomaly that is uncovered is that the number of values is different between the two fields. For `userid`, there are 9 non-null values and for the `date` field, there are 12 non-null values. For this dataset, we expect each row to have one value for both fields, but this command is telling us there are missing values. Let's run another command to identify which index/row has the missing data.

2. Run the `isnull()` command to confirm the data types and row counts and profile the DataFrame for more information:

```
In[]: pd.isnull(df_usage_patterns)
```

The results will look similar to the following table, where a list of `True` and `False` values is displayed by row and column:

Out[26]:

	userid	date
0	False	False
1	False	False
2	False	False
3	False	False
4	False	False
5	False	False
6	False	False
7	False	False
8	False	False
9	True	False
10	True	False
11	True	False

The record count looks okay but notice that there are null values (NaN) that exist in the `userid` field. A unique identifier for each row to help us to identify each user is critical for accurate analysis of this data. The reason why `userid` is blank would have to be explained by the producer of this data and may require additional engineering resources to help to investigate and troubleshoot the root cause of the issue. In some cases, it may be a simple technical hiccup during data source creation that requires a minor code change and reprocessing.

I always recommend cleaning data as close to the source as possible, which saves time by avoiding reworking by other data analysts or reporting systems.

Having nulls included in our analysis will impact our summary statistics and metrics. For example, the count of the average daily users would be lower on the dates where the null values exist. For the user churn analysis, the measure of the frequency of reporting users would be skewed because the NaN values could be one of the returning user_ids or a new user.

With any high volume transaction-based system, there could be a margin of error that you may need to account for. As a good data analyst, ask the question, *what is the cost of quality and of being one hundred percent accurate?* If the price is too high due to the time and resources required to change it, a good alternative is to exclude and isolate the missing data so it can be investigated later.

Note that if you end up adding isolated data back into your analysis, you will have to restate results and inform any consumers of the change to your metrics.

Let's walk through an example of how to isolate and exclude any missing data by identifying the NaN records and creating a new DataFrame that has them removed:

1. Create a new DataFrame by loading the data from the source DataFrame, except we will exclude the null values by adding the dropna() command:

```
In[]: df_user_churn_cleaned = df_usage_patterns.dropna()
```

2. To view and verify the results, you can run a simple head() command and confirm the NaN/null values have been removed:

```
In[]: df_user_churn_cleaned.head(10)
```

The results will look similar to the following table, where the new DataFrame has complete records with no missing values in either userid or date:

Out[11]:		userid	date
	0	1.0	1/1/2017
	1	2.0	1/2/2017
	2	3.0	1/3/2017
	3	4.0	1/1/2018
	4	5.0	1/2/2018
	5	6.0	1/3/2018
	6	1.0	1/1/2019
	7	3.0	1/2/2019
	8	6.0	1/3/2019

Combining and binning data

Combining multiple data sources is sometimes necessary for multiple reasons, which include the following:

- The source data is broken up into many different files with the same defined schema (tables and field names), but the number of rows will vary slightly. A common reason is for storage purposes, where it is easier to maintain multiple smaller file sizes versus one large file.
- The data is partitioned where one field is used to break apart the data for faster response time reading or writing to the source data. For example, HIVE/HDFS recommends storing data by a single date value so you can easily identify when it was processed and quickly extract data for a specific day.
- Historical data is stored in a different technology than more current data. For example, the engineering team changed the technology being used to manage the source data and it was decided not to import historical data beyond a specific date.

For any of the reasons defined here, combining data is a common practice in data analysis. I would define the process of combining data as when you are layering two or more data sources into one where the same fields/columns from all sources align. In SQL, this would be known as UNION ALL and in pandas, we use the concat() function to bring all of the data together.

A good visual example of how data is combined is in the following screenshot, where multiple source files are named `user_data_YYYY.cvs` and each year is defined as YYYY. These three files, which all have the same field names of `userid`, `date`, and `year`, are imported into one SQL table named `tbl_user_data_stage`, which is shown in the following screenshot. The target table that stores this information also includes a new field named `filesource` so the data lineage is more transparent to both the producer and the consumer:

user_data_2017.cvs		
userid	**date**	**year**
1	1/1/2017	2017
2	1/2/2017	2017
3	1/3/2017	2017

user_data_2018.cvs		
userid	**date**	**year**
4	1/1/2018	2018
5	1/2/2018	2018
6	1/3/2018	2018

user_data_2019.cvs		
userid	**date**	**year**
1	1/1/2019	2019
3	1/2/2019	2019
6	1/3/2019	2019

Once the data has been processed and persisted into a table named `tbl_user_data_stage`, all of the records from the three files are preserved as displayed in the following table. In this example, any duplicates would be preserved between what existed in the source files and the target table:

tbl_user_data_stage			
userid	date	year	filesource
1	1/1/2017	2017	user_data_2017.cvs
2	1/2/2017	2017	user_data_2017.cvs
3	1/3/2017	2017	user_data_2017.cvs
4	1/1/2018	2018	user_data_2018.cvs
5	1/2/2018	2018	user_data_2018.cvs
6	1/3/2018	2018	user_data_2018.cvs
1	1/1/2019	2019	user_data_2019.cvs
3	1/2/2019	2019	user_data_2019.cvs
6	1/3/2019	2019	user_data_2019.cvs

One of the reasons data engineering teams create `stage` tables is to help to build data ingestion pipelines and create business rules where duplicate records are removed.

To recreate the example in Jupyter, let's create a new notebook and name it `ch_07_combining_data`. There are more efficient ways to import multiple files but, in our example, we will import each one in separate DataFrames and then combine them into one:

1. Import the `pandas` library:

   ```
   In[]: import pandas as pd
   ```

   You will also need to copy the three CSV files to your local folder.

2. Import the first CSV file named `user_data_2017.csv`:

   ```
   In[]: df_user_data_2017 = pd.read_csv('user_data_2017.csv')
   ```

3. Run the `head()` command to verify the results:

   ```
   In[]: df_user_data_2017.head()
   ```

The results will look similar to the following screenshot, where the rows are displayed with a header row and index added starting with a value of 0:

In [3]:	df_user_data_2017.head()		
Out[3]:	**userid**	**date**	**year**
0	1	1/1/2017	2017
1	2	1/2/2017	2017
2	3	1/3/2017	2017

4. Repeat the process for the next CSV file, which is named `user_data_2018.csv`:

```
In[]: df_user_data_2018 = pd.read_csv('user_data_2018.csv')
```

5. Run the `head()` command to verify the results:

```
In[]: df_user_data_2018.head()
```

The results will look similar to the following screenshot, where the rows are displayed with a header row and index added starting with a value of 0:

In [4]:	df_user_data_2018 = pd.read_csv('user_data_2018.csv')		
In [17]:	df_user_data_2018.head()		
Out[17]:	**userid**	**date**	**year**
0	4	1/1/2018	2018
1	5	1/2/2018	2018
2	6	1/3/2018	2018

6. Repeat the process for the next CSV file, which is named `user_data_2019.csv`:

```
In[]: df_user_data_2019 = pd.read_csv('user_data_2019.csv')
```

7. Run the `head()` command to verify the results:

```
In[]: df_user_data_2019.head()
```

The results will look similar to the following screenshot, where the rows are displayed with a header row and index added starting with a value of 0:

```
In [5]: df_user_data_2019 = pd.read_csv('user_data_2019.csv')

In [18]: df_user_data_2019.head()
```

Out[18]:

	userid	date	year
0	1	1/1/2019	2019
1	3	1/2/2019	2019
2	6	1/3/2019	2019

8. The next step is to merge the DataFrames using the `concat()` function. We include the `ignore_index=True` parameter to create a new index value for all of the results:

```
In[]: df_user_data_combined = pd.concat([df_user_data_2017,
df_user_data_2018, df_user_data_2019], ignore_index=True)
```

9. Run the `head()` command to verify the results:

```
In[]: df_user_data_combined.head(10)
```

The results will look similar to the following screenshot, where the rows are displayed with a header row and index added starting with a value of 0:

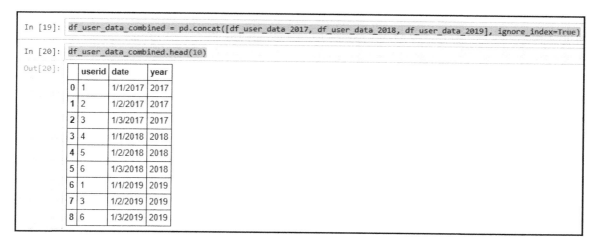

```
In [19]: df_user_data_combined = pd.concat([df_user_data_2017, df_user_data_2018, df_user_data_2019], ignore_index=True)

In [20]: df_user_data_combined.head(10)
```

Out[20]:

	userid	date	year
0	1	1/1/2017	2017
1	2	1/2/2017	2017
2	3	1/3/2017	2017
3	4	1/1/2018	2018
4	5	1/2/2018	2018
5	6	1/3/2018	2018
6	1	1/1/2019	2019
7	3	1/2/2019	2019
8	6	1/3/2019	2019

Binning

Binning is a very common analysis technique that allows you to group numeric data values based on one or more criteria. These groups become named categories; they are ordinal in nature and can have equal widths between the ranges or customized requirements. A good example is age ranges, which you commonly see on surveys such as that seen in the following screenshot:

Q: What is your age?

o Under 18 years old
o 18 – 24
o 15 – 44
o 45 – 74
o 75 years or older

In this example, a person's age range is the input, but what if we actually had the birthdate of each person available in the data? Then, we could calculate the age as of today and assign an age band based on the criteria in the preceding screenshot. This is the process of binning your data.

Another common example is weather data, where the assigned categories of *hot*, *warm*, or *cold* are assigned to ranges of Fahrenheit or Celsius temperature. Each bin value is defined by a condition that is arbitrarily decided by the data analyst.

For our user data, let's assign age bins based on when the user first appeared in our dataset. We will define three bins based on the requirements, which allows us the flexibility to adjust the assigned ranges. For our example, we define the bins as follows:

- Less than 1 year
- 1 to 2 years
- Greater than 3 years

The specific conditions on how to create the bins will be evident once we walk through the code.

Another cool feature of this type of analysis is the fact that our calculated age is based on the usage data and a point in time that's calculated each time we run the code. For example, if the date of the first time a user hits the website is *1/1/2017* and we did this analysis on December 3, 2018, the age in days of the user would be 360, which would be assigned to the *Less than 1 year* bin.

If we rerun this analysis at a later date such as November 18, 2019, the calculated age would change, so the new assigned bin would be *1 to 2 years*.

The decision on where to add the logic for each bin will vary. The most flexible to make changes to the assigned bins is to add the logic where you deliver the analytics. In our examples, that would be directly in the Jupyter notebook. However, in enterprise environments where many different technologies could be used to deliver the same analysis, it makes sense to move the binning logic closer to the source. In some cases of very large datasets stored in databases, using SQL or even having the schema changed in the table is a better option.

If you have the luxury of a skilled data engineering team and experience of working with big data like I had, the decision to move the binning logic closer to the data tables is easy. In SQL, you could use CASE Statement or if/then logic. Qlik has a function called class(), which will bin values based on a linear scale. In Microsoft Excel, a nested formula can be used to assign bins based on a mix of functions.

So, the concept of binning can be applied across different technologies and as a good data analyst, you now have a foundation of understanding how it can be done.

Let's reinforce the knowledge by walking through an example using our usage data and Jupyter Notebook.

Remember to copy any dependency CSV files into the working folder before walking through the following steps.

To recreate the example in Jupyter, let's create a new notebook and name it
ch_07_sifting_and_binning_data:

1. Import the pandas library:

   ```
   In[]: import pandas as pd
   ```

2. Read in the CSV file provided that includes additional data for this example and
   create a new DataFrame named df_user_churn_cleaned. We are also
   converting the date field found in the source CSV file into a data type of
   datetime64 while importing using the parse_dates parameter. This will make
   it easier to manipulate in the next few steps:

   ```
   In[]: df_user_churn_cleaned =
   pd.read_csv('user_hits_binning_import.csv', parse_dates=['date'])
   ```

3. Verify the DataFrame is valid using the head() function:

   ```
   In[]: df_user_churn_cleaned.head(10)
   ```

The output of the function will look similar to the following table, where the
DataFrame is loaded with two fields with the correct data types and is available
for analysis:

	userid	date
0	1	2017-01-01
1	2	2017-01-02
2	3	2017-01-03
3	4	2018-01-01
4	5	2018-01-02
5	6	2018-10-03
6	1	2019-10-01
7	3	2019-10-02
8	7	2019-10-03
9	8	2020-01-01

Out[231]:

4. Import the datetime and numpy libraries for reference later to calculate
   the age value of the userid field:

   ```
   In[]: from datetime import datetime
         import numpy as np
   ```

5. Create a new derived column named `age` by calculating the difference between the current date and time using the `now` function and the `date` field. To format the `age` field in days, we include the `dt.days` function, which will convert the values into a clean `"%d"` format:

```
In[]: #df_user_churn_cleaned['age'] = (datetime.now() -
pd.to_datetime(df_user_churn_cleaned['date'])).dt.days
df_user_churn_cleaned['age'] = (datetime(2020, 2, 28)   -
pd.to_datetime(df_user_churn_cleaned['date'])).dt.days
```

To match the screenshots, I explicitly defined the date value to 2020-02-28 with a date format of YYYY-MM-DD. You can uncomment the preceding line to calculate the current timestamp. Since the timestamp changes every time you run the function, the results will not match exactly to any image.

6. Verify that the new `age` column has been included in your DataFrame:

```
In[]: df_user_churn_cleaned.head()
```

The output of the function will look similar to the following table, where the DataFrame has been modified from its original import and includes a new field called `age`:

Out[214]:

	userid	date	age
0	1	2017-01-01	1153
1	2	2017-01-02	1152
2	3	2017-01-03	1151
3	4	2018-01-01	788
4	5	2018-01-02	787
5	6	2018-10-03	513
6	1	2019-10-01	150
7	3	2019-10-02	149
8	7	2019-10-03	148
9	8	2020-01-01	58
10	1	2020-01-02	57
11	2	2020-01-03	56

7. Create a new DataFrame called `df_ages` that groups the dimensions from the existing DataFrame and calculates the max `age` value by `userid`:

```
In[]: df_ages = df_user_churn_cleaned.groupby('userid').max()
```

The output will look similar to the following screenshot, where the number of rows has decreased from the source DateFrame. Only a distinct list of `userid` values will be displayed along with the maximum `age` when the first record was created by `userid`:

Out[216]:	userid	date	age
	1	2020-01-02	1153
	2	2020-01-03	1152
	3	2019-10-02	1151
	4	2018-01-01	788
	5	2018-01-02	787
	6	2018-10-03	513
	7	2019-10-03	148
	8	2020-01-01	58

8. Create a new `age_bin` column by using the `pandas` library's `cut()` function. This will thread each value from the `age` field between one of the assigned `bins` range we have assigned. We use the `labels` parameter to make the analysis easier to consume for any audience. Note that the value of `9999` was chosen to create a maximum boundary for the `age` value:

```
In[]: df_ages['age_bin'] = pd.cut(x=df_ages['age'], bins=[1, 365,
730, 9999], labels=['< 1 year', '1 to 2 years', '> 3 years'])
```

9. Display the DataFrame and validate the bin values displayed:

```
In[]: df_ages
```

The output of the function will look similar to the following screenshot, where the DataFrame has been modified and we now see the values in the `age_bin` field:

Out[218]:	userid	date	age	age_bin
	1	2020-01-02	1153	> 3 years
	2	2020-01-03	1152	> 3 years
	3	2019-10-02	1151	> 3 years
	4	2018-01-01	788	> 3 years
	5	2018-01-02	787	> 3 years
	6	2018-10-03	513	1 to 2 years
	7	2019-10-03	148	< 1 year
	8	2020-01-01	58	< 1 year

Summary

Congratulations, you have now increased your data literacy skills by working with data as both a consumer and producer of analytics. We covered some important topics, including essential skills to manipulate data by creating views of data, sorting, and querying tabular data from a SQL source. You now have a repeatable workflow for combining multiple data sources into one refined dataset.

We explored additional features of working with `pandas` DataFrames, showing how to restrict and sift data. We walked through real-world practical examples using the concept of *user churn* to answer key business questions about usage patterns by isolating specific users and dealing with missing values from the source data.

Our next chapter is `Chapter 8`, *Understanding Joins, Relationships, and Data Aggregates*. Along with creating a summary analysis using a concept called aggregation, we will also go into detail on how to join data with defined relationships.

Further reading

You can refer to the following links for more information on the topics of this chapter:

- A nice walk-through of filtering and grouping using DataFrames: `https://github.com/bhavaniravi/pandas_tutorial/blob/master/Pandas_Basics_To_Beyond.ipynb`
- Comparison of SQL features and their equivalent pandas functions: `https://pandas.pydata.org/pandas-docs/stable/getting_started/comparison/comparison_with_sql.html`
- Additional information on exporting data to Excel: `https://pandas.pydata.org/pandas-docs/stable/reference/api/pandas.DataFrame.to_excel.html#pandas.DataFrame.to_excel`
- Examples of SQL date and time functions: `https://www.postgresql.org/docs/8.1/functions-datetime.html`

8
Understanding Joins, Relationships, and Aggregates

I'm really excited about this chapter because we are going to learn about the foundation of blending multiple datasets. This concept has been around for decades using SQL and other technologies including R, pandas, Excel, Cognos, and Qlikview.

The ability to merge data is a powerful skill that applies across different technologies and helps you to answer complex questions such as how product sales can be impacted by weather forecasts. The data sources are mutually exclusive, but today, access to weather data can be added to your data model with a few joins based on geographic location and time of day. We will be covering how this can be done along with the different types of joins. Once exposed to this concept, you will learn what questions can be answered depending on the granularity of data available. For our weather and sales data example, the details become important to understand the level of analysis that can be done. If you wanted to know whether rain impacts sales, the more common fields available, such as date, day, and time, and geographic location tags, such as latitude and longitude, must be available in both sources for you to be accurate in your conclusions after joining the data together.

In this chapter, we will learn how to construct high-quality datasets for further analysis. We will continue to advance your hands-on data literacy skills by learning how to work with join relationships and how to create aggregate data for analysis.

In this chapter, we will cover the following topics:

- Foundations of join relationships
- Join types in action
- Explaining data aggregation
- Summary statistics and outliers

Technical requirements

Here's the GitHub repository of this book: `https://github.com/PacktPublishing/`
`Practical-Data-Analysis-using-Jupyter-Notebook/tree/master/Chapter08`.

You can download and install the required software from the following link: `https://www.`
`anaconda.com/products/individual`.

Foundations of join relationships

For anyone familiar with SQL, the concept of joining data together is well understood. The ability to join one or more tables together for the purpose of analytics has remained relevant throughout my 20+ year career of working with data and I hope it continues to be relevant.

In prior chapters, we introduced the concept of data models and the need for primary and foreign key fields to define relationships. We will now elaborate on these concepts by explaining joins and the different types of joins that exist in SQL and DataFrames.

Joining, in SQL, simply means merging two or more tables into a single dataset. The resulting size and shape of that single dataset will vary depending on the type of join that is used. Some key concepts you want to remember any time you are creating a join between datasets will be that the **common unique key** should always be used. Ideally, the key field functions as both the primary and foreign key but it can be derived using multiple fields to define a unique record for all rows of data.

We will go through the following types of join relationships in this section:

- One-to-one
- Many-to-many
- Left join
- Right join
- Inner join
- Outer join

With pandas DataFrames, the index in our examples has been the default or a single defined field because it has distinct values, but that is not always the case.

One-to-one relationships

A **one-to-one** relationship means the sources have common unique values by row and duplicates do not exist. A similar feature in Excel is the `vlookup` function with the exact match parameter enabled. When you use this Excel function, any matches to the source identifier return a distinct value from the target lookup. In SQL, one-to-one relationships ensure that the integrity between two tables is consistent. There are multiple reasons why these types of relationships are needed, but a good example is when a reference table that has the sales region is joined to a unique `Customer` table. In this example, a customer identifier (`ID`) field would exist in both tables and you would never have a sales region without a customer record and vice versa.

Many-to-one relationships

A **many-to-one relationship** means one of the sources can have duplicate rows but not both sources. You still need a unique key, index, or identifier between the sources. An example would be a lookup dimensional table joined to a fact table, which we covered in `Chapter 7`, *Exploring Cleaning, Refining, and Blending Datasets*.

A transaction fact table will have duplicate records because a user hit for a website or a product sale is recorded by date/time for each occurrence. The result will generate millions of rows with duplicate records in the `userid` field. When the join uses a common field such as `userid` between the fact table and the second table, the second table must be unique in each row. This second table will have additional attributes about `userid`, such as `city`, `state`, and `zip code`, which will offer richer analysis options. Once you understand that this type of join relationship exists between two source tables, you can confidently join them together.

Many-to-many relationship

A **many-to-many relationship** is when both sources have duplicate rows. Again, you should find a common unique key (one or more fields) or index between the sources. These types of joins are commonly referred to as *expensive* joins because the number of computing resources (memory and CPU) required will increase dramatically depending on the number of records and columns from both sources. A common example is a logical relationship between students and classes where many students can take many different classes. Conversely, many classes can have many different students. As a best practice, I would try to avoid direct many-to-many joins and use a bridge table to resolve them for analysis. For the students-to-classes example, you would need a roster table that marries together the unique list of one student per class, as in the following screenshot:

tbl_students				tbl_roster				tbl_classes		
student_id	student name	acceptance date		student_id	class_id	seminster date		class_id	class name	teacher_id
1	Mark Jo	9/1/2010		1	1	Fall 2012		1	Bio 101	1
2	Joe Smith	12/1/2009		2	1	Fall 2012		2	Econ 201	2
3	Roger Stein	6/1/2012		3	1	Fall 2012		3	English 102	1
				1	2	Fall 2012				
				2	2	Fall 2012				
				3	2	Fall 2012				
				1	3	Fall 2012				
				2	3	Fall 2012				
				3	3	Fall 2012				

For any join, you should avoid a **Cartesian product**, which is where all possible combinations of rows and columns exist as a result of the join. There are some cases where this might be useful in your analysis but be cautious, especially with big data volumes.

A Cartesian product is when all possible combinations of rows and columns are combined. For our example, if we joined `tbl_students` and `tbl_classes` without including `tbl_roster`, you would end up with students assigned to classes they never signed up for. There are occasions where I have deliberately constructed a Cartesian product because it was needed for certain types of analysis or a chart. For example, if you have a student ranking scale from 1 to 10 but none of the students achieved all of the possible values, you could create a Cartesian join to fill in the gaps of missing values.

Similar to concerns about exceeding memory and CPU utilization when working with many-to-many join types, a Cartesian product can easily consume all available memory, which could lead to a crash of your workstation or workspace.

Left join

Now that we have covered the key concepts, I'm going to begin with a visual representation of one of the most common types of joins used in analysis, which is called a **left join**. Let's start by looking at our source data for this example, which is represented in the following screenshot:

tbl_user_hits	
userid	date
1	1/1/2019
2	1/2/2019
3	1/3/2019

tbl_user_geo		
userid	city	state
1	Dover	DE
2	Orlando	FL
3	El Paso	TX
4	Lancaster	PA
5	Ewing	NJ

As you can see, we have tables named `tbl_user_hits` and `tbl_user_geo`. The width and length of `tbl_user_hits` is two columns and three rows. In `tbl_user_geo`, which represents the user's geographical location, we have three columns and five rows. We have a common field named `userid` in both tables, which I highlighted and will use to join the data. These tables have a primary and foreign key many-to-one relationship because not all of the records from one table exist in the other.

For this example, we want to keep all of the records in `tbl_user_hits` and enrich the data by blending together matching attributes such as city and state where `userid` exists only for the records in the user hits table. The result is in the following screenshot, where the original source, `tbl_user_hits`, has the same number of rows and but now includes the columns from the `tbl_user_geo` table:

Join Result			
userid	date	city	state
1	1/1/2019	Dover	DE
2	1/2/2019	Orlando	FL
3	1/3/2019	El Paso	TX

Why did the number of rows remain the same but the number of columns increase? A successful left join preserves the number of rows from the source and extends the number of columns.

The specific columns included in the join result can be defined but the default will include all of the columns.

Why are left joins common in analytics? That's because we are interested in adding more dimensional fields to answer more questions about the data that does not exist in a single table alone. Also, in your analysis, you typically don't want to include anything that doesn't match our source user hits. With this new join result, we can now answer questions such as which city has the highest number of users. Using a few date calculations, we can also provide monthly trends by state.

Right join

Next, we have a join type called a **right join**, which I find is less common. That is because there are not many use cases where the desire is to create gaps in the records of your merged data. A right join is where you want to preserve all of the columns and rows of the second table and fill in matching values from the first.

To understand the concept, start by referring back to our prior source tables, `tbl_user_hits`, and `tbl_user_geo`. The result of a successful right join is shown in the following screenshot, where the join result is shown with five rows and four columns. The date field from `tbl_user_hits` has been combined with the `tbl_user_geo` source but missing values will appear as `null()` or `NaN`. Note that if `tbl_user_hits` had thousands or millions of rows, the join result would increase the original size of `tbl_user_geo`:

Join Result			
userid	city	state	date
1	Dover	DE	1/1/2019
2	Orlando	FL	1/2/2019
3	El Paso	TX	1/3/2019
4	Lancaster	PA	
5	Ewing	NJ	

One advantage of using the right join is that now you can identify which cities and states do not have any user hits. This could be useful information and could be used for marketing campaigns.

Inner join

Next, we have an **inner join**. This is when only the exact values from both tables are returned along with all of the columns. To demonstrate the effect, I have made some adjustments to our source tables, which are shown in the following screenshot. The table names are the same but now some of the prior records are removed from tbl_user_geo. This could be due to a regulation request or the userid rows could have been determined to be invalid, so now we can use an inner join to remove them from tbl_user_hits:

tbl_user_hits			tbl_user_geo		
userid	date		userid	city	state
1	1/1/2019		1	Dover	DE
2	1/2/2019		3	El Paso	TX
3	1/3/2019		5	Ewing	NJ

The join results are shown in the following screenshot, where only the matching values found in the userid key field are displayed along with all of the combined columns between both source tables:

Join Result			
userid	date	city	state
1	1/1/2019	Dover	DE
3	1/3/2019	El Paso	TX

The pandas function for performing joins is called merge and an inner join is the default option.

Outer join

Finally, we have an **outer join**, which provides a comprehensive list of all rows and columns from both sources. Unlike a **Cartesian**, where any possible combination of values is created, an outer join reflects the truth from both source tables. For our example, we will use the same source as the following screenshot, where records from `tbl_user_geo` were removed. Unlike an inner join, the outer join results provide you with the ability to see any missing records as null in SQL or `NaN` in Python/pandas:

Join Result			
userid	date	city	state
1	1/1/2019	Dover	DE
2	1/2/2019		
3	1/3/2019	El Paso	TX
5		Ewing	NJ

While these concepts and common join types are not exhaustive, you now have a good foundational understanding of joining data sources together so we can move forward with walking through practical examples.

Join types in action

Unfortunately, the SQLite database that we use does not support all of the join options (right and outer), so I will provide only two examples of a join (left and inner) using SQL in this walk-through. The good news is that the `pandas` library supports all join types using the `merge()` function, so we can recreate all of the examples already discussed. Feel free to walk through the following code; I have placed a copy of the Jupyter Notebook code on GitHub for reference.

 Be sure to copy any dependencies files into your working folder before walking through all of the steps.

We will begin by launching a new Jupyter notebook and naming it `ch_08_exercises`:

1. Load a SQLite database connection:

```
In[]: import sqlite3
```

This library should already be available using Anaconda. Refer to `Chapter 2`, *Overview of Python and Installing Jupyter Notebook*, for help with setting up your environment.

2. Next, we need to assign a connection to a variable named `conn` and point to the location of the database file, which is named `user_hits.db`. Since we already imported the `sqlite3` library in the prior `In[]` line, we can use this built-in function to communicate with the database:

```
In[]: conn = sqlite3.connect('user_hits.db')
```

Be sure that you copied the `user_hits.db` file to the correct Jupyter folder directory to avoid errors with the connection.

3. Import the `pandas` library:

```
In[]: import pandas as pd
```

4. To run a SQL statement and assign the results to a DataFrame, we have to run this one line of code. The `pandas` library includes a `read_sql_query` function to make it easier to communicate with databases using SQL. It requires a connection parameter that we named `conn` in the previous steps. We assign the results to a new DataFrame as `df_left_join` to make it easier to identify:

```
In[]: df_left_join = pd.read_sql_query("select u.userid, u.date,
g.city, g.state from tbl_user_hits u left join tbl_user_geo g on
u.userid = g.userid;", conn)
```

SQL supports the concept of an alias for table names so you can shorten the syntax. In this example, `tbl_user_hits` has an alias of `u` and `tbl_user_geo` is `g`. This helps when explicitly calling field names that require a prefix of the table name.

5. Now that we have the results in a DataFrame, we can use all of the available `pandas` library commands against this data without going back to the database. To view the results, we can just run the `head()` command against this DataFrame using this code:

```
In[]: df_left_join.head()
```

The output will look like the following screenshot, where the SQL results have been loaded into a DataFrame with a labeled header row with the index column to the left starting with a value of `0`:

In [8]:	df_left_join.head()			
Out[8]:		userid	date	city	state
	0	1	1/1/2019	Dover	DE
	1	2	1/2/2019	None	None
	2	3	1/3/2019	El Paso	TX

6. The next join will be an inner and we will assign the results to a new DataFrame as `df_inner_join` to make it easier to identify:

```
df_inner_join = pd.read_sql_query("select u.userid, u.date, g.city,
g.state from tbl_user_hits u, tbl_user_geo g where u.userid =
g.userid;", conn)
```

7. Now that we have the results in a DataFrame, we can use all of the available `pandas` library commands against this data without going back to the database. To view the results, we can just run the `head()` command against this DataFrame using this code:

```
In[]: df_inner_join.head()
```

The output will look like the following screenshot, where the SQL results have been loaded into a DataFrame with a labeled header row with the index column to the left starting with a value of `0`:

In [11]:	df_inner_join.head()			
Out[11]:		userid	date	city	state
	0	1	1/1/2019	Dover	DE
	1	3	1/3/2019	El Paso	TX

We will continue the walk-through of the remaining exercise using the `merge()` function in pandas. I have a reference with more details about the function in the *Further reading* section, but using it is very straightforward. Once you have the two input tables stored as DataFrames, you can input them into the `merge()` function as parameters along with the join type you want to use, which is controlled using the `how` parameter. The default when you don't specify a parameter is an inner join, and it supports all of the SQL joins we have discussed, including left, right, and outer. The result of using the `merge()` function is to return a DataFrame with the source objects merged. Let's continue this walk-through exercise by loading our source SQL tables as DataFrames.

8. Create a new DataFrame called `df_user_hits`, which is a duplicate of the `tbl_user_hits` table, so we can use it later in the examples:

   ```
   In[]: df_user_hits = pd.read_sql_query("select * from
   tbl_user_hits;", conn)
   ```

9. To validate the results, you can run the `head()` function against this DataFrame using this code:

   ```
   In[]: df_user_hits.head()
   ```

   The output will look like the following screenshot, where the SQL results have been loaded into a DataFrame with a labeled header row with the index column to the left starting with a value of 0:

In [32]:	df_user_hits.head	
Out[32]:		
	userid	**date**
0	1	1/1/2019
1	2	1/2/2019
2	3	1/3/2019

10. Create a new DataFrame called `df_user_geo`, which is a duplicate of the `tbl_user_geo` table, so we can use it later in the examples:

    ```
    In[]: df_user_geo = pd.read_sql_query("select * from
    tbl_user_geo;", conn)
    ```

The output would look like the following screenshot, where the SQL results have been loaded into a DataFrame with a labeled header row with the index column to the left starting with a value of 0:

In [34]:	df_user_geo.head			
Out[34]:		userid	city	state
	0	1	Dover	DE
	1	3	El Paso	TX
	2	5	Ewing	NJ

11. It's a best practice to close the database connection since we no longer need to run any SQL queries and have retrieved all of the data. You would run this command to close it:

```
In[]: conn.close()
```

Now that we have all of the data loaded into pandas DataFrames, we can walk through the different join types by slightly modifying the parameters in the merge() function. The left and right parameters for all of the examples will be df_user_hits and df_user_geo respectively. The join fields are consistent, which is userid for both DataFrames. In this example, the source tables use the same common field name for their unique identifier, which is helpful.

The last parameter we will pass into the merge() function is named how which determines which type of join will be performed. We will start with my favorite, which is the left join.

12. Create a new DataFrame with the results of the pandas merge() function that creates a left join between the two DataFrames. In the next line, you can include the new DataFrame name, which will output the results similar to using the head() function:

```
In[]: df_left_join=pd.merge(left=df_user_hits, right=df_user_geo,
how='left', left_on='userid', right_on='userid')
df_left_join
```

The output will look like the following screenshot, where the merge() results have been loaded into a new DataFrame named df_left_join with a labeled header row with the index column to the left starting with a value of 0:

Out[36]:

	userid	date	city	state
0	1	1/1/2019	Dover	DE
1	2	1/2/2019	NaN	NaN
2	3	1/3/2019	El Paso	TX

The expected result, only `userid` from `df_user_hits`, will be displayed.

Notice the difference between SQL and pandas, where the blank `null()` values are replaced with **NaN**, which stands for **Not a Number**.

Next, we will create a right join, which has a slight variation to our prior syntax.

13. Create a new DataFrame with the results of the pandas `merge()` function that creates a right join between the two DataFrames. In the next line, you can include the new DataFrame name, which will output the results similar to using the `head()` function:

```
In[]: df_right_join=pd.merge(left=df_user_hits, right=df_user_geo,
how='right', left_on='userid', right_on='userid')
df_right_join
```

The output will look like the following screenshot, where the merge results have been loaded into a new DataFrame named `df_right_join` with a labeled header row with the index column to the left starting with a value of `0`:

Out[40]:

	userid	date	city	state
0	1.0	1/1/2019	Dover	DE
1	3.0	1/3/2019	El Paso	TX
2	5.0	NaN	Ewing	NJ

The expected result, only `userid` from `df_user_geo`, will be displayed.

Similar to our SQL example, we can perform an inner join using the merge function by using the default, which excludes the `how` parameter when passing it to the `merge()` function.

You can always explicitly include the `how` parameter if you want to be sure to define the type of join used.

14. Create a new DataFrame with the results of the pandas `merge()` function that creates an inner join between the two DataFrames. In the next line, you can include the new DataFrame name, which will output the results similar to using the `head()` function:

```
In[]: df_inner_join=pd.merge(left=df_user_hits, right=df_user_geo,
left_on='userid', right_on='userid')
df_inner_join
```

The output will look like the following screenshot, where the merge results have been loaded into a new DataFrame named `df_inner_join` with a labeled header row with the index column to the left starting with a value of `0`:

Out[41]:

	userid	date	city	state
0	1	1/1/2019	Dover	DE
1	3	1/3/2019	El Paso	TX

The expected result, only `userid` that exists in both DataFrames, will be displayed.

Finally, let's create an outer join using the `merge()` function by adding the `how` parameter and including the value of `outer`.

15. Create a new DataFrame with the results of the pandas `merge()` function that creates an outer join between the two DataFrames. In the next line, you can include the new DataFrame name, which will output the results similar to using the `head()` function:

```
In[]: df_outer_join=pd.merge(left=df_user_hits, right=df_user_geo,
how='outer', left_on='userid', right_on='userid')
df_outer_join
```

The output will look like the following screenshot, where the merge results have been loaded into a new DataFrame named df_outer_join with a labeled header row with the index column to the left starting with a value of 0:

Out[42]:		userid	date	city	state
	0	1.0	1/1/2019	Dover	DE
	1	2.0	1/2/2019	NaN	NaN
	2	3.0	1/3/2019	El Paso	TX
	3	5.0	NaN	Ewing	NJ

The expected result, all userid instances that exist in either DataFrame, will be displayed.

Excellent, we have successfully recreated all of the join types discussed throughout this chapter so far. Whether you feel more comfortable using SQL or pandas, the ability to join datasets together is a powerful skill and significantly increases your data literacy acumen.

Explaining data aggregation

Data aggregation is part of your daily life and you may or may not even realize it. When you pull up a review of a restaurant that uses one to five stars or if you purchase an item on Amazon because it has thousands of customer ratings, both examples are data aggregates. A data aggregate can be defined as a summary typically based on a significantly larger detail. In SQL, an aggregation is when a groupby command is applied against one or more tables, which includes a statistical calculation such as sum, average, min, or max against one or more fields.

Understanding the granularity of data

The aggregation of calculations would be known as the measure. When you are grouping by one or more fields to get their distinct values, they are classified as dimensions.

So, this should all sound very familiar because we introduced the concept of dimensions and measures in both `Chapter 5`, *Gathering and Loading Data in Python*, and `Chapter 6`, *Visualizing and Working with Time Series Data*, because it's the foundation for data modeling and visualizations. To reinforce the concept, let's see how a table or DataFrame gets summarized visually. As you can see in the following screenshot, an input table with any number of rows and columns can be summarized and reduced by many different types of aggregations, such as by a user or by date:

Source Table		Aggregation Example by User				Aggregation Example by Date		

tbl_user_hits

userid	date		userid	min_date	max_date	total_hits		date	user_count	total_hits
1	1/1/2019		1	1/1/2019	1/3/2019	3		1/1/2019	3	3
2	1/1/2019		2	1/1/2019	1/3/2019	3		1/2/2019	3	3
3	1/1/2019		3	1/1/2019	1/3/2019	3		1/3/2019	3	3
1	1/2/2019									
2	1/2/2019									
3	1/2/2019									
1	1/3/2019									
2	1/3/2019									
3	1/3/2019									

So, why are aggregations needed and important to analytics? First, as you can see in the preceding screenshot, the shape and size are significantly reduced, which helps large datasets to be manageable for ease of consumption by humans or machines.

For humans, when data is aggregated, it becomes easy to view and understand because the person does not have to visually sift through thousands of rows and columns. For machines, the reduction of very large data sources in both shape and size helps to reduce the file size, memory footprint, and input/output to process the data. When you see the sizes of structured data in **gigabytes (GB)**, the main factor impacting that size (either file, DataFrame, or database table) is the density of the data. The density of data is defined by each data point value within the rows and columns of the table or source file. When you aggregate data, the volume of data will be significantly reduced because one or more of the fields containing the distinct values are removed.

For example, if you have a high volume transaction table with millions of distinct `userid` values by timestamp, the daily number of records could be in the tens of millions if a user performs an action or event every few seconds. If your analysis requirement is to measure the average count of the number of users per day, you could create a daily snapshot table that has one row for each day. So, a simple aggregation reduced tens of millions of rows down to one per day! So, what's the catch? Well, first we lost all of the granularity of what actions each user was performing on each day. Another factor is the time to process and manage the aggregate table. Any data engineer will tell you that downtime and bugs occur, so they must keep the source table and any aggregate tables in sync and reinstate if the source changes.

To solve for any loss of granularity, you can create other aggregates based on different fields/dimensions, but that may create other problems if you add more attributes later after the aggregate table is created. For example, if you snapshot an aggregate table with average daily user counts by city and state for a year and then want the analysis by zip code, you would have to reprocess to backfill all of the history or have two different average granularities that change before and after a specific date.

Data aggregation in action

So, now that we have a better understanding of what aggregates exist and why, let's walk through how to create them in SQL and pandas. For this example, we will be working with a similar version of the user hits data named `tbl_user_geo_hits`. This table has the combined records from the sources we have been working with before, except we can now focus on the aggregation and `groupby` syntax. The SQL language can be complex and is robust enough to handle both joins and aggregation at the same time, but I find breaking down the process will make it easier to learn. Also, it is common to have persisted tables or views (database objects that behave like a table but are derived from one or more joins) available because of high data volumes and/or reporting.

We will begin by launching a new Jupyter notebook and naming it
`ch_08_sql_and_pandas_group_by`:

1. Load a SQLite database connection:

   ```
   In[]: import sqlite3
   ```

   This library should already be available using Anaconda. Refer to Chapter
   2, *Overview of Python and Installing Jupyter Notebook*, for help with setting up your
   environment.

2. Next, we need to assign a connection to a variable named `conn` and point to the
   location of the database file, which is named `user_hits.db`. Since we already
   imported the `sqlite3` library in the prior `In[]` line, we can use this built-in
   function to communicate with the database:

   ```
   In[]: conn = sqlite3.connect('user_hits.db')
   ```

   Be sure that you copied the `user_hits.db` file to the correct Jupyter folder
   directory to avoid errors with the connection.

3. Import the `pandas` library:

   ```
   In[]: import pandas as pd
   ```

4. To run a SQL statement and assign the results to a DataFrame, we have to run
   this one line of code. The `pandas` library includes a `read_sql_query` function to
   make it easier to communicate with databases using SQL. It requires a connection
   parameter that we named `conn` in the previous steps. We assign the results to a
   new DataFrame as `df_user_geo_hits` to make it easier to identify:

   ```
   In[]: df_user_geo_hits = pd.read_sql_query("select * from
   tbl_user_geo_hits;", conn)
   ```

5. To validate the results, you can run the `head()` function against this DataFrame
   using this code:

   ```
   In[]: df_user_geo_hits.head(10)
   ```

   The output will look like the following screenshot, where the merge results have
   been loaded into a new DataFrame named `df_user_geo_hits` with a labeled
   header row with the index column to the left starting with a value of `0`:

Out[6]:		userid	date	city	state
	0	1	1/1/2019	Dover	DE
	1	3	1/1/2019	El Paso	TX
	2	1	1/2/2019	Dover	DE
	3	2	1/2/2019	Philadelphia	PA
	4	3	1/2/2019	El Paso	TX
	5	1	1/3/2019	Dover	DE
	6	2	1/3/2019	Philadelphia	PA

So, we have user hits available and have previewed the data by loading it into a DataFrame. The advantage of a group by feature is that it allows us to ask specific questions about the data and return answers with some slight adjustments to the dimensions and aggregation used in the SQL syntax. How many user hits occurred by city and state across all time? To answer this question, let's identify what dimensions and measures are required. The dimensions are `city` and `state` and the measure is an aggregation created by counting the frequency of the occurrence of the number of records, which is represented by the function of `count (*)`. Since we have all of this information that we need in a single table, no join is required.

If we only included the one dimension of `city`, then we would combine any duplicate `city` names and misrepresent the data. For example, the city of `Dover` exists in multiple states, such as Delaware and New Jersey. This is where the granularity of the data could be lost by not including the right fields in the group by aggregation.

6. To run a SQL statement and assign the results to a DataFrame, we have to run this one line of code. The `pandas` library includes a `read_sql_query()` function to make it easier to communicate with databases using SQL. It requires a connection parameter that we named `conn` in the previous steps. We assign the results to a new DataFrame as `df_groupby_SQL` to make it easier to identify:

```
In[]: df_groupby_SQL=pd.read_sql_query("select city, state,
count(*) as hits from tbl_user_geo_hits group by 1, 2;", conn)
```

7. To validate the results, you can run the `head()` function against this DataFrame using this code:

```
[]: df_groupby_SQL.head()
```

The output will look like the following screenshot, where the merge results have been loaded into a new DataFrame named `df_groupby_SQL` with a labeled header row with the index column to the left starting with a value of 0:

In [20]:	df_groupby_SQL		
Out[20]:	**city**	**state**	**hits**
	0 Dover	DE	3
	1 El Paso	TX	2
	2 Philadelphia	PA	2

The SQL language supports shortcuts, so we use `group by 1, 2` to represent the two-dimensional fields of `city` and `state`. It also allows alias of field names, so `count (*) as hits` is used to make it easier to represent.

To recreate the SQL results using `pandas`, we can use the DataFrame we loaded and use the `groupby()` function with a few parameters. In our example, we pass the name of the columns we want to group by, which is both `city` and `state`. The measure will be similar to before by including `.count()`, and we include the field you want to perform the aggregation, which can be any field because we are counting the frequency. We use `userid` since the analysis is focused on the user.

8. To run a SQL statement and assign the results to a DataFrame, we have to run this one line of code. The `pandas` library includes a `read_sql_query` function to make it easier to communicate with databases using SQL. It requires a connection parameter that we named `conn` in the previous steps. We assign the results to a new DataFrame as `df_groupby_city_state` to make it easier to identify:

```
In[]: df_groupby_city_state=df_user_geo_hits.groupby(["city",
"state"]) ["userid"].count()
```

9. To validate the results, you can run the `head()` function against this DataFrame using this code:

```
In[]: df_groupby_city_state.head()
```

The output will look like the following screenshot, where the merge results have been loaded into a new DataFrame named `df_groupby_city_state`:

```
In [47]:   df_groupby_city_state.head
Out[47]:   city          state
           Dover         DE        3
           El Paso       TX        2
           Philadelphia  PA        2
           Name: userid, dtype: int64
```

10. It's a best practice to close the database connection since we no longer need to run any SQL queries and have retrieved all of the data. You would run this command to close it:

```
In[]: conn.close()
```

So, we have demonstrated the power of summarizing data by using an aggregation group in both `pandas` and SQL. Aggregation can be performed against a single table or a join between multiple tables. The common elements between using SQL or `pandas` are defining the dimension and measures, which are abstracted from the fields available in either a DataFrame or SQL object (table, join, or view). So far, we have only scratched the surface using one measure type, which has been count. There are more statistical functions available for data analysis. So, next, we will explore the differences between mean, median, and mode.

Summary statistics and outliers

We touched on the necessity of fundamental statistics when working with data in `Chapter 5`, *Gathering and Loading Data in Python*. Let's walk through the differences between mean, median, and mode in statistics as it applies to data analysis. The mean or average is when you sum the values of numeric values in a series divided by the count of those same numbers. The mean or average is a measure in analytics and is typically used to gauge performance over a period of time and define a comparison for each period of time.

For example, you see average daily temperatures all the time in the news—how is that calculated? Depending on your geographic location, the weather will have the temperature recorded in specific increments, such as hours. The **National Oceanic and Atmospheric Administration (NOAA)**, for example, uses stations and a scientific approach to calculate the minimum and maximum temperature values for each day and location. Those individual records are then used to create an average monthly temperature and 30-year averages by month.

Be sure to understand the lineage of your data, especially when working with averages, because an average of an average will limit how you can work with the data and is most likely a misuse of the metric. Ideally, have the lowest level of detail so you can re-calculate an average based on any period of time desired.

For the example that we have been working with throughout this chapter, calculating the average or mean would provide a standard that we can use for comparison. So, if we want to know the average number of hits per day, all we have to do is count all of the records and divide that by the distinct count of the values of date. From the `tbl_user_geo_hits` data, the average would be 2.3 hits per day because you had seven records with three distinct days. We can now use this as a litmus test to measure when each day has significant increases or decreases when compared to that mean value.

The median, a central value across a series of values, can be determined by finding the middle value, where fifty percent of the values are greater than or less than that specific data value. It is common to have those values ordered first to make it easier to identify that middle value. Identifying the mean is good for measuring the central tendency, which helps you to identify how the data values are distributed and is not affected by outlier data points. We will explore the shape of distributions in `Chapter 9`, *Plotting, Visualization, and Storytelling.*

Finally, we have the mode, which is the value in a series that occurs the most frequently. The mode is less commonly used in analytics and analysis but is useful when identifying outliers in your data. What is an outlier? Mathematically, it could be defined as a value that is multiple standard deviations from the mean. Practically, it's when a value or aggregated value is out of the normal pattern as compared to the rest of the data. A good way to visually identify outliers is to plot the values against a normal distribution or what is commonly known as a *bell curve*, which is represented in the following diagram as a dotted black line:

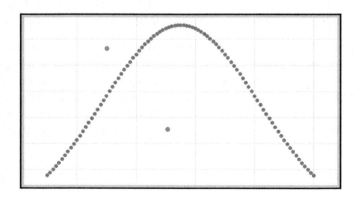

As you can see in the preceding diagram, the distribution line follows a shape based on the mean and standard deviation. A true normal distribution would have values where the mean, median, and mode are all equal. Left and right of that peak at the top of the line are based on one, two, or three standard deviations. A value plus or minus three standard deviations would represent only 99.7% of the population of values.

In practical terms, we are saying less than one percent of all of the data would be toward the min and max values. Having your data in a normal distribution may or may not be relevant but having this understanding helps to identify the shape of your data values. In the preceding example, there are red dots that fall significantly below and above the line, which are considered outliers. Having this visual representation of the outliers as compared to the normal distribution will help you as a data analyst to have a conversation with others about the data. This is the power of data literacy, where a visual representation can spark dialog and help to answer questions about what is expected or normal and what is an exception or an outlier.

Summary

Congratulations, we have covered the fundamentals of joining and merging data in both SQL and Python using pandas DataFrames. Throughout the process, we discussed practical examples of which joins to use along with why you should use them against user hits data. Enriching our data by blending multiple data tables allows deeper analysis and the ability to answer many more questions about the original single data source. After learning about joins and the `merge()` function, we uncovered the advantages and disadvantages of data aggregation. We walked through practical examples of using the `groupby` feature in both SQL and DataFrames. We walked through the differences between statistical functions and mean, median, and mode, along with tips for finding outliers in your data by comparing results to a normal distribution bell curve.

In our next chapter, we will be heading back to using plot libraries and visualizing data.

Further reading

For more information on the topics of this chapter, you can refer to the following links:

- **Guide to using the merge function:** `https://pandas.pydata.org/pandas-docs/stable/reference/api/pandas.DataFrame.merge.html`
- **NOAA weather data:** `https://www.ncdc.noaa.gov/cdo-web/datatools/records`
- **SQL join types:** `https://www.w3schools.com/sql/sql_join.asp`
- **Data Literacy Project – understanding aggregations:** `http://qcc.qlik.com/mod/url/view.php?id=5268`

Plotting, Visualization, and Storytelling

9

This chapter will teach you how to visualize data by exploring additional chart options such as histograms, box plots, and scatter plots to advance your data literacy skills. Storytelling with data starts with understanding the relationships that exist within the numbers, so we will learn about distribution curves and how they apply to analysis. During this discovery phase of analysis of your data, you will learn how to identify outliers and patterns along with best practices in visualizing geographic data. We will wrap up this chapter by learning the difference between correlation versus causation.

We will cover the following topics in this chapter:

- Explaining distribution analysis
- Understanding outliers and trends
- Geoanalytical techniques and tips
- Finding patterns in data

Technical requirements

The GitHub repository of this book can be found at `https://github.com/PacktPublishing/Practical-Data-Analysis-using-Jupyter-Notebook/tree/master/Chapter09`.

You can download and install the required software from `https://www.anaconda.com/products/individual`.

Explaining distribution analysis

I cannot recall a time in history where data, statistics, and science consumed daily lives as it does today. The news cycles are presenting a crisis as it unfolds in real time where changes to human behavior are happening and social norms are being redefined. As I'm writing this book, the concept of **flattening the curve** has gone mainstream and has become a globally understood concept because of the coronavirus (COVID-19) pandemic. You have probably seen something similar to what is shown in the following diagram, which was adapted from the **Centers for Disease Control and Prevention (CDC)**. These types of visualizations are commonly used to communicate the importance of preventing the spread of a disease. The following visualization has two curves, one in yellow labeled **No Intervention measures taken** and the other in blue named **"Flatten the Curve" using preventative measures**. A dotted reference line labeled **Healthcare capacity** is available for relative comparison between the two curves. From a data literacy perspective, we can identify them as distribution curves shown side by side to measure the **Daily # of Cases** on the y axis with a common dimension of duration, which is labeled as **Number of days since first Case** on the x axis. A distribution curve is common in data analysis and visually represents the numeric data values of a single variable:

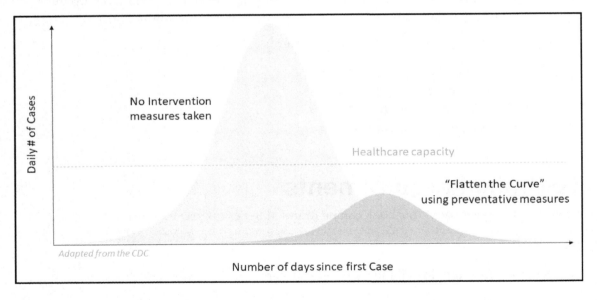

For reference, let's review the most well-known distribution curve, which is called a **Gaussian**, **normal**, or a **bell** curve because of the visual similarity to the shape of a physical bell. In a normal distribution, the values would be represented on the line with the highest point representing the mean or average of the sample or entire population of numeric values. As the line stretches away from the top in either direction, it shows how the numbers have variance from the mean. This spread or dispersion of the numbers from the average value is commonly known as the **Standard Deviation (SD)**. In a perfect distribution, the values would fall within plus or minus one, two, or three standard deviations from the mean, which creates symmetry in the line shape.

Some interesting facts to understand about a normal distribution are the following:

- About 68% of the population of data values fall within plus or minus one standard deviation.
- 96% of the data falls without plus or minus two standard deviation.
- 99.7% of the data falls within plus or minus three standard deviation.
- The calculated mean, median, and mode are all equal.
- There is a 50/50% split between the data left and right of the median.

Back to our example, in the first curve labeled **No Intervention measures taken**, the numbers actually double every few days, which creates a steep curve as it approaches the highest point. The second curve, which is identified as the "**Flatten the Curve**" using **preventative measures**, helps the consumer of this data to visualize the importance of stopping the spread of the virus because the height of the curve has been significantly reduced. I believe this chart became relevant to mass communications because of its simplicity of explaining a distribution curve without going into the statistics behind it. Even without showing the data behind the curves, anyone can visually understand the importance of this critical information.

At this point in time of writing this book, I do not know whether people around the world have successfully achieved the desired result of reducing the mortality rate of COVID-19. Furthermore, it is unknown at this time whether enough preventive measures such as social distancing are helping to **flatten the curve**. Many people all around the world have already suffered from the COVID-19 pandemic travesty. My heartfelt condolences go out to everyone who has suffered.

KYD

To see how the COVID-19 data is distributed, I have provided a snapshot CSV file that is available in the GitHub repository for this book. To support our data analyst **Know Your Data (KYD)** mantra, I'll provide some additional information on how the data was collected and its format. The `COVID-19 Cases.csv` file was collected from authoritative open source COVID-19 sources. A GitHub repository maintained by the **Center for Systems Science and Engineering (CSSE)** at Johns Hopkins University is available in the *Further reading* section. The CDC has also been distributing COVID-19 data for the greater good.

A sample of the first few records in the CSV file will look similar to the following screenshot, which was retrieved from authoritative sources found in the *Further reading* section:

```
1   Date,Country_Region,Province_State,Difference,Prep_Flow_Runtime,Latest_Date,Case_Type,Cases,Lat,Long
2   3/9/2020,India,N/A,0,3/24/2020 9:39:03 AM,3/23/2020,Deaths,0,21,78
3   3/8/2020,India,N/A,0,3/24/2020 9:39:03 AM,3/23/2020,Deaths,0,21,78
4   3/7/2020,India,N/A,0,3/24/2020 9:39:03 AM,3/23/2020,Deaths,0,21,78
5   3/6/2020,India,N/A,0,3/24/2020 9:39:03 AM,3/23/2020,Deaths,0,21,78
6   3/5/2020,India,N/A,0,3/24/2020 9:39:03 AM,3/23/2020,Deaths,0,21,78
7   3/4/2020,India,N/A,0,3/24/2020 9:39:03 AM,3/23/2020,Deaths,0,21,78
8   3/3/2020,India,N/A,0,3/24/2020 9:39:03 AM,3/23/2020,Deaths,0,21,78
9   3/23/2020,India,N/A,3,3/24/2020 9:39:03 AM,3/23/2020,Deaths,10,21,78
10  3/22/2020,India,N/A,3,3/24/2020 9:39:03 AM,3/23/2020,Deaths,7,21,78
```

This data source contains a daily snapshot of the COVID-19 cases by country. The key fields used in our analysis are as follows:

- `Date`, which formatted as `M/D/YYYY`, is the date a positive COVID-19 case was identified.
- `Country_Region` is the country of origin where the COVID-19 cases are tracked.
- The `Cases` field is the accumulated count of the number of COVID-19 cases by country and date.
- The `Difference` field is the daily number of COVID-19 cases by country and date.
- `Case_Type` is the type of case that is assigned to each value and is either `Confirmed` or `Deaths`.

From this data source, we can answer multiple questions about the data but will require some filtering to isolate records by `Country`, `Date`, and `Case_Type`.

Shape of the curve

Now that we have more information about the data, we can launch a new Jupyter Notebook for analysis to identify the shape of the curve.

Launch a new Jupyter Notebook and name it `ch_09_exercises`. To import the data from a CSV to a `pandas` DataFrame so we can create a histogram, we use the following steps:

1. Import the following libraries by adding the following codes in your Jupyter Notebook and run the cell. Feel free to follow along by creating your own Notebook; I have also placed a copy in GitHub for reference:

```
In[]: import pandas as pd
      import numpy as np
      import matplotlib.pyplot as plt
      %matplotlib inline
```

These libraries should already be available using Anaconda. Refer to `Chapter 2`, *Overview of Python and Installing Jupyter Notebook*, in case you need help with setting up your environment. `%matplotlib inline` is a magic command required to display the visual results inside your Jupyter Notebook after you run the cell.

2. Next, we create a new DataFrame by importing the CSV file:

```
In[]: covid_df = pd.read_csv("COVID-19 Cases.csv", header=0)
```

Be sure you copied the `COVID-19 Cases.csv` file to the correct Jupyter folder directory to avoid errors with the connection.

3. To verify the DataFrame has loaded correctly, we can run the `head()` function to display the first few records:

```
In[]: covid_df.head()
```

The output would look like the following screenshot where the source CSV file has been loaded into a DataFrame with a labeled header row with the index column to the left starting with a value of 0:

	Date	Country_Region	Province_State	Difference	Prep_Flow_Runtime	Latest_Date	Case_Type	Cases	Lat	Long
0	3/9/2020	India	NaN	0	3/24/2020 9:39:03 AM	3/23/2020	Deaths	0	21.0	78.0
1	3/8/2020	India	NaN	0	3/24/2020 9:39:03 AM	3/23/2020	Deaths	0	21.0	78.0
2	3/7/2020	India	NaN	0	3/24/2020 9:39:03 AM	3/23/2020	Deaths	0	21.0	78.0
3	3/6/2020	India	NaN	0	3/24/2020 9:39:03 AM	3/23/2020	Deaths	0	21.0	78.0
4	3/5/2020	India	NaN	0	3/24/2020 9:39:03 AM	3/23/2020	Deaths	0	21.0	78.0

4. Next, we will isolate the data we want to focus our attention on by creating a new DataFrame from the source and applying a few filters against it. We want to isolate the records where all of the following conditions are true. First, the daily `Difference` count is greater than zero. Next, the `Case_Type` should be `Confirmed`. Finally, the `Country_Region` should be only `Italy`:

```
In[]: df_results = covid_df[(covid_df.Difference >0) &
(covid_df.Case_Type == 'Confirmed') & (covid_df.Country_Region ==
'Italy')]
```

 The new `df_results` DataFrame will not display results in Jupyter Notebook by default.

5. To see the results sorted, we run the following command:

```
In[]: df_results.sort_values(by='Cases', ascending=False)
```

The output should look like the following screenshot, where a new `df_results` DataFrame is displayed with the values sorted by `Cases` in descending order:

	Date	Country_Region	Province_State	Difference	Prep_Flow_Runtime	Latest_Date	Case_Type	Cases	Lat	Long
28982	3/23/2020	Italy	NaN	4789	3/24/2020 9:39:03 AM	3/23/2020	Confirmed	63927	43.0	12.0
28983	3/22/2020	Italy	NaN	5560	3/24/2020 9:39:03 AM	3/23/2020	Confirmed	59138	43.0	12.0
28984	3/21/2020	Italy	NaN	6557	3/24/2020 9:39:03 AM	3/23/2020	Confirmed	53578	43.0	12.0
28985	3/20/2020	Italy	NaN	5986	3/24/2020 9:39:03 AM	3/23/2020	Confirmed	47021	43.0	12.0
28987	3/19/2020	Italy	NaN	5322	3/24/2020 9:39:03 AM	3/23/2020	Confirmed	41035	43.0	12.0
28988	3/18/2020	Italy	NaN	4207	3/24/2020 9:39:03 AM	3/23/2020	Confirmed	35713	43.0	12.0
28989	3/17/2020	Italy	NaN	3526	3/24/2020 9:39:03 AM	3/23/2020	Confirmed	31506	43.0	12.0

6. Now, we want to visually display the distribution of the values in the `Difference` column. We can pass an array of values into the default `hist()` plot using the following command:

```
In[]: df_results.hist(column='Difference');
```

The output would look like the following screenshot, where the array of values are displayed in a default histogram chart. The default settings bin the data values in equal sizes, which are displayed on the *x* axis. The frequency or count of the number of occurrences of the values falling inside of each bin are measured by the *y* axis:

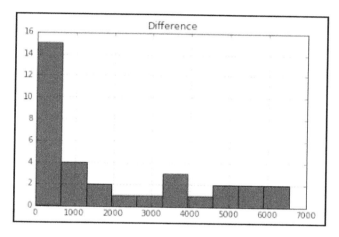

So, what does this histogram plot tell us about the data in the preceding chart at first glance? First, most of the data values are less than **1,000** since the highest bar is the first bar to the left. Second, we know the data is not a normal distribution based on the shape because we would have expected the most frequent results to be in the middle, closer to the mean of the data. How does this analysis apply to the COVID-19 data itself? This shape is good since the number of daily increases could be much larger.

To learn more details about the shape of this data, we can use the `describe()` function against this specific column in the DataFrame.

7. Use the `describe()` function against this DataFrame to see summary statistics. We can look at one column by explicitly passing it in the square brackets along with the column/field name in double quotes:

```
In[]: df_results["Difference"].describe()
```

The output would look like the following screenshot where summary statistics about the data in this specific field are displayed:

```
Out[98]:  count        33.000000
          mean       1937.181818
          std        2132.965299
          min           1.000000
          25%         202.000000
          50%         778.000000
          75%        3526.000000
          max        6557.000000
          Name: Difference, dtype: float64
```

In the preceding screenshot, we have identified some key statistics to help to better understand the shape of this data. There are `33` values that are identified as `count` in the summary table with a `mean` of `1937.181818` and a `std` (standard deviation) of `2132.965299`. The range of those thirty-three values is from `1` to `6557`, which is identified by `min` and `max`. With that high of a standard deviation value, we know the numbers are pretty spread out.

> The values will be displayed with a datatype of `float64` with a precision of six decimal places regardless of the source number value.

The **25%**, **50%**, and **75%** labels return the respective percentiles for the series of values in this field. These values are also known as the **Interquartile Range (IRQ)** with the 50% or second quartile equal to the **median**. Having the data in quartiles creates equal bins or buckets for the data values to help us understand how the numeric values are distributed. If a majority of the values fall into one specific bucket, you know the data is not evenly distributed. With our example, we have a large gap between our mean and median with our data (1937 versus 778) so we can classify this data as skewed. Having a skew in our data helps to understand that the visual shape of the distribution curve or histogram is not symmetrical. To help you to remember the distribution types and skewness, I have summarized them in the following graph. When the mean is greater than the median, it would have a positive skew and when the opposite is true, a negative skew exists. As described at the top of each visual trend in the following diagram, the type of skew (negative or positive) is directly correlated with the mean and median values. When all of the mean, median, and mode values are equal, you have a symmetrical distribution:

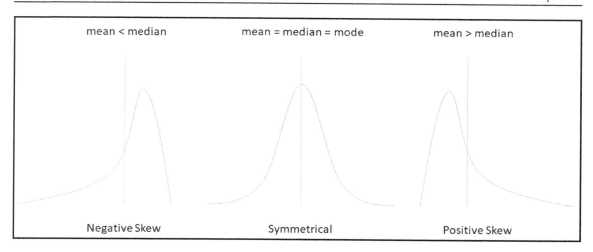

From a data analysis perspective, having these key statistics defined helps us to understand the spread of the data values. Calculating the mean, median, and mode against your data values are collectively known as the measures of **central tendency**, which we introduced in `Chapter 8`, *Understanding Joins, Relationships, and Aggregates*. A very important and practical use of central tendency is in data science models. In predictive regression models that use historical data, the ability to calculate a prediction is based on finding a *best fit* to the distribution curve. If the data has a dramatic positive or negative skew with *long tails*, which is when values trail off by multiple standard deviations from the central tendency, the algorithm becomes less accurate.

So, now we understand the importance of calculating central tendency and how symmetrical data is visually represented as a normal distribution curve. A normal distribution, also known as the Gaussian distribution and the bell curve, occurs when the mean (average) is equal to the median (middle) and is equal to the mode (most frequent). I find adding a normal distribution line useful as a reference to compare against the actual data results in charts. This helps the consumer of the analysis to visually compare the ideal shape of the data versus the actual results. So, what causes data to skew or not fit into a normal distribution? As a data analyst, your job is to find out why and the first step is to isolate outliers that may exist in the data. We will discuss this in the next section by understanding outliers and trends.

Understanding outliers and trends

Finding outliers begins by looking at the distribution curve but requires additional techniques that we will walk through together. Additionally, don't underestimate the need for soft skills where you must reach out to others to better understand why an outlier exists in your data. An outlier is commonly known as one or more data values that are significantly different than the rest of the data. Spotting outliers in data is easy depending on the data visualization used, but in many cases, especially when data volumes are very large, they can be obscured when data is aggregated. If you recall from Chapter 7, *Exploring Cleaning, Refining, and Blending Datasets*, we worked with hits created by a user for a website. A good example of obscuring outliers is when those user hits are aggregated by date. If a specific user has 1,000 hits per day when the average is 2, it would be difficult to identify that outlier user after the data was aggregated by week. So, what does an outlier look like visually in a series of data values? A good approach would be to use a box plot because it visually represents the data found in the describe() function:

As you can see in the preceding diagram, the box isolates the quartiles of **25%**, **50%**, and **75%**, and the min/max range of values is displayed at the most extreme vertical lines. The space between the box and the min/max lines is known as the whiskers of the box plot. If you see a plus symbol (+) displayed, they are known as fliers, which are outliers in this chart type.

 A box plot can be displayed horizontally or vertically and can include multiple dimensions so you can compare the distribution between them.

Let's continue to analyze our existing dataset and see how it would be visualized using a box plot. Similar to the prior example, we will load all of the data from the source into a single DataFrame and then create a subset DataFrame using filters. We will continue using the `ch_09_exercises` Jupyter Notebook:

1. Import the following libraries by adding the following command in your Jupyter Notebook and run the cell. Feel free to follow along by creating your own Notebook; I have placed a copy on GitHub for reference:

```
In[]: import pandas as pd
      import numpy as np
      import matplotlib.pyplot as plt
      %matplotlib inline
```

2. Create a new DataFrame by importing the CSV file:

```
In[]: covid_df = pd.read_csv("COVID-19 Cases.csv", header=0)
```

3. To verify the DataFrame has loaded correctly, we can run the `head()` function to display the first few records:

```
In[]: covid_df.head()
```

The output would look like the following screenshot where the source CSV file has been loaded into a DataFrame with a labeled header row with the index column to the left starting with a value of 0:

	Date	Country_Region	Province_State	Difference	Prep_Flow_Runtime	Latest_Date	Case_Type	Cases	Lat	Long
0	3/9/2020	India	NaN	0	3/24/2020 9:39:03 AM	3/23/2020	Deaths	0	21.0	78.0
1	3/8/2020	India	NaN	0	3/24/2020 9:39:03 AM	3/23/2020	Deaths	0	21.0	78.0
2	3/7/2020	India	NaN	0	3/24/2020 9:39:03 AM	3/23/2020	Deaths	0	21.0	78.0
3	3/6/2020	India	NaN	0	3/24/2020 9:39:03 AM	3/23/2020	Deaths	0	21.0	78.0
4	3/5/2020	India	NaN	0	3/24/2020 9:39:03 AM	3/23/2020	Deaths	0	21.0	78.0

Similar to the prior exercise, we will isolate the data we want to focus attention on by creating a new DataFrame from the source and applying a few filters against it. We want to isolate the records where all of the following conditions are true. First, the daily `Difference` count is greater than zero. Next, `Case_Type` should be `Confirmed`. Finally, we use the pipe symbol, `|`, to create an `or` condition to allow for multiple `Country_Region`:

```
In[]: df_results = covid_df[(covid_df.Difference >0) &
(covid_df.Case_Type == 'Confirmed') & ((covid_df.Country_Region ==
'Italy') | (covid_df.Country_Region == 'Spain') |
(covid_df.Country_Region == 'Germany'))]
```

The new `df_results` DataFrame will not display results in Jupyter Notebook by default.

4. To see the results, we run the following command:

```
In[]: df_results.head()
```

The output should look like the following screenshot where a new `df_results` DataFrame is displayed:

Out[78]:		Date	Country_Region	Province_State	Difference	Prep_Flow_Runtime	Latest_Date	Case_Type	Cases	Lat	Long
	20191	3/9/2020	Germany	NaN	136	3/24/2020 9:39:03 AM	3/23/2020	Confirmed	1176	51.0	9.0
	20192	3/8/2020	Germany	NaN	241	3/24/2020 9:39:03 AM	3/23/2020	Confirmed	1040	51.0	9.0
	20193	3/7/2020	Germany	NaN	129	3/24/2020 9:39:03 AM	3/23/2020	Confirmed	799	51.0	9.0
	20194	3/6/2020	Germany	NaN	188	3/24/2020 9:39:03 AM	3/23/2020	Confirmed	670	51.0	9.0
	20195	3/5/2020	Germany	NaN	220	3/24/2020 9:39:03 AM	3/23/2020	Confirmed	482	51.0	9.0

5. To display a box plot by `Country`, we use the following command. `boxplot()` has a few parameters such as `by=`, which allows us to group the data by `Country_Region`. We also include `column=` to isolate the values in the `Difference` field. Finally, we pass in `grid=False` to turn off the gridlines in the chart:

```
In[]: df_results.boxplot(by='Country_Region',
column=['Difference'], grid=False)
```

The output would look like the following screenshot where a box plot will be displayed:

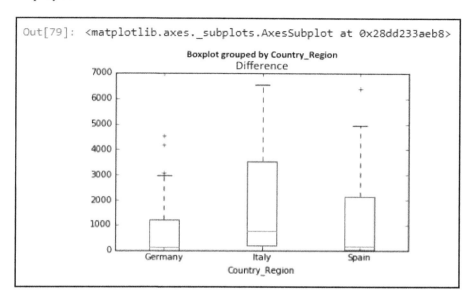

```
Out[79]:   <matplotlib.axes._subplots.AxesSubplot at 0x28dd233aeb8>
```

So, having the data limited to only three countries allows us to narrow our analysis, and having the data presented side by side in the box plot chart, as shown in the preceding screenshot, allows us to visually compare the results. First, we notice a few box sizes, which, if you recall, are the quartiles of the data and are different sizes depending on Country. Germany has a smaller box that is closer to a square than a rectangle, which typically tells us the data spread is much tighter. Another observation we can identify in this chart is we have multiple plus symbols (+) displayed; these highlight outliers that exist in the countries of Germany and Spain.

Analyzing data by country and other attributes related to geography is a common requirement today for a data analyst. Next, we will explore best practices related to visually representing data in maps and spatial data, which is known as geoanalytics.

Geoanalytical techniques and tips

For a data analyst, the concept of geoanalytics is a relatively new technique applied to spatial data to understand where data is geographically located. However, cartography, which is the study of maps, has been around for centuries and traditionally requires training, expertise, and niche software to provided insights from data by location. Today, there are multiple add-on modules and software available to create charts and visualizations that use maps to visualize data in exciting ways that provide a different perspective.

First, you need to understand the grain of the data you have available. Having precision of the exact latitude and longitude available in your source data is a luxury unless the source system was built to capture that information. For example, mobile app source data will commonly have this level of detail available because a smartphone can track your location. However, if we go back to our COVID-19 source data, the individual cases' lowest level of detail available is by `Province_State` so you lose the ability to display data below that level.

Next, if your source data does not include latitude and longitude values, you will have to add it, which sounds simple at first but usually has some challenges that you will have to overcome. When you profile the data, ensure it has conformity and consistency in specific fields such as `Country`, `City`, `Parcel`, or `Zip Code`. If the `Country` values exist, do they have **International Organization for Standardization (ISO)** codes so you can join the data to commonly available sources? If so, I have included a source a link to the World Bank data source in the *Further reading* section.

Finally, I find including a world or regional map as a good complement to, but not a replacement for, good data analysis solutions. In many cases, having a single map chart even with color gradients does not provide enough answers to common questions. For example, let's look at the following screenshot, which shows a global map of the COVID-19 outbreak found on the HealthMap site:

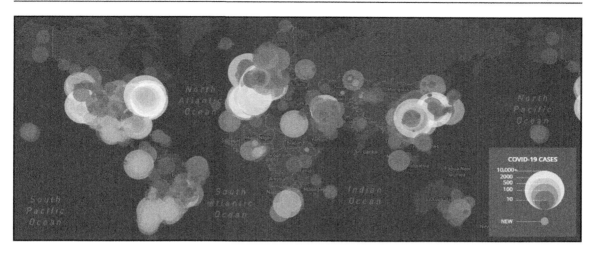

As displayed in the preceding screenshot, the legend at the bottom right of the chart provides insights on the outbreak by location using the color and size of the bubbles. If you look at this visualization as a static map, it leaves the audience asking more questions about the overlap of the bubbles with colors. For example, how do you distinguish between the details of closely clustered cities such as New York and Philadelphia? Also, the consumer of this geoanalytic chart might want to know whether the number of cases is accelerating per location, which is unclear.

However, these criticisms change once you visit the site, which allows the user to interact with the map.

When you use the HealthMap site created for the COVID-19 outbreak, you are offered a solution that provides the following features:

- Zoom capabilities to drill down to the lowest level of detail and zoom out to compare results across different locations
- Mouse hover over the circles that provide aggregated counts by location along with the context of which location is selected or has the focus
- A timeline feature that allows the user to see before and after results

Once you appreciate having any or all of these features available in geoanalytics data, you expect it for any solution you are building as a data producer. If you are missing the data or tools to create it, I would recommend creating a complementary chart to support it. For example, in the following screenshot, we have a horizontal bar chart sorted in descending order by country:

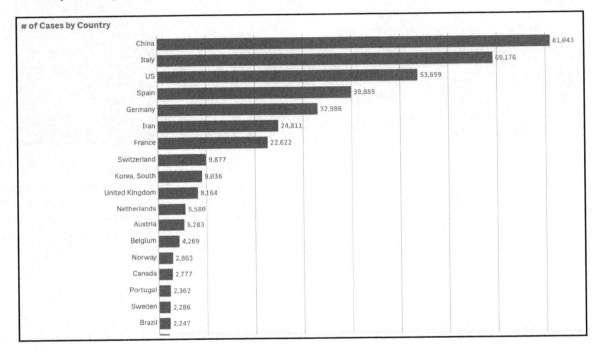

The legend at the top of the chart indicates the measure used, which is titled **# of Cases by Country**, to help the consumer of the data easily answer questions such as which country has the highest number of cases as of a specific date. When you bring together multiple charts that complement each other, they provide context to the consumer of the geographic data.

Be sure the common join key between the data sources behind these charts is consistent. If you select a country on the map, the bar chart should filter to match along with any date selections.

Using multiple charts in tandem helps to tell a story with the information to build a connection with the audience. The consumers of data today are sophisticated so telling the same story over and over will not be effective. I recommend using time-honored techniques such as having a lesson or moral for the story to work well and you should feel empowered to adjust to include your own personal style.

I find creative inspiration from art and learning more about the masters of their craft. For example, the artist Pablo Picasso is well known for works created during his **Blue Period**, which defined a time in his life when all variations of the color blue were the primary color used commonly across different subjects he painted. This period lasted a few years and reflected his personal struggles living with depression and financial distress. In comparison, the COVID-19 pandemic is creating personal struggles for people all around the world. The high levels of mortality related to the COVID-19 data are causing global financial distress and numerous stories of personal loss. Picasso produced a staggering volume of work during his lifetime, with well over 100,000 pieces over a 70 plus year timeframe. Even during times of emotional distress, Picasso continued to find the strength to create new works of art and master his craft. I can relate to his struggles during this pandemic and am inspired to spend time on my data craft to help me through these trying times.

The power of storytelling with data becomes a critical skill to build trust with your audience so they can understand the information. Using data visualizations breaks down the technical barriers that can exist when working with data. As a person fluent in data literacy, you now have the additional skills required to create your own story using data.

Now that you understand the geographic techniques that are effective in data storytelling, let's focus our attention on identifying patterns within data.

Finding patterns in data

Now that we have a better understanding of distribution curves and spotting outliers that can exist in your data, let's break down how to find patterns in your data. In my experience, as you work with more and more data, you will start to develop a **sixth sense** that will help you identify patterns faster, for example, the following diagram may appear like a random list of numbers where no distinguishing pattern is obvious, until you make some minor changes to make it easier to identify:

8	3	8	7	4	3	7	4

Having the data sorted allows you to see groupings and clusters that exist within the data values. In this case, we have pairings of numbers that were not as evident until you sorted them together. With a quick sort, we can now see all of the numbers are duplicated, as in the following diagram:

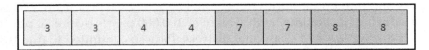

To hammer this point home, look at the following diagram where those same numbers from the preceding two diagrams are now colored by pairs, which creates a pattern to make it easier to visually identify:

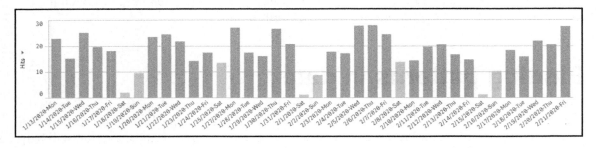

Data visualizations and charts will help you to identify these patterns as well, but some charts are better suited than others depending on the data. For example, to see patterns in the data over time, a line or bar chart will display the trends better and help to create recognizable patterns in your data. A good example of that can be seen in the following screenshot, which is a bar chart with a measure of **Hits** on the *y* axis and a dimension of date with the day of the week in the `dtype` format of `M/DD/YYYY-DDD` displayed on the *x* axis:

In the preceding screenshot, we have a trend chart that displays a pattern of web hit usage over each date. What becomes more evident when you look at this data sorted is the peaks and valleys that naturally appear every few days. Even without understanding all of the details behind it, having this pattern suggests our weekday data usage is higher than weekends, which I highlighted in a different color to make it more obvious.

During this time of analysis and identifying patterns, you will find yourself coming to conclusions about the data. Doing this is natural and if based on business or domain expertise, is viable. If you find patterns in your data that apply to multiple dimensions or variables, you can identify a correlation between them. Correlations are common in data, especially when overlaying patterns over the same timeframe. A more formal definition is when one variable or series of values increase or decrease, a second variable will follow in parallel. A common example of a correlation between two values would be ice-cream store sales and the weather. If the weather has snow or heavy rain or is cold, ice-cream sales are typically lower. If the weather is warm and sunny, sales would be higher. Based on this information, you could say there is a **positive** correlation between the variables of sales and weather over the same period of time.

If the opposite relationship exists, where the inverse pattern between the two variables occurs, this would be considered a **negative** correlation.

To determine whether two variables are statically correlated, there is a concept called the **correlation coefficient.** This is a measurement that falls between 1 and –1 and is denoted by *r*. If the value is 0, there is no correlation between the two variables. The closer the values are to 1, they have a positive correlation, which means when one variable's value changes, the other will trend in the same direction. The opposite is true when the values are closer to –1, where a negative correlation creates an inverse relationship between the two variables. So, can we visually see a correlation and pattern with data? A good approach would be to use a scatter plot.

Let's continue to analyze our existing dataset and see how it would be visualized using the scatter plot. Similar to the prior example, we will load all of the data from the source into a single DataFrame and then create a subset DataFrame using filters. In this example, we are going to create two subsets to allow for comparisons. We will continue using the ch_09_exercises Jupyter Notebook:

1. Import the following libraries by adding the following command in your Jupyter Notebook and run the cell. Feel free to follow along by creating your own Notebook; I have placed a copy on GitHub for reference:

```
In[]: import pandas as pd
import numpy as np
import matplotlib.pyplot as plt
%matplotlib inline
```

2. Create a new DataFrame by importing the CSV file:

```
In[]: covid_df = pd.read_csv("COVID-19 Cases.csv", header=0)
```

3. We will now create two new DataFrames, which will be subsets from the original source. The advantage of naming them generically as `df_results_1` and `df_results_2` is that it allows you to adjust the filters such as `Country_Region` used in this one line without changing any other code in the additional steps:

```
In[]: df_results_1 = covid_df[(covid_df.Case_Type == 'Confirmed') &
(covid_df.Country_Region == 'Germany')]
```

4. Run the `head()` function to validate the results:

```
In[]: df_results_1.head()
```

The output will look like the following table where a new `df_results_1` DataFrame is displayed:

Out[78]:

	Date	Country_Region	Province_State	Difference	Prep_Flow_Runtime	Latest_Date	Case_Type	Cases	Lat	Long
20191	3/9/2020	Germany	NaN	136	3/24/2020 9:39:03 AM	3/23/2020	Confirmed	1176	51.0	9.0
20192	3/8/2020	Germany	NaN	241	3/24/2020 9:39:03 AM	3/23/2020	Confirmed	1040	51.0	9.0
20193	3/7/2020	Germany	NaN	129	3/24/2020 9:39:03 AM	3/23/2020	Confirmed	799	51.0	9.0
20194	3/6/2020	Germany	NaN	188	3/24/2020 9:39:03 AM	3/23/2020	Confirmed	670	51.0	9.0
20195	3/5/2020	Germany	NaN	220	3/24/2020 9:39:03 AM	3/23/2020	Confirmed	482	51.0	9.0

5. We will load the second DataFrame that we will use to compare with the first using the following commands:

```
In[]: df_results_2 = covid_df[(covid_df.Case_Type == 'Confirmed') &
(covid_df.Country_Region == 'Italy')]
```

6. Run the `head()` function to validate the results:

```
In[]: df_results_2.head()
```

The output would look like the following table where a new `df_results_2` DataFrame is displayed:

Out[43]:

	Date	Country_Region	Province_State	Difference	Prep_Flow_Runtime	Latest_Date	Case_Type	Cases	Lat	Long
28975	3/9/2020	Italy	NaN	1797	3/24/2020 9:39:03 AM	3/23/2020	Confirmed	9172	43.0	12.0
28976	3/8/2020	Italy	NaN	1492	3/24/2020 9:39:03 AM	3/23/2020	Confirmed	7375	43.0	12.0
28977	3/7/2020	Italy	NaN	1247	3/24/2020 9:39:03 AM	3/23/2020	Confirmed	5883	43.0	12.0
28978	3/6/2020	Italy	NaN	778	3/24/2020 9:39:03 AM	3/23/2020	Confirmed	4636	43.0	12.0
28979	3/5/2020	Italy	NaN	769	3/24/2020 9:39:03 AM	3/23/2020	Confirmed	3858	43.0	12.0

7. Let's profile the data in each DataFrame to better understand it. We use the `describe()` function to better identify key statistics and how the data is distributed. First, we look at the contents of the first DataFrame:

```
In[]: df_results_1["Cases"].describe()
```

The output will look like the following screenshot where results are displayed:

```
Out[50]:  count       61.000000
          mean      2707.491803
          std       6468.499823
          min          0.000000
          25%         13.000000
          50%         16.000000
          75%       1040.000000
          max      29056.000000
          Name: Cases, dtype: float64
```

8. Then, we look at the contents of the second DataFrame:

```
In[]: df_results_2["Cases"].describe()
```

The output will look like the following screenshot where results are displayed:

```
Out[51]:  count       61.000000
          mean      8241.770492
          std      15956.982677
          min          0.000000
          25%          3.000000
          50%         62.000000
          75%       7375.000000
          max      63927.000000
          Name: Cases, dtype: float64
```

Based on the results of the `describe()` function run against each DataFrame, we have a basis for comparison. First, we have the count, which is the same value of 61 values. This is important when creating a scatter plot since the size of the data is required to be the same. Another common value between the two data series is the minimum, which is at 0. However, the maximum values are different, which are slightly larger than double (29,056 versus 63,927). Next, we have the mean, which is vastly different. The first results have a rounded mean value of 2,707.49 and the second is 8,241.77. Finally, the standard deviation (**std**) is different as well so we know the shape and size of the distribution curves will be different.

The question we want to answer is: are these values correlated? To confirm this visually, we continue by creating a scatter plot with a few simple commands. The scatter plot will have *x* and *y* axes and plot the values in a grid with dots representing where the values align to the axis.

9. We use the `plt.scatter()` function to create the visualization. It requires two parameters, which are the *x* and *y* axes values separated by a comma. We are passing the common series of values found in the `Cases` column from each DataFrame. We also include labels and a title to help the audience to understand the chart:

```
In[]: plt.scatter(df_results_1["Cases"], df_results_2["Cases"]);
plt.title("# of Cases")
plt.xlabel("Germany Cases")
plt.ylabel("Italy Cases");
```

The output would look like the following graph where results are displayed:

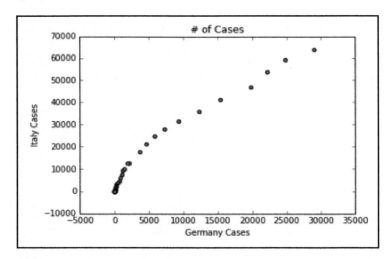

The result of our scatter plot does have a correlation where the values closer to 0 on either axis cluster together, which are shown with overlapping blue dots on the chart. You can also observe a natural straight-line alignment between the values as the # **of Cases** increase.

With every correlation comes the inevitable expectation that one variable is dependent on the other and is the cause. Causation is when one variable directly impacts the direction of another. Cause and effect or root cause analysis are common analysis techniques. Identifying causation between only two variables is rare and requires deeper analysis to understand all of the factors that directly and indirectly impact the change. The first point to understand is that *correlation doesn't always equal causation*. A good example is our ice-cream store sales and the weather. We know that eating more ice-cream would never improve the weather but if you look purely at the data, you might accidentally come to that kind of conclusion if the data is highly correlated. Another point when analyzing data to determine whether correlation and causation are related is based on the sample size of the data. I would recommend being a **data skeptic** and question a causative conclusion if the population of data is incomplete or covers a small window of time. Finally, we have walked through the value of joining data for data analysis but that invites the opportunity to come to conclusions about data that didn't exist independently. Be sure to add assumptions and be transparent with the methods of how you joined the data so the correlations can be peer-reviewed.

Summary

Congratulations, we have now learned some essential skills for making various plots that visualize the distribution of data. We discussed key statistics related to the central tendency of data by calculating the standard deviation, mean, median, and mode of a series of data values. We looked at normal distributions and how data values can be skewed positively or negatively. When data has symmetry, it becomes easier to work with some algorithms found in predictive analytics. We reviewed patterns and outliers that are common when working with datasets, along with how to use a box plot chart to visualize outliers.

We discussed best practices and tips for working with geospatial data, along with how it can be used to help to tell a story with data. Finally, we discussed the difference between correlation versus causation along with the importance of the correlation coefficient, so you can understand the relationships between two variables/series of data values.

In our next chapter, we will be switching to working with unstructured data sources and best practices when working with free text data.

Further reading

For more information on the relative topics of this chapter, you can visit the following links:

- Authoritative sources for COVID-19 data: `https://github.com/CSSEGISandData/COVID-19`
- Centers for Disease Control and Prevention COVID-19 data: `https://www.cdc.gov/coronavirus/2019-ncov/`
- Cheatsheets to help to create data visuals using Python: `https://python-graph-gallery.com/cheat-sheets/`
- The World Bank ISO country data: `https://datahelpdesk.worldbank.org/knowledgebase/articles/898590-country-api-queries`
- Open source mapping software: `https://www.openstreetmap.org/`
- HealthMap geoanalytics example of COVID-19: `https://www.healthmap.org/covid-19/`

3
Section 3: Working with Unstructured Big Data

Now that the foundations for data analysis have been established using structured data, in this section, the exciting frontier of unstructured social media and textual data will be explored. Here, we will learn about the various elements of supervised **Natural Language Processing** (**NLP**) and how to use a basic sentiment analysis model. Finally, we'll wrap up this book with a capstone project using open source data to provide insights.

This section includes the following chapters:

10
Exploring Text Data and Unstructured Data

The need to become literate with both structured and unstructured data continues to evolve. Working with structured data has well-established techniques such as merging and uniform data types, which we have reviewed in prior chapters. However, working with unstructured data is a relatively new concept and is rapidly turning into a must-have skill in data analysis. **Natural Language Processing (NLP)** has evolved into an essential skill, so this chapter introduces the concepts and tools available to analyze narrative free text. As technology has advanced, using these techniques can help you to provide transparency to unstructured data, which would have been difficult to uncover only a few years ago.

We will cover the following topics in this chapter:

- Preparing to work with unstructured data
- Tokenization explained
- Counting words and exploring results
- Normalizing text techniques
- Excluding words from analysis

Technical requirements

The GitHub repository of this book is at `https://github.com/PacktPublishing/Practical-Data-Analysis-using-Jupyter-Notebook/tree/master/Chapter10`.

You can download and install the required software from `https://www.anaconda.com/products/individual`.

Preparing to work with unstructured data

Today, we are living in a digital age where data is entangled into our lives in ways not technically possible or even imaginable before. From social media to mobile to the **Internet of Things (IoT)**, humanity is living in what is commonly known as the information age. This age is where an exponentially growing of data about you is available to you instantaneously anywhere in the world. What has made this possible has been a combination of people and technology, including contributions from the **Evolution of Data Analysis**, which was introduced in `Chapter 1`, *Fundamentals of Data Analysis*.

It is commonly predicted by multiple sources that 80 percent of all of the data created around the world will be unstructured over the next few years. If you recall from `Chapter 1`, *Fundamentals of Data Analysis*., unstructured data is commonly defined as information that does not offer uniformity and pre-defined organization. Examples of unstructured data include free text, chatbots, **Artificial Intelligence (AI)**, photos, videos, and audio files. Social media, of course, produces the highest volume, velocity, and variety of unstructured data. So, we're going to focus our examples on those data sources, but you can apply the concepts learned in this chapter to any narrative-based text data sources such as help desk ticket logs or email communications.

What's important to understand about working with unstructured data is that it's inherently messy. Without structure, defined data types, and conformity applied to data when it's captured, uncertainty is created. This should not prohibit or discourage you from working with the data, but just being conscious that precision is going to be a luxury in some cases. For example, words in a sentence can and will be misspelled. The meaning of a word or phrase can be misrepresented and the context is sometimes lost. With all of these shortcomings, the technology continues to be improved to a point where you will find it being used in everyday life. For example, chatbots are now replacing many customer service solutions so you may think you're talking with an agent but it is actually software with NLP algorithms installed.

The concepts of NLP have been around for decades. Using NLP concepts have some fundamentals that you may have already used in the past such as rule-based conditions or tags. A rule-based example would be when a specific keyword or collection of words is found in a dataset with a flag field used to identify it, similar to the following table where we have three columns with five rows including a header row to identify the purpose of each record:

id	phrase	key_word_found_flag
1	Automated client-driven internet solution is balanced	1
2	Configurable balanced content-based toolset	1
3	Balanced 5th generation pricing structure	1
4	Virtual bandwidth-monitored website is well-balanced	1
5	Visionary needs-based balancing act	1

In the table, I have changed the font color for any variation of the keyword `balanced` to make it easier to identify. As you can observe from the table, the word does have minor variations that would seem obvious to a human but must be programmed as a rule to account for the differences. So, to identify any variation of the keyword such as whether it is capitalized or conjugated, it must be accounted for using conditional logic. In this example, a conditional field named `key_word_found_flag` is used to determine whether the phrase field contains the keyword, which is using a value of `1` to identify a true case.

Rule-based NLP has evolved from earlier concepts that used basic wildcard searches and ASCII character identification to machine-learned statistical models. I don't plan on going into all of the details behind the mathematical models used by NLP, but I encourage you to explore the subject. I will focus, in this chapter, on using predefined NLP libraries as is without adjusting or training the models. The intention is to help you to gain some confidence in when, where, and how it can be used. Over the last few years, I have been impressed by the level of accuracy behind solutions that leverage NLP, but I recognize it is an evolving technology. I was reminded of this when I interacted with Alexa the other day when it told me it could not understand my question regardless of how I phrased it.

Anytime you use or create solutions with NLP, the potential for a **False Positive (FP)** or **False Negative (FN)** exists. An FP or FN is when the NLP algorithm has incorrectly predicted the output. When the output returns true, but the actual result is false, it is considered an FP. When the model returns false or was missing but the correct result was to return true, it is called an FN. Conversely, when the algorithm or model correctly predicts the output, this is called either a **True Positive (TP)** or **True Negative (TN)**. It is common to use a confusion matrix to identify and train the model to reduce FPs and FNs.

I created a version of a confusion matrix found in the following screenshot to help to identify NLP predictions where the results for positive are in green and negative in red. What determines the color and designation is comparing the actual verse in the predicted output. For example, if a computer model is used to predict the outcome of testing a person for a disease, a **TP** or **TN** would indicate the model either accurately predicted that the person has the disease or verified they do not have the disease. For those cases, the green color boxes indicate a match to the actual outcomes. For any other outcome, the boxes are colored in red because the prediction inaccurately returned a false result:

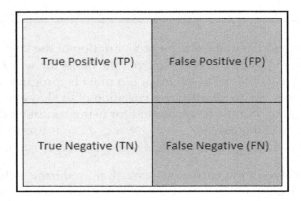

Validating the results of NLP models can and should be done by a human when the data volumes are small. This will ensure trust exists with the code behind the algorithm. However, when data volumes are large, this becomes a time-consuming task, and in many cases, unrealistic to verify without alternative solutions such as crowd-sourcing. Crowd-sourcing solutions are when humans are used for data entry in the process, but at a large scale by breaking up tasks and distributing them to a population of people to validate data.

Typical NLP or data science models will use supervised learning techniques where training sets of data are used to teach the model to be accurate in its prediction output. The labeled data used for training will be a small population of data classified by a person or people with an accurate outcome. So, the statistical models used to accurately predict the results are based on teaching the NLP model based on trained data. Using mislabeled training data in supervised NLP models will result in more false positives and inaccurate results. If you work with a data scientist or data engineering team using supervised learning, you can showcase your data literacy knowledge by asking what process is used to retrain and re-evaluate the accuracy of the model.

Now that we have some fundamental understanding of working with unstructured data, let's walk through how to gather it from its source. For social media data from platforms such as Twitter, using their API connection would be an option and allows you to consume data in near real time by streaming the data into your Jupyter notebook. Using any social media's APIs will require you to set up a user account and create a secret key so you can use a REST client connection via HTTP.

 Depending on the network connection used by your workstation, you may need to adjust your firewall or proxy settings to allow you access to consume data via APIs and REST.

Because there are restrictions and different API limits on exporting social media data by platform, we will be using the sample data pre-installed with the packages from the Python libraries. The **Natural Language Toolkit (NLTK)** package is available to help us to work with unstructured data in multiple use cases. The software is open source and contains dozens of modules to support NLP using a concept called a corpus. A corpus creates a taxonomy that can be used by linguists, computer scientists, and machine learning enthusiasts. A taxonomy is a breakdown of the language of a body of a text into its fundamental elements. Examples include the American Heritage Dictionary and Wikipedia. It also serves as the foundation for counting and searching words when using software.

Corpus in action

For our first example, we are going to use the Brown Corpus, which contains hundreds of sample language text categorized by an eclectic mix of subjects such as mystery short stories, political press releases, and religion. The original collection had over a million words defined and tagged with a part of speech such as noun, verb, and preposition. To install the Brown Corpus and use it in your Jupyter notebook, use the following steps:

1. Launch a new Jupyter notebook and name it `ch_10_exercises`.
2. Import the following libraries by adding the following command in your Jupyter notebook and running the cell. Feel free to follow along by creating your own notebook (I have placed a copy in GitHub for reference):

```
In[]: import nltk
```

The library should already be available using Anaconda. Refer to `Chapter 2`, *Overview of Python and Installing Jupyter Notebook*, for help with setting up your environment. If you are behind a firewall, there is an `nltk.set_proxy` option available. Check the documentation at `http://www.nltk.org/` for more details.

3. Next, we download the specific corpus we want to use. Alternatively, you can download all of the packages using the `all` parameter:

```
In[]: nltk.download('brown')
```

The output would look like the following screenshot where the package download is confirmed and the output is verified with `True`:

```
In [2]:  nltk.download('brown')

         [nltk_data] Downloading package brown to /home/nbuser/nltk_data...
         [nltk_data]    Unzipping corpora/brown.zip.
Out[2]:  True
```

4. To confirm the package is available in your Jupyter notebook, we can use the following command to reference the corpus using a common alias of `brown` for reference:

```
In[]: from nltk.corpus import brown
```

5. To display a list of the few words available in the Brown Corpus, use the following command:

```
In[]: brown.words()
```

The output would look like the following screenshot where six words in single quotes are displayed along with an ellipsis inside square brackets:

```
In [4]:  from nltk.corpus import brown

In [5]:  brown.words()
Out[5]:  ['The', 'Fulton', 'County', 'Grand', 'Jury', 'said', ...]
```

6. To count all of the words available, we can use the `len()` function, which counts the length of a string or the number of items in an object such as an array of values. Since our values are separated by commas, it will count all of the words available. To make it easier to format, let's assign the output to a variable called `count_of_words`, which we can use in the next step:

   ```
   In[]: count_of_words = len(brown.words())
   ```

7. To make the output easier to understand for the consumer of this data, we use the `print()` and `format()` functions to display the results using the following command:

   ```
   In[]: print('Count of all the words found the Brown Corpus
   =',format(count_of_words,',d'))
   ```

   The output would look like the following screenshot where a sentence will appear that includes a dynamic count of all of the words assigned to the `count_of_words` variable. We also formatted the value to display with a comma:

```
In [15]:  count_of_words = len(brown.words())

In [16]:  print('Count of all the words found the Brown Corpus =',format(count_of_words,',d'))
          Count of all the words found the Brown Corpus = 1,161,192
```

Excellent, you have now successfully loaded your first NLP library and were able to run a few commands against a popular corpus package. Let's continue dissecting the different elements of NLP by explaining why tokenization is important.

Tokenization explained

Tokenization is the process of breaking unstructured text such as paragraphs, sentences, or phrases down into a list of text values called tokens. A token is the lowest unit used by NLP functions to help to identify and work with the data. The process creates a natural hierarchy to help to identify the relationship from the highest to the lowest unit. Depending on the source data, the token could represent a word, sentence, or individual character.

The process to tokenize a body of text, sentence, or phrase, typically starts with breaking apart words using the white space in between them. However, to correctly identify each token accurately requires the library package to account for exceptions such as hyphens, apostrophes, and a language dictionary, to ensure the value is properly identified. Hence, tokenization requires the language of origin of the text to be known to process it. Google Translate, for example, is an NLP solution that can identify the language, but still has the option for users to define it to ensure the translation is accurate.

This is one of the reasons why tokenization is an evolving process. For example, as new words are added to the English language, the NLP reference libraries require an update. Handling sarcasm, dual meanings, and catchphrases may get lost in translation when using NLP solutions such as Alexa or Siri. For example, the phrase **social ambassador** has an obvious meaning to a human but would require the library to be trained to identify it as a token phrase.

There are a few techniques used by NLP to address this issue. The first is called n-grams, which is the process of combining words within the same sentence as a group, typically of two or three words, to create a pattern that is recognizable by the NLP library. Acronyms can also be used in n-grams but require identification or training to be effective. An n-gram could then be used to identify **social ambassador** to understand these two values can be used together.

 Another common reference for an n-gram is a bi-gram, which only uses two words. The **n** denotes the number of grams so a uni-gram stands for one gram, a bi-gram is for two, a tri-gram is for three, and so on.

Another concept is called a **bag of words**, which is when a high occurrence of specific words exist in the source data. The use of a **bag of words** is another helpful way to identify patterns and key term searches against large text sources of data. For example, a prediction model to improve response time from system outages can use historical text logs found in help desk tickets. The **bag of words** technique can be used to create multiple flag fields (yes or no) as inputs into the algorithm.

So, the study of tokenization and NLP is a deep subject that will remain an evolving science. I recommend continuing to research the subject in more detail. The Stanford University NLP site is a fantastic source of information that I have added to the *Further reading* section.

Let's explore the additional features available in the NLTK library in our Jupyter notebook. Another downloadable library available is called **Punkt**, which is used to tokenize sentences into words. I have included a link to the downloads available from NLTK in the *Further reading* section. The code behind the algorithm requires a high volume of text so the model can be trained but the NLTK data package includes a pre-trained option in English that we can use.

Tokenize in action

You will continue by going back into the ch_10_exercises notebook in Jupyter:

1. Import the following libraries by adding the following command in your Jupyter notebook and run the cell. Feel free to follow along by creating your own notebook (I have placed a copy on GitHub for reference):

   ```
   In[]: nltk.download('punkt')
   ```

   The output would look like the following screenshot where the package download is confirmed and the output is verified with True:

   ```
   In [20]:  nltk.download('punkt')

             [nltk_data] Downloading package punkt to /home/nbuser/nltk_data...
             [nltk_data]   Unzipping tokenizers/punkt.zip.
   Out[20]:  True
   ```

2. Next, we will create a new variable called input_sentence and assign it to a free-form text sentence that must be encapsulated in double quotes and on a single line input. There will be no input after you run the cell:

   ```
   In[]: input_sentence = "Seth and Becca love to run down to the
   playground when the weather is nice."
   ```

3. Next, we will use the word_tokenize() function that is available in the NLTK library to break up the individual words and any punctuation:

   ```
   In[]: nltk.word_tokenize(input_sentence)
   ```

The output would look like the following screenshot where the individual words are broken out from the sentence as an array of values with single quotes around each text value surrounded by square brackets:

```
In [24]:  input_sentence = "Seth and Becca love to run down to the playground when the weather is nice."

In [26]:  nltk.word_tokenize(input_sentence)

Out[26]:  ['Seth',
          'and',
          'Becca',
          'love',
          'to',
          'run',
          'down',
          'to',
          'the',
          'playground',
          'when',
          'the',
          'weather',
          'is',
          'nice',
          '.']
```

4. Next, let's tokenize by sentence, which requires you to import the `sent_tokenize` option from the NLTK `tokenize` library using the following command:

```
In[]: from nltk.tokenize import sent_tokenize
```

5. Now, let's assign a new variable called `input_data` to a collection of sentences that we can use later in our code. There will be no input after you run the cell:

```
In[]: input_data = "Seth and Becca love the playground.  When it
sunny, they head down there to play."
```

6. Then, we will pass the `input_data` variable as a parameter to the `sent_tokenize()` function, which will look at the string of text and break it down into individual token values. We wrap the output with the `print()` function to display the results cleanly in the notebook:

```
In[]: print(sent_tokenize(input_data))
```

The output would look like the following screenshot where the individual sentences are broken down as an array of string values with single quotes around them surrounded by square brackets:

```
In [38]:  from nltk.tokenize import sent_tokenize

In [41]:  input_data = "Seth and Becca love the playground.  When it sunny, they head down there to play."

In [42]:  print(sent_tokenize(input_data))
          ['Seth and Becca love the playground.', 'When it sunny, they head down there to play.']
```

So, now you can see that having these NLTK library features can help you to work with unstructured data by breaking down language into foundational pieces. As a data analyst, you will be faced with free text in many different forms, so now you have some additional resources to leverage. Once you have the data tokenized, additional options are available that we will explore in the next section, such as counting the frequency of words to identify patterns within the underlying source.

Counting words and exploring results

Counting word frequency will provide initial metadata about the unstructured source text. Exposing the count of the occurrence of a word or when specific words are missing within a body of text is known as **text mining**. Text mining will provide analytics about the data, so a data analyst can determine the value of a data asset along with how it can be used to answer business questions. Likewise, you can identify keyword patterns that occur during unexpected outages that impact users by looking at application system logs. Once those words or phrases are identified, you can work with the developers to identify the root cause and reduce the impact on your application users.

A popular option available for text analysis is the use of regular expressions or **regex** for short. The regex concept is when you use a combination of rules and search patterns to extract features from very large, unstructured text. Regex becomes useful when reading the text line by line would be unreasonable, based on the amount of time and number of people required. Regex has a wide range of applications including how to separate emails, phone numbers, and hashtags from the source text. If you are working with help desk ticket logs, for example, you would tag successful matches to the regex rules with a unique ticket ID so you can join the unstructured data back to the data model.

Regex covers a variety of techniques including wildcard character searches, pattern matching based on qualifiers, and anchors used to identify the beginning or end of textual data. Regex rules are usually combined with standard software engineering, so the code can be modular and automated when looking at high-frequency data sources such as a chatbot or system logs. For example, if you created a regex rule against any combination of the keyword `frustrated` in a customer service system, you can create a flag field named `is_customer_frustrated_yes_no` with a value of 1 for true and 0 for false. Regex rules can and should evolve over time, based on the data and validation, the rules that are accurate is important. This can be done with a random sampling of data by manually validating the conditions exist and returning the correct result.

Counting words

Before we explore those options, let's continue with the Jupyter notebook exercise and walk through how to count the frequency of words from a population of free text.

You will continue by going back into the `ch_10_exercises` notebook in Jupyter:

1. Import the probability module available in the NTLK library to count the frequency of the words available in a body of text. There will be no result returned after you run the cell:

   ```
   In[]: from nltk.probability import FreqDist
   ```

2. Next, explore a large body of text using the Brown Corpus. To do this, we assign the population of all of the token words available by using the `FreqDist()` function and assigning it to a variable named `input_data`. To see the results of the processing of this data, we can print the variable:

   ```
   In[]: input_data = FreqDist(brown.words())
   print(input_data)
   ```

   The output would look like the following screenshot where the frequency distribution results are calculated and printed using the `print()` function against the assigned variable, `input_data`:

   ```
   In [29]:  input_data = FreqDist(brown.words())
             print(input_data)

             <FreqDist with 56057 samples and 1161192 outcomes>
   ```

3. To see a list of the most common words that exist in `input_data`, we can use the `most_common()` function along with a parameter to control how many are displayed. In this case, we want to see the top 10:

```
In[]: input_data.most_common(10)
```

The output would look like the following screenshot where a list of name-value pairs are displayed like a two-column table with ten rows to show each token, which can be a word, punctuation mark, or character enclosed with single quotes along with an integer value that provides the cumulative count of the times the word appears in the source data:

```
In [25]:  input_data.most_common(10)

Out[25]:  [('the', 62713),
           (',', 58334),
           ('.', 49346),
           ('of', 36080),
           ('and', 27915),
           ('to', 25732),
           ('a', 21881),
           ('in', 19536),
           ('that', 10237),
           ('is', 10011)]
```

Through this exercise, we can identify and extract words from a body of unstructured text, which is the foundation for creating regex rules. The next section will focus on normalizing words for consistency to improve the accuracy of NLP model predictions.

Normalizing text techniques

In most cases, making the regex rules **smarter** by adding new code logic or libraries will be required. One such way to do this is by using the concepts behind normalizing your text called stemming and lemmatization. Both terms are rooted in the study of linguistics, and how they are adopted to be used in technology has exploded due to integrating NLP solutions into everything, from customer service to speech-to-text features.

When applied to NLP, stemming is when any word is programmatically identified to its common root form. In this process, any suffix, plural form, or synonym that exists for the word is identified. Stemmers require a reference dictionary or lookup to be accurate, so the source language is required. Lemmatization takes into account all of the variations of a word so it can be rooted back to a dictionary source. From my research, both stemming and lemmatization are used together in NLP and you can start by using the open source libraries available, which I included in the *Further reading* section. These libraries should be sufficient to cover common words but analogies or custom-defined lingo in your organization will require a new corpus. Simple examples of using stemming or a lemma include identifying when the word **fishes** appears, and returning **fish,** or **geese** returning **goose**.

The subject for both concepts is pretty vast, so I encourage you to continue learning about it, but the bottom line is the benefits of using these concepts will help to clean and normalize data for analysis. Having the data normalized where multiple similar values are grouped together as a single value is necessary. It reduces the volume of data you are analyzing and prepares the results for deeper analytics such as creating a data science or machine learning model.

Stemming and lemmatization in action

For our exercises, we will use the Porter Stemmer, which is commonly used to help to prepare text data and normalize data in NLP.

Let's continue by going back to the `ch_10_exercises` notebook in Jupyter:

1. Import the `PorterStemmer` module available in the NTLK library to normalize a word. There will be no result returned after you run the cell:

   ```
   In[]: from nltk.stem import PorterStemmer
   ```

2. To import an instance of this feature so it can be referenced later in the code, we use the following code. There will be no result returned after you run the cell:

   ```
   In[]: my_word_stemmer = PorterStemmer()
   ```

3. Now, you can pass individual words into the instance to see how the word would be normalized:

   ```
   In[]: my_word_stemmer.stem('fishing')
   ```

The output will look like the following screenshot where the stem of the word fishing will be displayed as fish:

```
In [61]: my_word_stemmer.stem('fishing')
Out[61]: 'fish'
```

4. To use lemma features, we need to download the WordNet corpus using the following command:

```
In[]: nltk.download('wordnet')
```

5. To import an instance of this feature so it can be referenced later in the code, we use the following code. There will be no result returned after you run the cell:

```
In[]: from nltk.stem import WordNetLemmatizer
my_word_lemmatizer = WordNetLemmatizer()
```

6. To see how the lemma would output for the same word we used a stem for earlier, we pass the same word into the lemmatize() function:

```
In[]: my_word_lemmatizer.lemmatize('fishing')
```

The output would look like the following screenshot where the lemma of the word fishing will be displayed as fishing:

```
In [78]: my_word_lemmatizer.lemmatize('fishing')
Out[78]: 'fishing'
```

So, why are the results different? The algorithms used by each of the NLTK corpora apply different approaches to normalize the words. Lemmatization will adjust to the form or structure of the word as it is defined in the dictionary that is included in the WordNet corpus whereas stemming is intended to break down the word to its root. Each is a tool that is available and, depending on the use case, you may need to adjust which approach to use to normalize the data for analysis.

To take it one step forward, let's pass a list of words into each instance using a loop and print out the results to see how they compare to the original word. We will use a sample from the Brown words by limiting the results.

If you pass all over a million words into the loop in your Jupyter Notebook session, it will take much longer to run and take up resources (RAM and CPU) to process.

7. To create a list but limit the words to only a sample by assigning it to a variable, we use the following command. There will be no result returned after you run the cell:

```
In[]: my_list_of_words = brown.words()[:10]
```

8. Now, we create a loop against each value in the list and print the results. We include some formatting to make it easier to understand the results for each row. Be sure to include a carriage return to create a new line to use the print() function without errors:

```
In[]: for x in my_list_of_words :
    print('word =', x, ': stem =', my_word_stemmer.stem(x), ':
lemma =', my_word_lemmatizer.lemmatize(x))
```

The output will look like the following screenshot where ten lines are printed with a colon delimiter used to separate the results for the original word, the stem of the word, and the lemma of the word:

```
In [113]: for x in my_list_of_words :
    print('word =', x, ': stem =', my_word_stemmer.stem(x), ': lemma =', my_word_lemmatizer.lemmatize(x))

word = The : stem = The : lemma = The
word = Fulton : stem = Fulton : lemma = Fulton
word = County : stem = Counti : lemma = County
word = Grand : stem = Grand : lemma = Grand
word = Jury : stem = Juri : lemma = Jury
word = said : stem = said : lemma = said
word = Friday : stem = Friday : lemma = Friday
word = an : stem = an : lemma = an
word = investigation : stem = investig : lemma = investigation
word = of : stem = of : lemma = of
```

Now that we learned how to normalize the words within your unstructured data, let's find out how to exclude words or phrases from your data to reduce the noise so we can focus on valuable keywords that can provide insight.

Excluding words from analysis

Visually sifting through millions of words is impractical in data analysis because language includes many linking verbs that are repeated throughout the body of a text. Common words such as **am**, **is**, **are**, **was**, **were**, **being**, and **been** would be at the top of the `most_common()` list when you apply NLP against the source data even after it has been normalized. In the evolution of improving NLP libraries, a dictionary of **stopwords** was created to include a more comprehensive list of words that provide less value in text analytics. Example **stopwords** include linking verbs along with words such as **the**, **an**, **a**, and **until**. The goal is to create a subset of data that you can focus your analysis on after filtering out these stopwords from your token values.

NLP can require high CPU and RAM resources especially working with a large collection of words, so you may need to break up your data into logical chucks, such as alphabetically, to complete your analysis.

You will continue by going back to the `ch_10_exercises` notebook in Jupyter:

1. Download the `stopwords` corpus from the NLTK library using the following command:

   ```
   In[]: nltk.download('stopwords')
   ```

2. Next, import the stopwords and `word_tokenize` features so they can be used later in the exercise:

   ```
   In[]: from nltk.corpus import stopwords
   from nltk.tokenize import word_tokenize
   ```

3. Now, let's assign a new variable called `input_data` to a collection of sentences that we can use later in our code. There will be no input after you run the cell:

   ```
   In[]: input_data = "Seth and Becca love the playground.  When it's
   sunny, they head down there to play."
   ```

4. We will assign object variables called `stop_words` and `word_tokens` so they can be referenced later in the code:

   ```
   In[]: stop_words = set(stopwords.words('english'))word_tokens =
   word_tokenize(input_data)
   ```

5. Finally, we have a few lines of code that will loop through the word tokens from `input_data` and compare them to `stop_words`. If they match, they will be excluded. The final result prints the original `input_data`, which has been tokenized along with the results after the stopwords have been removed. Be sure to use the correct indentation when entering the code:

```
In[]: input_data_cleaned = [x for x in word_tokens if not x in
stop_words]
input_data_cleaned = []

for x in word_tokens:
    if x not in stop_words:
        input_data_cleaned.append(x)
print(word_tokens)
print(input_data_cleaned)
```

The output would look like the following screenshot where the original sentence is displayed as tokens that include all words. The second line of the output will have fewer token words because stopwords such as `the` have been removed:

```
In [11]:  input_data_cleaned = [x for x in word_tokens if not x in stop_words]
          input_data_cleaned = []

          for x in word_tokens:
              if x not in stop_words:
                  input_data_cleaned.append(x)

          print(word_tokens)
          print(input_data_cleaned)
          ['Seth', 'and', 'Becca', 'love', 'the', 'playground', '.', 'When', 'it', 'sunny', ',', 'they', 'head', 'down', 'there', 'to',
          'play', '.']
          ['Seth', 'Becca', 'love', 'playground', '.', 'When', 'sunny', ',', 'head', 'play', '.']
```

Excellent, we have learned now to exclude common words, which removes the noise from large volumes of text. The focus of your analysis will be on keywords and phrases to provide context within the text without reading through the entire body of unstructured data.

Summary

Congratulations, you have successfully walked through the foundations of **Natural Language Processing** (**NLP**), along with key features that are available when working with unstructured data. We explored the **Natural Language Toolkit** (**NLTK**) Python library, which offers many options to work with free text by downloading different corpora to analyze large bodies of text. We learned how to split raw text into meaningful units called tokens so it can be interpreted and refined. We learned about regex and pattern matching using words as it applies to NLP. We also explored how to count the frequency of words in a collection of text using probability and statistical modules. Next, we learned how to normalize words using stemming and lemmatization functions, which shows how variations in words can impact your data analysis. We explained the concepts of n-grams and how to use `stopwords` to remove the noise that is common when working with large bodies of free text data.

In the next chapter, `Chapter 11`, *Practical Sentiment Analysis*, we will show how prediction models can be applied to unstructured data.

Further reading

For more information on the relative topics of this chapter, you can refer to the following links:

- Creating random sample data: `https://www.mockaroo.com/`
- The NLTK source code and documentation: `https://www.nltk.org/`
- NLP Stanford University reference: `https://nlp.stanford.edu/`

11
Practical Sentiment Analysis

This is going to be a fun chapter. In this chapter, we will explore and demonstrate some practical examples of using **Natural Language Processing** (**NLP**) concepts to understand how unstructured text can be turned into insights. In Chapter 10, *Exploring Text Data and Unstructured Data*, we explored the **Natural Language Toolkit** (**NLTK**) library and some fundamental features of working with identifying words, phrases, and sentences. In that process of tokenizing, we learned how to work with data and classify text, but did not go beyond that. In this chapter, we will learn about sentiment analysis, which predicts the underlying tone of text that's input into an algorithm. We will break down the elements that make up an NLP model and the packages used for sentiment analysis before walking through an example together.

In this chapter, we will cover the following topics:

- Why sentiment analysis is important
- Elements of an NLP model
- Sentiment analysis packages
- Sentiment analysis in action

Let's get started.

Technical requirements

You can find the GitHub repository for this book at https://github.com/ PacktPublishing/Practical-Data-Analysis-using-Jupyter-Notebook/tree/master/ Chapter11.

You can download and install the required software for this chapter from the following link: https://www.anaconda.com/products/individual.

Why sentiment analysis is important

Today, we are all living in a digital age where data is entangled in our daily lives. However, since most of this data is unstructured and the volume of it is large, it requires statistical libraries and **machine learning** (**ML**) to apply it to technology solutions. The NLTK libraries serve as a framework for us to work with unstructured data, and sentiment analysis serves as a practical use case in NLP. **Sentiment analysis**, or opinion mining, is a type of supervised ML that requires a training dataset to accurately predict an input sentence, phrase, headline, or even tweet is positive, negative, or neutral. Once the model has been trained, you can pass unstructured data into it, like a function, and it will return a value between negative one and positive one. The number will output decimals, and the closer it is to an integer, the more confident the model's accuracy will be. Sentiment analysis is an evolving science, so our focus will be on using the NLTK corpus libraries. As with any NLP model, you will find inaccuracies in the predicted output if you don't have a good sample for the input training data.

Also, note that NLP and sentiment analysis is a deep subject and should be validated by a data scientist or ML engineering team if you plan on implementing your own models using internal company data sources. That being said, you will notice sentiment analysis in many different applications today, and the exercises in this chapter provide you with another tool for data analysis. Another benefit of learning about how to use sentiment analysis is that it allows you to argue about the data that's output from a model. The ability to defend the accuracy and predictive nature of working with unstructured data will increase your data literacy skills. For example, let's say you are analyzing a population of tweets about a restaurant for a marketing campaign that had a mix of positive and negative reviews in the past. If the results of your analysis come back as 100% positive, you should start questioning the training data, the source of the data, and the model itself. Of course, it's possible for all the tweets to be positive, especially against a small population of data, but is it likely that every single one has a positive sentiment?

This is why **Knowing Your Data** (**KYD**) remains important, as covered in `Chapter 1`, *Fundamentals of Data Analysis*, regardless of the technology and tools being used to analyze it. However, why sentiment analysis is important today needs to be stated. First, the accuracy of the models has significantly improved because the more training data there is, the better the prediction's output. The second point is that NLP models can scale beyond what a human can process in the same amount of time. Finally, the alternatives to sentiment analysis available today, such as expert systems, are more costly because of the time and resources required to implement them. Expert system development using text-based logic and wildcard keyword searches is rigid and difficult to maintain.

Now, let's explore what makes up the elements of NLP and the process of how it is used in sentiment analysis.

Elements of an NLP model

To summarize the process required to use an NLP supervised ML model for sentiment analysis, I have created the following diagram, which shows the elements in a logical progression indicated by the letters **A** through **E**:

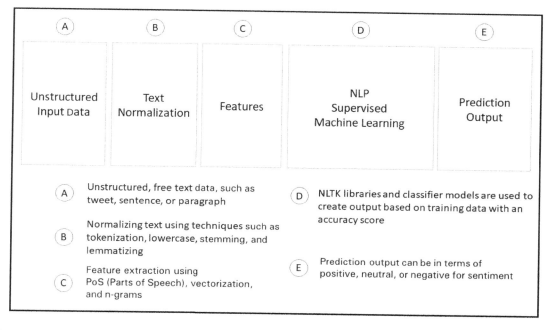

The process begins with our source **Unstructured Input Data**, which is represented in the preceding diagram with the letter **A**. Since unstructured data has different formats, structures, and forms such as a tweet, sentence, or paragraph, we need to perform extra steps to work with the data to gain any insights.

The next element is titled **Text Normalization** and is represented by the letter **B** in the preceding diagram, and involves concepts such as tokenization, n-grams, and **bag-of-words (BoW)**, which were introduced in `Chapter 10`, *Exploring Text Data and Unstructured Data*. Let's explore them in more detail so that we can learn how they are applied in sentiment analysis. BoW is when a string of text such as a sentence or paragraph is broken down to determine how many times a word occurs. In the process of **tokenizing** to create the bag-of-words representation, the location of where the word appears in a sentence, tweet, or paragraph becomes less relevant. How each word is classified, categorized, and defined using a classifier will serve as input to the next process.

Think of tokens and bag-of-words as raw ingredients to the sentiment analysis recipe; as in cooking, the ingredients take additional steps of refinement. Hence, the concept of classification becomes important. This is considered a **Features** and is represented by the letter **C** in the preceding diagram. Because tokens are nothing more than ASCII characters to a computer, word embedding and tagging is the process of converting the words into an input for an ML model. An example would be to classify each word with a pair value such as a one or zero to represent true or false. This process also includes finding similar words or groupings in order to interpret the context.

Creating **Features** is known as feature engineering, which is the foundation of supervised ML. Feature engineering is the process of transforming unstructured data elements into specific inputs for the prediction model. Models are abstractions where the output is only as accurate as the input data behind it. This means models need training data with extracted features to improve their accuracy. Without feature engineering, the results of a model would be random guesses.

Creating a prediction output

To see how **features** can be extracted from unstructured data, let's walk through the NLTK gender feature, which includes some minor modifications from the original example. You can find the original source in the *Further reading* section.

Launch a new Jupyter Notebook and name it ch_11_exercises. Now, follow these steps:

1. Import the following libraries by adding the following command to your Jupyter Notebook and run the cell. Feel free to follow along by creating your own Notebook. I have placed a copy in this book's GitHub repository for reference:

   ```
   In[]: import nltk
   ```

   The library should already be available using Anaconda. Refer to Chapter 2, *Overview of Python and Installing Jupyter Notebook*, for help with setting up your environment.

2. Next, we need to download the specific corpus we want to use. Alternatively, you can download all the packages using the all parameter. If you are behind a firewall, there is an nltk.set_proxy option available. Check the documentation at nltk.org for more details:

   ```
   In[]: nltk.download("names")
   ```

The output will look as follows, where the package download is confirmed and the output is verified as `True`:

```
In [19]: nltk.download("names")

         [nltk_data] Downloading package names to /home/nbuser/nltk_data...
         [nltk_data]   Package names is already up-to-date!

Out[19]: True
```

3. We can use the following command to reference the corpus:

```
In[]: from nltk.corpus import names
```

4. To explore the data available in this corpus, let's run the `print` command against the two input sources, `male.txt` and `female.txt`:

```
In[]: print("Count of Words in male.txt:",
len(names.words('male.txt')))
print("Count of Words in female.txt:",
len(names.words('female.txt')))
```

The output will look as follows, where a count of the number of words found in each source file is printed in the Notebook:

```
In [37]: print("Count of Words in male.txt:", len(names.words('male.txt')))
         print("Count of Words in female.txt:", len(names.words('female.txt')))

         Count of Words in male.txt: 2943
         Count of Words in female.txt: 5001
```

We now have a better understanding of the size of the data due to counting the number of words found in each source file. Let's continue by looking at the contents within each source, taking a look at a few samples from each gender file.

5. To see a list of the first few words found in each source, let's run the `print` command against the two input sources, `male.txt` and `female.txt`:

```
In[]: print("Sample list Male names:",
names.words('male.txt')[0:5])
print("Sample list Female names:", names.words('female.txt')[0:5])
```

The output will look as follows, where a list of words found in each source file is printed in the Notebook:

```
In [40]: print("Sample list Male names:", names.words('male.txt')[0:5])
         print("Sample list Female names:", names.words('female.txt')[0:5])

         Sample list Male names: ['Aamir', 'Aaron', 'Abbey', 'Abbie', 'Abbot']
         Sample list Female names: ['Abagael', 'Abagail', 'Abbe', 'Abbey', 'Abbi']
```

Remember that the computer has no idea if a name actually returns a value of `male` or `female`. The corpus has defined them as two different source files as a list of values that the NLTK library has identified as words because they have been defined as such. With thousands of names defined as either male or female, you can use this data as input for sentiment analysis. However, identifying gender alone will not determine whether the sentiment is positive or negative, so additional elements are required.

The next element, labeled **D** in the first diagram, is the actual **NLP supervised ML** algorithm. Remember, building an accurate model involves using feature engineering, along with NLTK libraries and classifier models. When used correctly, the output will be based on the input **training** and **test** data. Models should always be validated and the accuracy should be measured. For our example, which is building a basic gender determination model, we are going to use `NaiveBayesClassifier`, which is available in the NLKT libraries. The Naïve Bayes Classifier is an ML model created from Bayes theorem that is used to determine the probability of an event happening based on how often another similar event has occurred. A classifier is a process that chooses the correct tag value or label based on an inputted feature dataset. The mathematical concepts behind these models and libraries are vast, so I have added some links in the *Further reading* section for additional reference. To complete the elements of sentiment analysis summarized in the first diagram, we will create a prediction output, so let's continue in our Jupyter Notebook session:

1. Create a `gender_features` function that returns the last letter of any input word. The model will use this classifier feature as input to predict the output, which, based on the concept that first names that end in the letters **A**, **E**, and **I** are more likely to be female, while first names ending in **K**, **O**, **R**, **S**, or **T** are more likely to be male. There will be no output after you run the cell:

```
In[]: def gender_features(word):
    return {'last_letter': word[-1]}
```

Remember to indent the second line in your cell so that Python can process the function.

2. To confirm the function will return a value, enter the following command, which prints the last character of any inputted name or word:

```
In[]: gender_features('Debra')
```

The output will look as follows, where the last character from the inputted word Debra is printed in the Notebook with Out[]:

```
In [16]:  gender_features('Debra')
Out[16]:  {'last_letter': 'a'}
```

3. Create a new variable named labeled_names that loops through both source gender files and assigns a **name-value pair** so that it can be identified as either male or female to be input into the model. To see the results after the loop has completed, we print the first few values to verify that the labeled_names variable contains data:

```
In[]: labeled_names = ([(name, 'male') for name in
names.words('male.txt')] + [(name, 'female') for name in
names.words('female.txt')])
print(labeled_names[0:5])
```

The output will look as follows, where each name value from the source file will be combined with a tag of male or female, depending on which text file source it came from:

```
In [44]:  labeled_names = ([(name, 'male') for name in names.words('male.txt')] +
                           [(name, 'female') for name in names.words('female.txt')])
          print(labeled_names[0:5])

          [('Aamir', 'male'), ('Aaron', 'male'), ('Abbey', 'male'), ('Abbie', 'male'), ('Abbot', 'male')]
```

4. Since the model should be trained using a random list of values to avoid any bias, we will input the random function and shuffle all the name and gender combinations, which will change the sequence of how they are stored in the `labeled_names` variable. I added a `print()` statement so that you can see the difference from the output created in the prior step:

```
In[]: import random
random.shuffle(labeled_names)
print(labeled_names[0:5])
```

The output will look as follows, where each name value from the source file will be combined with a tag of `male` or `female`, depending on which text file source it came from:

```
In [46]: import random
random.shuffle(labeled_names)
print(labeled_names[0:5])

[('Lindie', 'female'), ('Krysta', 'female'), ('Cathy', 'female'), ('Orin', 'male'), ('Siouxie', 'female')]
```

 Note because the `random()` function is used, the results of the `print()` function will always change each time you run the cell.

5. Next, we are going to train the model by creating features for each gender using the last letter from each name in the `labeled_names` variable. We will print the new variable called `featuresets` so that you can see how the feature will be used in the next step:

```
In[]: featuresets = [(gender_features(n), gender) for (n, gender)
in labeled_names]
print(featuresets[0:5])
```

The output will look as follows, where each combination of the last letter from the names is assigned to a gender value, thereby creating a list of name-value pairs:

```
In [61]: featuresets = [(gender_features(n), gender) for (n, gender) in labeled_names]
print(featuresets[0:5])

[({'last_letter': 'e'}, 'female'), ({'last_letter': 'a'}, 'female'), ({'last_letter': 'y'},
'female'), ({'last_letter': 'n'}, 'male'), ({'last_letter': 'e'}, 'female')]
```

6. Next, we are going to slice the data from the `featuresets` variable list into two input datasets called `train_set` and `test_set`. Once we have those datasets separated, we can use `train_set` as an input for the classifier. We use the `len()` function to give us a sense of the size of each dataset:

```
In[]: train_set, test_set = featuresets[500:], featuresets[:500]
print("Count of features in Training Set:", len(train_set))
print("Count of features in Test Set:", len(test_set))
```

The output will look as follows, where the results of the `len()` function provide context as to how large each dataset is compared to the others:

```
In [96]:  train_set, test_set = featuresets[500:], featuresets[:500]
          print("Count of features in Training Set:", len(train_set))
          print("Count of features in Test Set:", len(test_set))

          Count of features in Training Set: 7444
          Count of features in Test Set: 500
```

7. We will now pass the `train_set` variable as input to the NLTK Naïve Bayes classifier. The model is assigned the name `classifier`, so you can call it like a function in the next step. There will be no output once you run the cell:

```
In[]: classifier = nltk.NaiveBayesClassifier.train(train_set)
```

8. Now, we will validate the results of the model by sending random names into the model using the following commands:

```
In[]: classifier.classify(gender_features('Aaron'))
classifier.classify(gender_features('Marc'))
classifier.classify(gender_features('Debra'))
classifier.classify(gender_features('Deb'))
classifier.classify(gender_features('Seth'))
```

The output will look as follows, where the gender values of either `male` or `female` will be displayed after each name is passed as a parameter in the `classifier` model:

```
In [103]: classifier = nltk.NaiveBayesClassifier.train(train_set)

In [104]: classifier.classify(gender_features('Aaron'))
Out[104]: 'male'

In [105]: classifier.classify(gender_features('Marc'))
Out[105]: 'male'

In [106]: classifier.classify(gender_features('Debra'))
Out[106]: 'female'

In [107]: classifier.classify(gender_features('Deb'))
Out[107]: 'male'

In [108]: classifier.classify(gender_features('Seth'))
Out[108]: 'female'
```

Congratulations – you have successfully created your first supervised ML model! As you can see, the **classifier** model has some accuracy issues and returns incorrect values in some cases. For example, when you pass in the values of `Aaron`, `Marc`, or `Debra`, the gender results are predicted correctly. The name `Aaron` was found in the training data, so that was no surprise. However, the model shows signs of being incomplete or requiring additional features because it returns the incorrect gender when using the nickname of `Deb` for `Debra` and for the name `Seth`, who is male.

How do we solve this problem? There are a few approaches that can be used, all of which we will explore next.

Sentiment analysis packages

The NLTK libraries include a few packages to help solve the issues we experienced in the gender classifier model. The first is the `SentimentAnalyzer` module, which allows you to include additional features using built-in functions. What's special about these packages is that they go beyond traditional functions where defined parameters are passed in. In Python, arguments (`args`) and keyword arguments (`kwargs`) allow us to pass name-value pairs and multiple argument values into a function. These are represented with asterisks; for example, `*args` or `**kwargs`. The NLTK `SentimentAnalyzer` module is a useful utility for teaching purposes, so let's continue by walking through the features that are available within it.

The second is called **VADER**, which stands for **Valence Aware Dictionary and Sentiment Reasoner**. It was built to handle social media data. The VADER sentiment library has a dictionary known as a **lexicon** and includes a rule-based algorithm specifically built to process acronyms, emoticons, and slang. A nice feature available from VADER is that it already includes training data and we can use a built-in function called `polarity_scores()` that returns key insights in the output that's displayed. The first is a compound score that is between negative one and positive one. This provides you with a normalized sum of VADER's lexicon ratings in a single score. For example, if the output returns `0.703`, this would be an extremely positive sentence, while a compound score of `-0.5719` would be interpreted as negative. The next output from the VADER tool is a distribution score in terms of how positive, negative, or neutral the input is from zero to one.

For example, the sentence `I HATE my school!` would return the results shown in the following screenshot:

```
In [34]: my_input_sentence = "I HATE my school!"
         my_analyzer.polarity_scores(my_input_sentence)
Out[34]: {'compound': -0.6932, 'neg': 0.703, 'neu': 0.297, 'pos': 0.0}
```

As you can see, a compound value of -0.6932 is returned, which validates the VADER model is accurately predicting the sentiment as very negative. On the same output line, you can see `'neg'`, `'neu'`, and `'pos'`, which are short for negative, neutral, and positive, respectively. Each metric next to the values provides a little more detail about how the compound score was derived. In the preceding screenshot, we can see a value of 0.703, which means that the model prediction is 70.3% negative, with the remaining 29.7% being neutral. The model returned a value of 0.0 next to `pos`, so there is a 0% positive sentiment based on the built-in VADER training dataset.

Note that the VADER sentiment analysis scoring methodology has been trained to handle social media data and informal proper grammar. For example, if a tweet includes multiple exclamation points for emphasis, the compound score will increase. Capitalization, the use of conjunctions, and the use of swear words will all be accounted for in the output from the model. So, the main benefit of using VADER is that it already includes those extra steps required to feature and train the model, but you lose the ability to customize it with additional features.

Now that we have a better understanding of the VADER tool, let's walk through an example of using it.

Sentiment analysis in action

Let's continue with our Jupyter Notebook session and walk through how to install and use the VADER sentiment analysis library. First, we will walk through an example of using manual input and then learn how to load data from a file.

Manual input

Follow these steps to learn how to use manual input in VADER:

1. Import the NLTK library and download the `vader_lexicon` library so that all the necessary functions and features will be available:

   ```
   In[]: import nltk
   nltk.download('vader_lexicon')
   ```

   The output will look as follows, where the package download will be confirmed and the output is verified as `True`:

```
In [21]:  import nltk

In [22]:  nltk.download('vader_lexicon')

          [nltk_data] Downloading package vader_lexicon to
          [nltk_data]     /home/nbuser/nltk_data...
          [nltk_data]   Package vader_lexicon is already up-to-date!

Out[22]:  True
```

2. Import `SentimentIntensityAnalyzer` from the NLTK Vader library. There will be no output when you run the cell:

```
In[]:from nltk.sentiment.vader import SentimentIntensityAnalyzer
```

3. To make it easier, we will assign a variable object called `my_ analyzer` and assign it to the `SentimentIntensityAnalyzer()` model. There will be no output after you run the cell:

```
In[]:my_analyzer = SentimentIntensityAnalyzer()
```

4. Next, we will create a variable named `my_input_sentence` and assign it a string value of `I HATE my school!`. On the second line, we will call the model and pass the variable as an argument to the `polarity_scores()` function:

```
In[]:my_input_sentence = "I HATE my school!"
my_analyzer.polarity_scores(my_input_sentence)
```

The output will look as follows, where we can see the result of the VADER sentiment analysis model:

```
In [34]:  my_input_sentence = "I HATE my school!"
          my_analyzer.polarity_scores(my_input_sentence)

Out[34]:  {'compound': -0.6932, 'neg': 0.703, 'neu': 0.297, 'pos': 0.0}
```

Excellent—you have now utilized the VADER sentiment analysis model and returned results to determine whether a sentence is positive or negative. Now that we understand how the model works with individual input sentences, let's demonstrate how to work with a sample social media file and combine it with what we have learned using the `pandas` and `matplotlib` libraries.

In the next exercise, we are going to work with a text file source that you will need to import into your Jupyter Notebook. This is a small sample CSV file containing example social media type free text, including a hashtag, informal grammar, and extra punctuation.

It has 2 columns and 10 rows of content, with a header row for easy reference, as shown in the following screenshot:

```
id,text
1,I Hate my School!!!
2,@socialmediahandle I learned something new today
3,I need to take a cool trip to Austraila!
4,The restaurant service was amazing!
5,I will never go back there again!
6,You learn something new every day – this place is great
7,First Impressions – this is good but then it went downhill from there
8,A bit pricey
9,Love them
10,meh
```

Social media file input

Let's continue working with our Jupyter Notebook session and walk through how to work with this source file so that it includes a VADER sentiment and then analyze the results:

1. We are going to import some additional libraries so that we can work with and analyze the results, as follows:

```
In[]:import pandas as pd
import numpy as np
%matplotlib inline
```

2. We also have to install a new library named `twython`. Use the following command to install it in your Notebook session. The `twython` library includes features to make it easier to read social media data:

```
In[]:!pip install twython
```

The output will look as follows, where the resulting installation will be displayed. If you need to upgrade `pip`, you may need to run additional commands:

```
In [30]: !pip install twython
         Requirement already satisfied: twython in /home/nbuser/anaconda3_420/lib/python3.5/site-packages (3.8.2)
         Requirement already satisfied: requests>=2.1.0 in /home/nbuser/anaconda3_420/lib/python3.5/site-packages (from twython) (2.14.
         2)
         Requirement already satisfied: requests-oauthlib>=0.4.0 in /home/nbuser/anaconda3_420/lib/python3.5/site-packages (from twytho
         n) (1.3.0)
         Requirement already satisfied: oauthlib>=3.0.0 in /home/nbuser/anaconda3_420/lib/python3.5/site-packages (from requests-oauthli
         b>=0.4.0->twython) (3.1.0)
         WARNING: You are using pip version 19.3.1; however, version 20.1 is available.
         You should consider upgrading via the 'pip install --upgrade pip' command.
```

3. If required, re-import the NLTK library and import the
   SentimentIntensityAnalyzer module. No output will be displayed after you
   run the cell:

   ```
   In[]:import nltk
   from nltk.sentiment.vader import SentimentIntensityAnalyzer
   ```

4. Define a variable as analyzer to make it easier to reference later in the code. No
   output will be displayed after you run the cell:

   ```
   In[]:analyzer = SentimentIntensityAnalyzer()
   ```

5. If required, redownload the NLTK vader_lexicon:

   ```
   In[]:nltk.download('vader_lexicon')
   ```

   The output will look as follows, where the download result will be displayed:

```
In [33]:  nltk.download('vader_lexicon')

          [nltk_data] Downloading package vader_lexicon to
          [nltk_data]     /home/nbuser/nltk_data...
          [nltk_data]   Package vader_lexicon is already up-to-date!

Out[33]:  True
```

6. Now, we will read in the .csv file using the pandas library and assign the result
   to a variable named sentences. To validate the results, you can run the len()
   function:

   ```
   In[]:sentences = pd.read_csv('social_media_sample_file.csv')
   len(sentences)
   ```

TIP

> Be sure to upload the source CSV file in the correct file location so that you can reference it in your Jupyter Notebook.

The output will look as follows, where the value of 10 will be displayed. This matches the number of records in the source CSV file:

```
In [34]: sentences = pd.read_csv('social_media_sample_file.csv')
         len(sentences)

Out[34]: 10
```

7. To preview the data and verify that your DataFrame is loaded correctly, you can run the head() command:

```
In[]:sentences.head()
```

The output will look as follows, where the results of the head() function are displayed to verify that the source file is now a DataFrame:

```
In [35]: sentences.head()

Out[35]:
            id                                              text
         0  1                                  I Hate my School!!!
         1  2   @socialmediahandle I learned something new today
         2  3               I need to take a cool trip to Austraila!
         3  4                 The restaurant service was amazing!
         4  5                    I will never go back there again!
```

8. The following block of code includes a few steps that look through the DataFrame, analyze the text source, apply the VADER sentiment metrics, and assign the results to a numpy array for easier usage. No output will be displayed after you run the cell:

```
In[]:i=0 #reset counter for loop

#initialize variables
my_vader_score_compound = [ ]
my_vader_score_positive = [ ]
```

```
my_vader_score_negative = [ ]
my_vader_score_neutral = [ ]

while (i<len(sentences)):

    my_analyzer =
analyzer.polarity_scores(sentences.iloc[i]['text'])
    my_vader_score_compound.append(my_analyzer['compound'])
    my_vader_score_positive.append(my_analyzer['pos'])
    my_vader_score_negative.append(my_analyzer['neg'])
    my_vader_score_neutral.append(my_analyzer['neu'])
    i = i+1
#converting sentiment values to numpy for easier usage
my_vader_score_compound = np.array(my_vader_score_compound)
my_vader_score_positive = np.array(my_vader_score_positive)
my_vader_score_negative = np.array(my_vader_score_negative)
my_vader_score_neutral = np.array(my_vader_score_neutral)
```

Be sure to double-check your indentations when entering multiple commands in the Jupyter Notebook input cell.

9. Now, we can extend the source DataFrame so that it includes the results from the VADER sentiment model. This will create four new columns. No output will be displayed after you run the cell:

```
In[]:sentences['my VADER Score'] = my_vader_score_compound
sentences['my VADER score - positive'] = my_vader_score_positive
sentences['my VADER score - negative'] = my_vader_score_negative
sentences['my VADER score - neutral'] = my_vader_score_neutral
```

10. To see the changes, run the head() function again:

```
In[]:sentences.head(10)
```

The output will look as follows, where the results of the `head()` function are displayed to verify that the DataFrame now includes the new columns that were created from the loop in the previous step:

```
In [40]:  sentences.head(10)
```

	id	text	my VADER Score	my VADER score - positive	my VADER score - negative	my VADER score - neutral
0	1	I Hate my School!!!	-0.6784	0.000	0.696	0.304
1	2	@socialmediahandle I learned something new today	0.0000	0.000	0.000	1.000
2	3	I need to take a cool trip to Austraila!	0.3802	0.302	0.000	0.698
3	4	The restaurant service was amazing!	0.6239	0.506	0.000	0.494
4	5	I will never go back there again!	0.0000	0.000	0.000	1.000
5	6	You learn something new every day - this place...	0.6249	0.313	0.000	0.687
6	7	First Impressions - this is good but then it w...	0.3400	0.254	0.000	0.746
7	8	A bit pricey	0.0000	0.000	0.000	1.000
8	9	Love them	0.6369	0.808	0.000	0.192
9	10	meh	-0.0772	0.000	1.000	0.000

11. While this information is useful, it still requires the user to scan through the results row by row. Let's make it easier to analyze and summarize the results by creating a new column that categorizes the compound score results. No output will be displayed after you run the cell:

```
In[]:i=0 #reset counter for loop

#initialize variables
my_prediction = [ ]

while (i<len(sentences)):
    if ((sentences.iloc[i]['my VADER Score'] >= 0.3)):
        my_prediction.append('positive')
    elif ((sentences.iloc[i]['my VADER Score'] >= 0) &
(sentences.iloc[i]['my VADER Score'] < 0.3)):
        my_prediction.append('neutral')
    elif ((sentences.iloc[i]['my VADER Score'] < 0)):
        my_prediction.append('negative')
    i = i+1
```

12. Similar to before, we will take the results and add a new column to our DataFrame called `my prediction sentiment`. No output will be displayed after you run the cell:

```
In[]:sentences['my predicted sentiment'] = my_prediction
```

13. To see the changes, run the `head()` function again:

```
In[]:sentences.head(10)
```

The output will look as follows, where the results of the `head()` function are displayed to verify that the DataFrame now includes the new column that was created from the loop in the previous step:

```
In [62]:   sentences.head(10)
```

Out[62]:	id	text	my VADER Score	my VADER score - positive	my VADER score - negative	my VADER score - neutral	predicted sentiment	my predicted sentiment
0	1	I Hate my School!!!	-0.6784	0.000	0.696	0.304	negative	negative
1	2	@socialmediahandle I learned something new today	0.0000	0.000	0.000	1.000	neutral	neutral
2	3	I need to take a cool trip to Austraila!	0.3802	0.302	0.000	0.698	positive	positive
3	4	The restaurant service was amazing!	0.6239	0.506	0.000	0.494	positive	positive
4	5	I will never go back there again!	0.0000	0.000	0.000	1.000	neutral	neutral
5	6	You learn something new every day - this place...	0.6249	0.313	0.000	0.687	positive	positive
6	7	First Impressions - this is good but then it w...	0.3400	0.254	0.000	0.746	positive	positive
7	8	A bit pricey	0.0000	0.000	0.000	1.000	neutral	neutral
8	9	Love them	0.6369	0.808	0.000	0.192	positive	positive
9	10	meh	-0.0772	0.000	1.000	0.000	negative	negative

14. To make it easier to interpret the results, let's create a data visualization against the DataFrame by summarizing the results using an aggregate `groupby`. We'll use the `plot()` function from the `matplotlib` library to display a horizontal bar chart:

```
In[]:sentences.groupby('my predicted
sentiment').size().plot(kind='barh');
```

The output will look as follows, where a horizontal bar chart will be displayed showing a summary of the count of the text by sentiment in terms of positive, negative, and neutral:

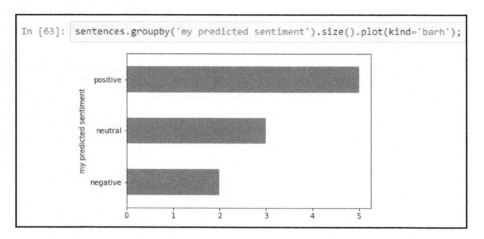

```
In [63]:  sentences.groupby('my predicted sentiment').size().plot(kind='barh');
```

As you can see, we have more positive opinions in our data source. It was much faster to interpret the results like this because we visualized the results to make it easier to consume them visually. We now have a reusable workflow to analyze much larger volumes of unstructured data by looking at a source data file and applying the VADER sentiment analysis model to each record. If you replace the sample CSV file with any social media source, you can rerun the same steps and see how the analysis changes.

 The accuracy score for VADER models is around 96%, which has been proven to be more accurate than a human interpretation according to research on the subject.

There is some bias in the analysis since the bins of **positive**, **negative**, and **neutral** can be adjusted in the code. As a good data analyst, understanding the bias can help you either adjust it for your specific needs or be able to communicate the challenges of working with free text data.

Summary

Congratulations—you have successfully walked through the foundations of NLP and should have a high-level understanding of supervised ML using the NLTK libraries! Sentiment analysis is a fascinating and evolving science that has many different moving parts. I hope this introduction is a good start to your continued research so that you can utilize it in your data analysis. In this chapter, we learned about the various elements of sentiment analysis, such as feature engineering, along with the process of how an NLP ML algorithm works. We also learned how to install NLP libraries in Jupyter to work with unstructured data, along with how to analyze the results created by a classifier model. With this knowledge, we walked through an example of how to use the VADER sentiment analysis model and visualized the results for analysis.

In our last chapter, Chapter 12, *Bringing it all Together*, we will bring together all the concepts we've covered in this book and walk through some real-world examples.

Further reading

- NLTK sentiment analysis example: https://www.nltk.org/howto/sentiment.html
- The source code for VADER and its documentation: https://github.com/cjhutto/vaderSentiment
- Bayes theorem explained: https://plato.stanford.edu/entries/bayes-theorem/
- VADER sentiment analysis research: http://comp.social.gatech.edu/papers/icwsm14.vader.hutto.pdf

12
Bringing It All Together

Welcome to the capstone chapter, where we'll walk through some examples to show you how the skills learned you've throughout this book can be applied. In this chapter, we will learn about open source real-world datasets, some tips on how to report results, and a capstone project that blends, transforms, and visualizes data from multiple sources. Data analysis is a craft and a journey rewarded by the fact that you never stop learning new ways to work with data, provide insights, and answer questions. The **data literacy** skills of reading, working with, analyzing, and arguing with data is agnostic to any technology, but in my experience, nothing replaces the experience of using a specific technology head down and hands-on. Our tool of choice in this book was Jupyter Notebook, along with the extendable libraries available when using the Python ecosystem, such as pandas, NumPy, and NTLK. As you continue to practice and apply these skills, you will become a fungible asset who can solve problems using data personally and professionally.

In this chapter, we will cover the following topics:

- Discovering real-world datasets
- Reporting results
- Capstone project

Let's get started!

Technical requirements

The GitHub repository for this book can be found at `https://github.com/PacktPublishing/Practical-Data-Analysis-using-Jupyter-Notebook/tree/master/Chapter12`.

Furthermore, you can download and install the required software for this chapter from: `https://www.anaconda.com/products/individual`.

Discovering real-world datasets

Throughout this book, I have emphasized that the power of analytics comes from blending data together from multiple sources. An individual data source alone rarely includes all the fields required to answer key questions. For example, if you have a timestamp field but not a geographic field about a user, you can't answer any questions about the data related to where an event took place.

As a good data analyst, always offer up creative solutions that have filled data gaps or offer a different perspective by including an external data source. Finding new data sources is much easier today than ever before. Let's go over a few examples.

Data.gov

Data.gov is managed by the United States General Services Administration, which offers hundreds of thousands of datasets regarding various topics at the State and Federal levels. Most are curated from specific agencies and posted for public use. They are open source with limited restrictions. What I like about using data.gov is its catalog, which allows you to search across all the topics, tags, formats, and organizations. The site was created using open source technologies, including CKAN.org, which stands for Comprehensive Knowledge Archive Network. This is a platform explicitly built as an open data portal for organizations to host datasets and make them transparent. This process democratizes datasets and creates standards for publishers to follow, such as exposing data formats (CSV, API, and XML, for example) of the source and providing details about how often the data is refreshed.

The following is a screenshot from the data.gov website where you can search for open source datasets from the United States government:

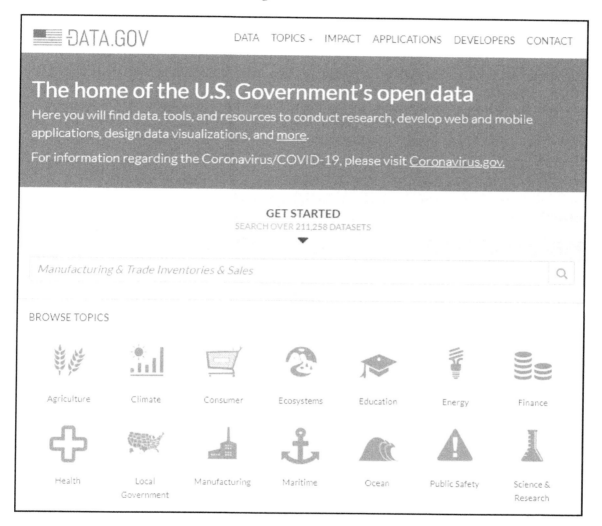

The DATA.GOV (`data.gov`) site is a good starting point but it can be overwhelming to find specific data elements. I find the next example easier and faster to OVind and use datasets.

The Humanitarian Data Exchange

The Humanitarian Data Exchange (HDX) has become topical due to the COVID-19 pandemic but has been sponsoring open source datasets for years. These datasets contain health-specific statistics from around the world with a focus on helping humanity. This is a true example of what is commonly known as **Data for Good** because the site provides transparency on the impact it has on people for free. What I like about this site is how it integrates the Creative Commons License into the data catalog so that you can understand any limitations around reusing or distributing the data from the source. Part of their terms of service is to restrict the use of any **Personally Identifiable Information** (PII) so that the data already adheres to regulations that support protecting individuals from being directly identified.

The following is a screenshot from The Humanitarian Data Exchange website (`data.humdata.org`), where you can search for humanitarian datasets about locations all around the world:

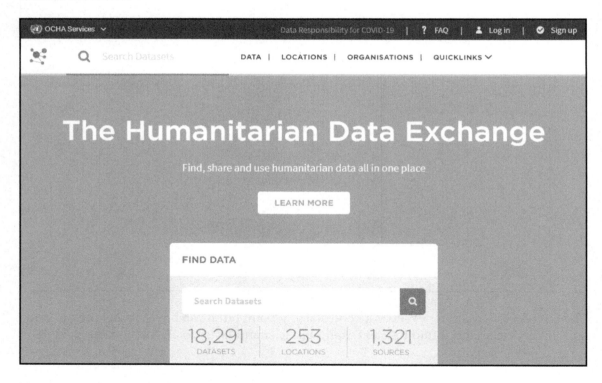

If you are searching for financial data elements categorized by global statistical measures, You can begin your search at **The World Bank** data portal.

The World Bank

The World Bank has an open data repository that includes thousands of datasets categorized and conformed by country with metrics classified as indicators. The site allows you to compare your data to global baseline metrics such as **Gross Domestic Product (GDP)**, which creates thresholds and performance metrics for your analysis. I find that the website is easy to navigate and is quick to identify datasets that can easily be joined to other datasets because it includes defined data type values such as ISO country codes.

The following is a screenshot from the World Bank Open Data website (`data.worldbank.org`), where you can search for financially focused datasets as they impact countries around the world:

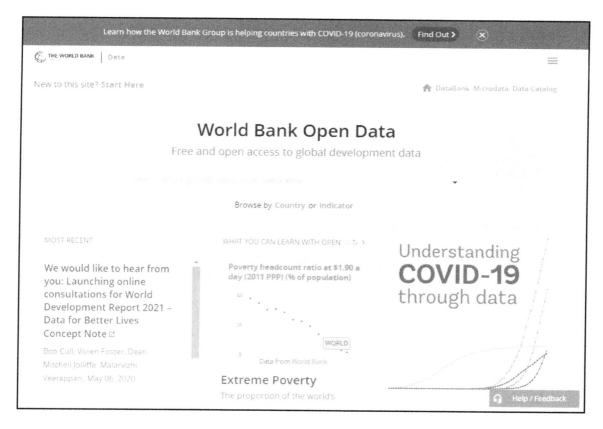

The World Bank data portal has many rich examples that include data visualizations for quick analysis and preview before you start using them. The next site we will look at, **Our World in Data**, has similar usability features.

Our World in Data

The **Our World in Data** site started with research data from Oxford University but has evolved into an online publication based on scientific studies focused on helping the world solve problems using data. I enjoy the site because you can uncover historical trends that provide context regarding how humanity is improving in many cases, but not at the same pace when you look at different countries. I also find their data visualizations easy to use and navigate; for example, you can filter and compare results between different countries or regions. Their data and site have become invaluable during the COVID-19 pandemic as you can track cases and compare progress between different countries and within the United States.

The following is a screenshot from the Our World in Data website (`ourworldindata.org`), where you can explore thousands of charts and open source data focused on helping solve global problems:

With only the few examples I showcased here, you can see that you have access to thousands of datasets available to use for research, blending, or learning. Be mindful of the open source licenses that may restrict distribution or limit how often you can extract the data. This becomes important when building any automated data pipelines or using APIs to pull data on demand. You will probably have to find alternative paid data companies in those situations. In either case, even when the source data is conformed and structured, it may not answer all the questions required for your analysis. Another point to note is that the aggregation level of the data might not be very high. For example, if data is aggregated by country, you can't join the data by city. In those situations, being transparent in terms of how you are using the data from external sources is important, along with quoting the source and providing a disclaimer stating that external data is being used.

Next, we will cover some best practices that can be used to report the results from your analysis.

Reporting results

How to present your analysis results will vary by the audience, the time available, and the level of detail required to tell a story about the data. Your data may have an inherent bias, be incomplete, or require more attributes in order to create a complete picture, so don't be afraid to include this information in your analysis. For example, if you have done some research on climate change, which is a very broad topic, presenting the consumers of your analysis with a narrow scope of assumptions specific to your dataset is important. How and where you include this information is not as important as ensuring it is available for peer review.

Storytelling

Storytelling with data requires some practice and you need time to sell your message to the audience. Like any good story, presenting the data results in a cadence with a beginning, middle, and end will help with the flow of the analysis being consumed. I also find using analogies to compare your findings will offer some connectivity between the data and the intended consumers. Knowing who you are presenting the results of your analysis to is just as important as understanding the data itself.

For example, in poker, knowing the probability of your hand and your bankroll are not the only factors for success. Who you are playing against is a contributing factor to how much you will win or lose. So, understanding the reactions of the players at the table will help you make decisions to fold, call, or raise during the game.

So, when presenting results, think like a poker player and be mindful of who you are presenting your data to in order to convince the audience about your conclusions. For example, if you are presenting to senior management, time is limited, so being direct, brief, and skipping to the summary results is suggested. If the audience is your peers, then walking through the journey of how you came to your conclusions will resonate because it builds credibility and trust.

Regardless of the audience, if you present a chart with trends becoming higher over time, be prepared to offer proof of the underlining source, along with how the metric was calculated. Without that information, doubt about the ability to recreate your findings will lead to your analysis being dismissed.

A good data analyst will be able to **read the room** and understand how much detail is required when presenting results. There have been plenty of times when I have presented findings where I had to cut my message short because when I looked up to see how engaged the people were, I realized they were lost. Rather than continuing, I stopped and offered up questions so I could provide more clarity. Just changing the format to offer time for questions in the middle of the presentation helped both the audience and myself refocus our attention on the conclusions.

So, be authentic and provide transparency in your analysis. If you make a mistake or misinterpret the data, the audience will be forgiving as long as you continue to improve and avoid repeating a missed step. I find having peers, mentors, and managers who can provide honest and constructive feedback before you present yourself, helps improve your messaging and presentation of the data artifacts.

From a **data literacy** perspective, focus less on the technology used and more on the insights gained in your analysis. Realize that the people interpreting your results will come from a diverse set of perspectives. A CEO can understand a chart of the balance sheet of company financial data but probably does not care which NumPy library was used for your analysis. In our final exercise in this book, we will create a capstone project with a focus on answering a real-world question using data from multiple sources.

The Capstone project

For our real-world dataset example, we are going to use two different sources and blend them together using the techniques we've learned throughout this book. Since **Know Your Data (KYD)** still applies, let's walk through the sources.

KYD sources

The first source is from the World Bank and is a list of green bonds, which are used to fund the reduction of carbon emissions and climate-related projects. It was downloaded from the website, so it's a snapshot based on a point in time stored as a CSV file with 115 rows and 10 columns, including a header.

A visual preview of the data in Microsoft Excel can be seen in the following screenshot:

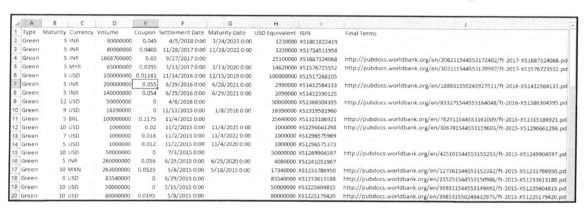

The source data has some insights that we can mine through *as is*, such as the following:

- How many **bonds** are issued by **Currency?**
- What is the total distribution of the bonds by **Currency**?
- Which **bonds** are maturing in the next 3, 5, 7, or 10 years?

However, we have a data gap for the questions related to the local currency for the country of issuance. Since currency exchange rates fluctuate daily, there are more questions we could answer if we had that information available to join by the **Currency** field. So, our second source of data that we want to work with is from the **Humanitarian Data Exchange (HDX)** site. This includes the **Foreign Exchange (FX)** rate by country designated by the currency as it relates to the **United States Dollar (USD)** by date from 1/4/1999 to 5/7/2020 in the date format of **M/D/YYYY**. This is another CSV file that can be downloaded with 5,465 rows and 34 columns on a specific date. There is a header row, and the first record of data includes metadata tags prefixed with a hash sign, #, which is used by the HDX site for metadata management and cataloging.

A visual preview of the data in Microsoft Excel can be seen in the following screenshot:

	A	B	C	D	E	F	G	H	I	J
1	Date	EUR	JPY	BGN	CZK	DKK	GBP	HUF	PLN	RON
2	#date	#value+eur	#value+jpy	#value+bgn	#value+czk	#value+dkk	#value+gbp	#value+huf	#value+pln	#value+ron
3	5/7/2020	1.0783	0.009383866	0.551334492	0.039704691	0.144534549	1.232652781	0.003086501	0.237161018	0.223551363
4	5/6/2020	1.0807	0.009426079	0.552561612	0.040045207	0.144831006	1.238582054	0.003091336	0.238071111	0.224058217
5	5/5/2020	1.0843	0.009370841	0.554402291	0.040192008	0.145325149	1.245462899	0.003095612	0.239275311	0.224678823
6	5/4/2020	1.0942	0.009364944	0.559464158	0.040348095	0.14663236	1.244851988	0.003097348	0.239598844	0.22622395
7	4/30/2020	1.0876	0.009386381	0.55608958	0.040137285	0.14582216	1.251481503	0.003083466	0.239897653	0.22456691
8	4/29/2020	1.0842	0.009385388	0.554351161	0.039970507	0.14539164	1.240815766	0.00304936	0.238589851	0.223846392
9	4/28/2020	1.0877	0.009371877	0.55614071	0.039949315	0.145862948	1.249109993	0.003055852	0.23922319	0.224522655
10	4/27/2020	1.0852	0.009337463	0.55486246	0.039920541	0.145486721	1.243596943	0.003060609	0.239627266	0.224353938
11	4/24/2020	1.08	0.009292721	0.552203702	0.039545954	0.144816767	1.234313927	0.003040626	0.238494833	0.223052934
12	4/23/2020	1.0772	0.009306263	0.550772063	0.039098399	0.144441316	1.235321101	0.003013063	0.237378523	0.222447083
13	4/22/2020	1.0867	0.00928724	0.55562941	0.039467567	0.145691724	1.236010009	0.003060179	0.239630422	0.224566552
14	4/21/2020	1.0837	0.009310937	0.554095511	0.039483368	0.145303156	1.229800272	0.003052504	0.239274911	0.224029934
15	4/20/2020	1.086	0.009273333	0.5552715	0.039739461	0.145607637	1.243373825	0.003062865	0.239883372	0.224486843
16	4/17/2020	1.086	0.009293171	0.5552715	0.039980856	0.145570553	1.248591598	0.003086893	0.240345247	0.224584333
17	4/16/2020	1.0888	0.009296448	0.556703139	0.040246923	0.145914579	1.249153884	0.003114773	0.240416887	0.225084241
18	4/15/2020	1.0903	0.009309255	0.557470089	0.040394946	0.146080362	1.247696973	0.003112475	0.240254732	0.225371036
19	4/14/2020	1.0963	0.009317525	0.560537887	0.040809261	0.14691181	1.256461096	0.003126034	0.241088118	0.226775335
20	4/9/2020	1.0867	0.009183639	0.55562941	0.040384258	0.145559023	1.241020956	0.003063198	0.238384592	0.22484999

Previewing data in Microsoft Excel or any spreadsheet tool is a best practice if you wish to visually understand the structure of the data before working with it in Jupyter Notebook. If the data volumes are large, break off a sample so it can be loaded on your workstation.

So, our bonds data with currencies lists the values by rows and our FX rate data is listing the values for each currency by column with a value assigned for each specific date. There are a few ways to solve this but for our example, we are interested in blending the latest FX rate by currency to our bond data so that we can convert the **USD Equivalent** value into the **Local CCY Equivalent**. That way, we can perform analysis of the data in either USD or the respective country's currency and report the findings.

Exercise

Let's open a new Jupyter Notebook session and get started:

1. We are going to import the libraries required to work with and analyze the results by including the following commands:

```
In[]:import pandas as pd
import numpy as np
%matplotlib inline
```

2. We will read in the first `.csv` file using the `pandas` library and assign the result to a variable named `df_greenbonds`:

> In[]:df_greenbonds = pd.read_csv('Green_Bonds_since_2008.csv')

Be sure to upload the source CSV file in the correct file location so that you can reference it in your Jupyter Notebook.

3. To validate all the records have loaded successfully, we need to run a `shape()` function against the DataFrame:

> In[]:df_greenbonds.shape

The output will look as follows, where the values `115` and `10` will be displayed. These match the number of rows and columns in the source CSV file:

```
In [132]: df_greenbonds.shape
Out[132]: (115, 10)
```

4. To preview the DataFrame, we can run the following `head()` function:

> In[]:df_greenbonds.head()

The output will look as follows, where the DataFrame results will be displayed in the Notebook:

```
In [134]: df_greenbonds.head
Out[134]:
```

	Type	Maturity	Currency	Volume	Coupon	Settlement Date	Maturity Date	USD Equivalent	ISIN	Final Terms
0	Green	5	INR	80000000	0.04500	04/05/2018 12:00:00 AM	03/24/2023 12:00:00 AM	1230000	XS1801822419	NaN
1	Green	5	INR	80000000	0.04050	11/28/2017 12:00:00 AM	11/28/2022 12:00:00 AM	1230000	XS1724511958	NaN
2	Green	5	INR	1608700000	0.05000	09/27/2017 12:00:00 AM	NaN	25100000	XS1687324068	http://pubdocs.worldbank.org/en/20621154455
3	Green	3	MYR	65000000	0.02950	03/13/2017 12:00:00 AM	03/13/2020 12:00:00 AM	14620000	XS1576723552	http://pubdocs.worldbank.org/en/30221154455
4	Green	3	USD	100000000	0.01181	11/14/2016 12:00:00 AM	12/15/2019 12:00:00 AM	100000000	XS1517268105	NaN

5. We will read in the second CSV file using the `pandas` library and assign the result to a variable named `df_fx_rates`:

   ```
   In[]:df_fx_rates = pd.read_csv('ECB_FX_USD-quote.csv')
   ```

Be sure to upload the source CSV file to the correct file location so that you can reference it in your Jupyter Notebook.

6. To validate all the records have loaded successfully, run a `shape()` function against the DataFrame:

   ```
   In[]:df_fx_rates.shape
   ```

The output will look as follows, where the values `5464` and `34` will be displayed in parentheses. These match the number of rows and columns in the source CSV file:

```
In [136]:   df_fx_rates.shape
Out[136]:   (5464, 34)
```

7. To preview the DataFrame, we can run the following `head()` function:

   ```
   In[]:df_fx_rates.head()
   ```

The output will look as follows, where the DataFrame results will be displayed in the Notebook:

```
In [138]:   df_fx_rates.head()
Out[138]:
```

	Date	EUR	JPY	BGN	CZK	DKK	GBP	HUF
0	#date	#value+eur	#value+jpy	#value+bgn	#value+czk	#value+dkk	#value+gbp	#value+huf
1	2020-05-07	1.0783	0.009383865633974415	0.5513344922793741	0.039704691067088888	0.14453454862274648	1.2326527812707195	0.003086501
2	2020-05-06	1.0807	0.009426079372001744	0.5525616116167297	0.04004520695149517	0.1448310059235037	1.2385820544852326	0.003091335
3	2020-05-05	1.0843	0.009370840895341804	0.5544022906227631	0.0419200830306175	0.14532514876963493	1.2454628991500114	0.003095611
4	2020-05-04	1.0942	0.00936494351249572	0.5594641578893548	0.04034809543124747	0.14663236042990002	1.244851987531002	0.003097347

5 rows × 34 columns

8. Since we know from the prior chapters that data is inherently messy and requires some cleanup, we will delete the first row because it contains the HDX hashtag metadata values, which are not required for our analysis:

```
In[]:df_fx_rates = df_fx_rates.drop(0)
df_fx_rates.head()
```

It is recommended that you clean up as you go through the analysis step by step in case you need to troubleshoot and recreate any prior steps in the data analysis workflow.

The output will look as follows, where the DataFrame results will be displayed in the Notebook:

```
In [139]: # Delete first row because it contains hdx hashtag metadata values
df_fx_rates = df_fx_rates.drop(0)
df_fx_rates.head
```

	Date	EUR	JPY	BGN	CZK	DKK	GBP	HUF
1	2020-05-07	1.0783	0.009383865633974415	0.5513344922793741	0.0397046910670888	0.14453454862274648	1.2326527812707195	0.003086501030
2	2020-05-06	1.0807	0.00942607937200174	0.5525616116167297	0.04004520695149517	0.1448310059235037	1.2385820544852326	0.003091335564
3	2020-05-05	1.0843	0.009370840895341804	0.5544022906227631	0.04019200830306175	0.14532514876963493	1.2454628991500114	0.003095611956
4	2020-05-04	1.0942	0.00936494351249572	0.5594641578893548	0.04034809543124747	0.14663236042990002	1.244851987531002	0.003097347637
5	2020-04-30	1.0876	0.009386381289376024	0.5560895797116269	0.04013728457024762	0.14582216024884692	1.2514815027904032	0.003083465638

5 rows × 34 columns

9. For our analysis, we want to focus on the latest FX rate available in the file. You could take the first row available in the DataFrame, but a more robust method would be to use the `max()` function so that how the data is sorted becomes irrelevant. To verify that the correct value will work before we filter the DataFrame, use the following command:

```
In[]:df_fx_rates['Date'].max()
```

The output will look as follows, where the results from the command will be displayed in the Notebook. In this dataset, the max date at the time of download is 2020-05-07, with the date format as YYYY-MM-DD:

```
In [10]: df_fx_rates['Date'].max()
Out[10]: '2020-05-07'
```

10. From the prior step, we are confident that our filter will use the correct `Date` value, so we will create a new DataFrame with only one specific date value so that we can join the results in later steps. The new DataFrame is named `df_fx_rates_max_date` and is a result of filtering the original DataFrame, named `df_fx_rates`, by the `Date` field, where only the calculated max `Date` value will be returned. We will add the following `head()` function to validate the results in the Notebook:

```
In[]:df_fx_rates_max_date =
df_fx_rates[df_fx_rates.Date==df_fx_rates['Date'].max()]
df_fx_rates_max_date.head()
```

The output will look as follows, where the results from the command will be displayed in the Notebook. The new DataFrame, named `df_fx_rates_max_date`, will only have one record with a header containing 34 columns. Each column will represent the latest available currency value using the three-letter country's designation, such as `EUR`:

```
In [11]: df_fx_rates_max_date = df_fx_rates[df_fx_rates.Date==df_fx_rates['Date'].max()]
         df_fx_rates_max_date.head()
```

Out[11]:

	Date	EUR	JPY	BGN	CZK	DKK	GBP	HUF
1	2020-05-07	1.0783	0.009383865633974415	0.5513344922793741	0.03970469106708888	0.14453454862274648	1.2326527812707195	0.003086501030

1 rows × 34 columns

11. We still have more work to do in order to join this data to our original bond DataFrame. We need to transform it using the `transpose()` function, which will change all the columns into rows. In other technologies, this concept is called a pivot, crosstab, or crosstable; this was covered in more detail in Chapter 4, *Creating Your First pandas DataFrame*. The results are stored in a new DataFrame called `df_rates_transposed`. We rename the columns to make it easier to work with them. We also need to run the following `head()` command to preview the results:

```
In[]:df_rates_transposed = df_fx_rates_max_date.transpose()
df_rates_transposed.columns.name = 'Currency'
df_rates_transposed.columns = ['Currency_Value']
df_rates_transposed.head(10)
```

The output will look as follows, where the new DataFrame, named `df_rates_transposed`, is displayed. Here, all the columns have been converted into rows:

```
In [39]:  df_rates_transposed = df_fx_rates_max_date.transpose()
          df_rates_transposed.columns.name = 'Currency'
          df_rates_transposed.columns = ['Currency_Value']
          df_rates_transposed.head(10)
```

Out[39]:

	Currency_Value
Date	2020-05-07
EUR	1.0783
JPY	0.009383865633974415
BGN	0.5513344922793741
CZK	0.03970469106708888
DKK	0.14453454862274648
GBP	1.2326527812707195
HUF	0.0030865010304556902
PLN	0.23716101788110056
RON	0.2235513631180678

12. The goal is for our reference table to have all the FX rates by currency values in the same format. However, notice that, on the first row in the following diagram, the `Date` value is mixed with `Currency_values`, which need to have the same data type. The need to have conformed and consistent data values represented in structured data has been reinforced throughout this book, so we will clean up the DataFrame by dropping the `Date` record. We will also use the `reindex()` function to make it easier to join in the next step and then run the following `head()` command to verify the results:

```
In[]:df_rates_transposed = df_rates_transposed.drop('Date')
df_rates_transposed = df_rates_transposed.reindex()
df_rates_transposed.head()
```

The output will look as follows, where the new DataFrame, named `df_rates_transposed`, is displayed as before, except now, the `Date` record has been deleted. This means the first row will be EUR with a `Currency_Value` of `1.0783`:

```
In [46]: df_rates_transposed = df_rates_transposed.drop('Date')
         df_rates_transposed = df_rates_transposed.reindex()
         df_rates_transposed.head()
```

Out[46]:

	Currency_Value
EUR	1.0783
JPY	0.0093838656633974415
BGN	0.55133449227937741
CZK	0.039704691067088888
DKK	0.14453454862274648

13. We are now ready to join the transformed and cleaned FX rates to our original bonds source using the common `Currency` join key field. Because we want all the records from the `df_greenbonds` source and only the matching values from `df_rates_transposed`, we will use a left join. To display and verify the results, we use the following `head()` command:

```
In[]:df_greenbonds_revised =
df_greenbonds.merge(df_rates_transposed, how='left',
left_on='Currency', right_index=True)
df_greenbonds_revised.head()
```

The output will look as follows, where the results of the left join are stored in the `df_greenbonds_revised` DataFrame. The following screenshot shows a table with 5 rows and 11 columns. It includes a header row and index values that are not labeled:

```
In [59]:  df_greenbonds_revised = df_greenbonds.merge(df_rates_transposed, how='left', left_on='Currency', right_index=True)
          df_greenbonds_revised.head
```

Out[59]:

Volume	Coupon	Settlement Date	Maturity Date	USD Equivalent	ISIN	Final Terms	Currency_Value
80000000	0.04500	04/05/2018 12:00:00 AM	03/24/2023 12:00:00 AM	1230000	XS1801822419	NaN	0.013187229801207066
80000000	0.04050	11/28/2017 12:00:00 AM	11/28/2022 12:00:00 AM	1230000	XS1724511958	NaN	0.013187229801207066
1608700000	0.05000	09/27/2017 12:00:00 AM	NaN	25100000	XS1687324068	http://pubdocs.worldbank.org/en/20621154455317...	0.013187229801207066
65000000	0.02950	03/13/2017 12:00:00 AM	03/13/2020 12:00:00 AM	14620000	XS1576723552	http://pubdocs.worldbank.org/en/30221154455317...	0.23124101992236926
100000000	0.01181	11/14/2016 12:00:00 AM	12/15/2019 12:00:00 AM	100000000	XS1517268105	NaN	NaN

Like in the preceding diagram, be sure to scroll to the right to see that a new column called Currency_Value is included.

14. An advantage of constantly running the head() command to validate results in each step is that you can make observations about the data as you prepare and clean it for further analysis. In the preceding screenshot , we can see a null() value in Currency_Value, which is displayed as NaN. We covered working with NaN values in Chapter 5, *Gathering and Loading Data in Python*. This is a result of the left join and is expected because there was no value of USD in the FX rates source data. This makes sense because you don't need to convert the currency of USD. However, this will have an impact when we attempt to create calculations from the values in this column. The solution, in this case, is to just convert all the NaN values to 1 because the FX rate conversion for USD is 1. There will be no output after running this command:

```
In[]:df_greenbonds_revised["Currency_Value"].fillna(1,
inplace=True)
```

15. Since our CSV file sources do not include a data dictionary, the defined data type for each field is unknown. We can solve any inconsistencies within the data values by applying the `astype()` function. We will focus on the two columns we used for calculating the local currency rate by converting them into a `dtype` of the `float` type. There will be no output after running this command:

```
In[]:df_greenbonds_revised["Currency_Value"] =
df_greenbonds_revised.Currency_Value.astype(float)
df_greenbonds_revised["USD Equivalent"] =
df_greenbonds_revised["USD Equivalent"].astype(float)
```

16. We are now ready to create a new calculated column in our existing DataFrame that will divide the `USD Equivalent` column by `Currency_Value`. The result will be stored in a new column named `Local CCY` in the same DataFrame. There will be no output after running this command:

```
In[]:df_greenbonds_revised['Local CCY'] =
df_greenbonds_revised['USD
Equivalent']/df_greenbonds_revised['Currency_Value']
```

17. Now, we can convert the data types of the specific columns back into integers and focus our attention on the key columns by explicitly identifying them. We can do this by using the following commands:

```
In[]:df_greenbonds_revised['Local CCY'] =
df_greenbonds_revised['Local CCY'].astype(int)
df_greenbonds_revised['USD Equivalent'] =
df_greenbonds_revised['USD Equivalent'].astype(int)
df_greenbonds_revised[['ISIN', 'Currency', 'USD Equivalent',
'Currency_Value', 'Local CCY']]
```

The output will look as follows, where the results from the preceding commands will be displayed in the Notebook. The original column, `USD Equivalent`, is displayed as an integer and we now have the `Local CCY` column available to the right of `Currency_Value`:

```
In [95]:  df_greenbonds_revised['Local CCY'] = df_greenbonds_revised['Local CCY'].astype(int)
          df_greenbonds_revised['USD Equivalent'] = df_greenbonds_revised['USD Equivalent'].astype(int)
          df_greenbonds_revised ['ISIN', 'Currency', 'USD Equivalent', 'Currency_Value', 'Local CCY'] |
```

Out[95]:

	ISIN	Currency	USD Equivalent	Currency_Value	Local CCY
0	XS1801822419	INR	1230000	0.013187	93272053
1	XS1724511958	INR	1230000	0.013187	93272053
2	XS1687324068	INR	25100000	0.013187	1903356533
3	XS1576723552	MYR	14620000	0.231241	63224076
4	XS1517268105	USD	100000000	1.000000	100000000
5	XS1432564133	INR	2990000	0.013187	226734503
6	XS1432390125	INR	2090000	0.013187	158486659
7	XS1386304395	USD	50000000	1.000000	50000000
8	XS1319581960	USD	16390000	1.000000	16390000
9	XS1315186921	BRL	25640000	0.173162	148069038
10	XS1296661298	USD	1000000	1.000000	1000000

18. To analyze the results, let's group the data by `Currency` and only sum the values for both the `USD Equivalent` and `Local CCY` fields using the following commands:

```
In[]:df_greenbonds_revised[['Currency', 'USD Equivalent', 'Local
CCY']].groupby(['Currency']).sum().astype(int)
```

The output will look as follows, where the data is now aggregated by `Currency`, with the total sum of `USD Equivalent` and `Local CCY` also being displayed:

```
In [109]:  df_greenbonds_revised[['Currency', 'USD Equivalent', 'Local CCY']].groupby(['Currency']).sum().astype(int)
```

Out[109]:

	USD Equivalent	Local CCY
Currency		
AUD	606880000	940120883
BRL	288510000	1666123174
CAD	10570000	14877203
COP	12910000	12910000
EUR	758690000	703598253

19. Another type of analysis would be to see how the data is distributed by `Currency` visually by creating a horizontal bar chart using the `matplotlib` library's `plot()` function:

```
In[]:df_greenbonds_revised[['Currency', 'USD
Equivalent']].groupby(['Currency']).size().plot(kind='barh');
```

The output will look as follows:

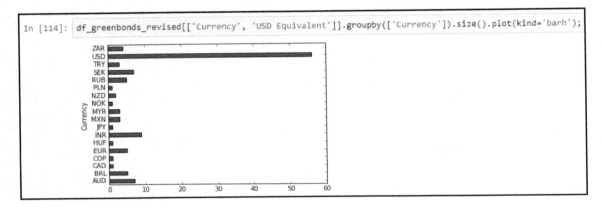

As you can see, an overwhelming number of green bonds have been issued in USD because it has the largest bar by a large margin compared to the other currencies. The reason why this is the case is not evident by looking exclusively at this data, so additional analysis will need to be done. When you present your findings to others within the organization, this is often the reality, where blending data together offers more insights but then leads to more unanswered questions. This, in turn, leads to the need for more data to be added to your existing sources. Finding a balance between when to stop blending more and more data together is challenging, so adding incremental milestones to present your findings is encouraged.

Summary

With that, we have walked through many of the different concepts we covered throughout this book in one comprehensive exercise. In this chapter, we learned more about real-world data sources that can be used for analysis. We also created a repeatable workflow that can be summarized as a workflow that collects external data sources, joins them together, and then analyzes the results. Since we know the reality of working with data is never that straightforward, we walked through some inherent challenges of working with it. We have broken down the steps of collecting multiple sources, transforming them, and cleansing, joining, grouping, and visualizing the results. The more you work hands-on with data, the easier it is to apply these concepts to any dataset with the foundation remaining constant. As you increase your data literacy skills when it comes to working with data, you will notice the syntax and tools will change but that the challenges and opportunities to solve problems remain the same. I encourage you to continue investing in yourself by continuously learning more about data. I hope you find it as fulfilling a journey as I do!

Further reading

- The Humanitarian Data Exchange site: https://data.humdata.org/
- Data.gov – the US government's open data: https://www.data.gov/
- The Creative Commons site: https://creativecommons.org/
- The Open Data Commons site: https://opendatacommons.org/
- The Our World in Data site: https://ourworldindata.org/
- The World Bank Open Data site: https://data.worldbank.org/

Works Cited

The works cited in the book are taken from the following sources:

- Belle Selene Xia, Peng Gong (2015), *Review of business intelligence through data analysis*, Benchmarking, 21(2), 300-311. DOI:10.1108/BIJ-08-2012-0050
- Edward Loper, Ewan Klein, and Steven Bird, *Natural Language Processing with Python*, O'Reilly Media, 978-0-596-51649-9
- W. Francis, and H. Kucera. Department of Linguistics, *Brown Corpus Manual* Brown University, Providence, Rhode Island, US, (1979)
- Buneman Peter, *Semistructured Data*: https://homepages.inf.ed.ac.uk/opb/papers/PODS1997a.pdf.
- Roy Thomas Fielding, *Architectural Styles and the Design of Network-based Software Architectures*: https://www.ics.uci.edu/~fielding/pubs/dissertation/top.htm, Accessed 23 Dec. 2019.
- C.J. Hutto & Eric Gilbert, *VADER: A Parsimonious Rule-based Model for Sentiment Analysis of Social Media Text*. Eighth International Conference on Weblogs and Social Media (ICWSM-14). Ann Arbor, MI, June 2014.
- Wes McKinney, *Data Structures for Statistical Computing in Python*. Proceedings of the 9th Python in Science Conference. Vol. 445. 2010.
- *Python | Pandas DataFrame*, GeeksforGeeks: A Computer Science Portal for Geeks: www.geeksforgeeks.org/python-pandas-dataframe/
- Christopher C. Shilakes and Julie Tylman, *Enterprise Information Portals* (PDF): https://web.archive.org/web/20110724175845/http://ikt.hia.no/perep/eip_ind.pdf. 16 Nov 1998.

Other Books You May Enjoy

If you enjoyed this book, you may be interested in these other books by Packt:

Hands-On Exploratory Data Analysis with Python
Suresh Kumar Mukhiya, Usman Ahmed

ISBN: 978-1-78953-725-3

- Import, clean, and explore data to perform preliminary analysis using powerful Python packages
- Identify and transform erroneous data using different data wrangling techniques
- Explore the use of multiple regression to describe non-linear relationships
- Discover hypothesis testing and explore techniques of time-series analysis
- Understand and interpret results obtained from graphical analysis
- Build, train, and optimize predictive models to estimate results
- Perform complex EDA techniques on open source datasets

Hands-On Data Analysis with Pandas

Stefanie Molin

ISBN: 978-1-78961-532-6

- Understand how data analysts and scientists gather and analyze data
- Perform data analysis and data wrangling using Python
- Combine, group, and aggregate data from multiple sources
- Create data visualizations with pandas, matplotlib, and seaborn
- Apply machine learning (ML) algorithms to identify patterns and make predictions
- Use Python data science libraries to analyze real-world datasets
- Use pandas to solve common data representation and analysis problems
- Build Python scripts, modules, and packages for reusable analysis code

Leave a review - let other readers know what you think

Please share your thoughts on this book with others by leaving a review on the site that you bought it from. If you purchased the book from Amazon, please leave us an honest review on this book's Amazon page. This is vital so that other potential readers can see and use your unbiased opinion to make purchasing decisions, we can understand what our customers think about our products, and our authors can see your feedback on the title that they have worked with Packt to create. It will only take a few minutes of your time, but is valuable to other potential customers, our authors, and Packt. Thank you!

Index

Entity Relationship Diagram (ERD) 109, 130
Entity-Relationship (ER) 18
Extract, Transform, and Load (ETL) 122

F

False Negative (FN) 235
False Positive (FP) 235
feature engineering 256
FiveThirtyEight
  reference link 30
flattening the curve 208
Foreign Exchange (FX) 283
foreign key 19
free text 17
fundamental statistics
  of data 114, 115, 117, 118

G

Gaussian curve 209
Gaussian distribution 215
geoanalytics
  techniques 220, 221, 222, 223
  tips 220, 221, 222, 223
good data analyst
  qualities 14
grain of data 197, 199
Graphical User Interface (GUI) 35
Gross Domestic Product (GDP) 279

H

Hadoop Distributed File System (HDFS) 107
Hello World!
  about 45, 46, 47, 48
  file, uploading 50, 51
horizontal bar charts
  advantages 139
  example 140
human resources (HR) 132
Humanitarian Data Exchange (HDX) 278, 283

I

Information Technology (IT) 168
inner join 189
Integrated Development Environment (IDE) 35

International Organization for Standardization
    (ISO) 106, 220
Internet of Things (IoT) 234
Interquartile Range (IRQ) 214
interval data 23

J

join relationships
  about 184
  inner join 189
  left join 187, 188
  many-to-many relationship 186
  many-to-one relationships 185
  one-to-one relationships 185
  outer join 190
  right join 188, 189
join types
  working 190, 191, 192, 193, 194, 195, 196,
    197
JSON 93, 94
Jupyter Notebook
  using 34
Jupyter
  running 39, 40, 41, 42

K

Kaggle
  reference link 29
key-value pairs 18
Know Your Data (KYD) 14, 95, 109, 167, 210,
    254, 282
KYD sources
  using 283, 284

L

left join 187, 188
lemmatization 245, 247
lexicon 263
line feed (LF) 90
lists 60
Logo 60
loop
  used, for assigning values to array 72, 74, 75,
    76

M

manual input
  using, in VADER 264
  using, in VADER sentiment analysis 265, 266
many-to-many relationship 186
many-to-one relationships 185
Master Data Management (MDM) 96
Matplotlib 54
matrix 61, 62
measures 27, 130, 131, 133, 134, 135, 137
measures of central tendency 215
metadata 118, 119, 121

N

n-dimensional array 62, 63
National Association of Securities Dealers
  Automated Quotations (NASDAQ) 67, 147
National Oceanic and Atmospheric Administration
  (NOAA) 203
Natural Language Toolkit (NLTK) 237
NLP model
  elements 255, 256
nominal data 23
normal curve 209
normal distribution 209
normalizing text techniques
  about 245, 246
  lemmatization 247
  stemming 246
Not a Number (NaN) 85
Numerical Python 60
NumPy array
  about 60
  creating 63, 64
  examples 61
  features 62
  functions 64, 65, 66
  importance 61
  use cases 68
  using 62
NumPy
  checking for 53
  use cases 67

O

one-to-one relationships 185
Open Database Connectivity (ODBC) 107
ordinal data 23
Our World in Data 280, 281
outer join 190
outliers 203, 204, 205, 216, 218, 219

P

pandas 52
pandas DataFrames 109, 110, 111, 112, 113, 114
pandas library 83, 84
panel data
  about 80
  example 81
parent-child relationship 92
patterns
  finding, in data 223, 224, 225, 226, 227, 228, 229
personally identifiable information (PII) 278
pie charts
  unpopularity 139
  usage 140
prediction output
  creating 256, 257, 258, 259, 260, 261, 262
primary key 19
Punkt 241
Python code
  running 45, 46, 47, 48
Python packages
  exploring 51
  installing, for data analysis 39, 40, 41, 42
Python
  installing 34, 35
  used, for cleaning tabular data 167, 168, 169, 170
  used, for purifying tabular data 167, 168, 169, 170
  used, for refining tabular data 167, 168, 169, 170

Q

QlikView Data (QVD) 84

R

ratio data 24
real-world dataset, example
  exercise 294
real-world datasets
  discovering 276
regex 243
Relational Database Management System
  (RDBMS) 84, 107
relational databases 106, 107, 108, 109
right join 188, 189

S

schema on read 94
science
  about 142
  versus art 141, 142
SciPy 55
semi-structured data 17, 18
sentiment analysis packages 264
sentiment analysis
  need for 254
server 93
shape of the curve 147, 211, 212, 213, 214, 215
single arrays
  versus multiple dimensional arrays 61, 62, 63
sklearn 54
social media file input
  handling, in VADER sentiment analysis 266,
  267, 268, 269, 270, 272
Software Development Life Cycle (SDLC) 15
Standard Deviation (SD) 209
star schema relationship 134
stateless 93
statistics 203, 204, 205
stemming 245, 246
structured data 18
Structured Query Language (SQL) 106, 107, 108,
  109
Subject Matter Expert (SME) 20, 121

T

tabular data
  about 80

binning 176, 177, 178, 179, 180
cleaning, with Python 167, 168, 169, 170
combining 171, 172, 173, 174, 175
filtering 162
purifying, with Python 167, 168, 169, 170
refining, with Python 167, 168, 169, 170
restricting 162, 163, 164
retrieving 158, 159, 160
sifting 166, 167
sorting 164, 165
storing 158, 159, 161, 162
techniques, for manipulating 80, 81, 82, 83
viewing 158, 159, 160, 161
text mining 243
The World Bank
  reference link 30
time data 25
time series chart
  creating 148, 149, 150, 151, 152, 154
token 239
tokenization 239
tokenize
  working 241, 242
tokenizing process 255
trends 216, 218, 219
True Positive (TP) 235
two-dimensional array 61, 62

U

Unicode Transformation Format (UTF-8) 89
United States Dollar (USD) 283
unstructured data
  about 17
  working with 234, 235, 236

V

VADER sentiment analysis
  about 263
  manual input, using 264, 265, 266
  social media file input, handling 266, 267, 268,
  269, 270, 272
  working 264
Valence Aware Dictionary and Sentiment Reasoner
  (VADER) 263
Voice of the Customer (VOC) 15

W

X

Made in the USA
Columbia, SC
02 February 2022

55227411R00176